Education for equality

Written by people with wide experience in education, this collection of essays tackles the issues of class, gender, and 'race' in education today. It is a detailed, practical guide on how to undermine inequalities, whatever their basis and at whatever level, from pre-school to higher education.

Looking at class, gender, and 'race' from a theoretical perspective, the contributors consider how theory can inform practice. They examine the relationship between reform and fundamental change, and discuss how to change a whole institution around so as to promote equality. They describe how to establish equal opportunities policies and keep them, and how to set up materials, resources, and methods conducive to good practice. Teacher education is also covered, and specific curriculum subjects are discussed. In addition, the 'hidden curriculum' is explored, and topics such as stereotyping, use of language, outside influences, and existing educational hierarchies are explored.

The Editor

Mike Cole is Senior Lecturer in Sociology in the faculties of Education and Health at Brighton Polytechnic.

Education for equality

Some guidelines for good practice

Edited by

MIKE COLE

ROUTLEDGE
London and New York

First published 1989
by Routledge
11 New Fetter Lane, London EC4P 4EE
29 West 35th Street, New York, NY 10001

© 1989 Mike Cole

Printed and bound in Great Britain by
Biddles Ltd, Guildford and King's Lynn

British Library Cataloguing in Publication Data

Education for equality: some guidelines for
  good practice
  1. Great Britain. Education. Equality of
  opportunity
  I. Cole, Mike, *1946– .*
  370'.941

ISBN 0-415-00546-9
ISBN 0-415-00547-7 Pbk

Library of Congress Cataloging in Publication Data

Education for equality: some guidelines for good practice / edited by
  Mike Cole.
      p. cm.
    Bibliography: p.
    Includes index.
    ISBN 0-415-00546-9. — ISBN 0-415-00547-7 (pbk.)
    1. Discrimination in education. 2. Educational equalization.
  I. Cole, Mike, 1956–
  LC212.E38 1989
  370.19–dc19   88-32169
                                                      CIP

To Jordan Alexandrov

Stoimenov

CONTENTS

LIST OF CONTRIBUTORS

Mike Cole is a Lecturer in sociology in the Faculties of Education and Health at Brighton Polytechnic. Before that, he taught in Inner London schools for five years.

Chris Gaine is a Senior Lecturer at the West Sussex Institute of Higher Education with special responsibility for the issue of 'race' in initial and in-service teacher education. He is involved with school developments in several local education authorities. Until three years ago he was a faculty head in a large Wiltshire comprehensive.

Pauline Lyseight-Jones is an Education Inspector for the London Borough of Ealing. Prior to this appointment she was a Senior Lecturer at Bulmershe College of Higher Education in Reading. Before that she taught for a number of years in primary and secondary schools. She was also a part-time adult literacy tutor for mentally handicapped adults for five years.

Robin Richardson is Principal Adviser for Brent Education Authority. Previously, in the period 1979-85, he was adviser for multicultural education in Berkshire. In the period 1973-9 he was Director of the World Studies Project.

Jane Lane taught in further education and now works as an Education Officer at the Commission for Racial Equality.

The Anti-Sexist Working Party (ASWP) is a group of primary school teachers whose priority is girls and equality. They have held meetings at local Teachers' Centres, provided in-service training, given talks to governors, parents, and deputy heads and have held seminars for student teachers and union groups, as well as a workshop for ancillary staff. They can be contacted through Jackie Granados Johnson at Grazebrook Primary School, Lordship Road, London N16.

Muriel Robinson is a Lecturer in language and literacy in Primary Education at Brighton Polytechnic. From 1976 to 1985 she worked for the Inner London Education Authority, teaching in a variety of Lambeth primary schools and spending a year as teacher fellow at Avery Hill College of Education.

Europe Singh currently teaches at South West London College. He has been a mathematics teacher with the Inner London Education Authority (ILEA) for seventeen years. He was one of the original members of the ILEA antiracist strategies team.

Doug Holly has been a Lecturer in Education at Leicester University for twenty-one years. He specializes in training postgraduates to teach on integrated humanities courses. Before that he trained primary teachers for a while in Birmingham. Originally he taught English, first at a secondary modern school then, for nearly ten years, at a London comprehensive.

Ahmed Gurnah taught Social Science in general and Sociology in particular for several years in adult education and at Sheffield Polytechnic. His main interests are in social philosophy and issues concerning black and Third World people. Currently he works for Sheffield Local Education Authority.

Beverley Bryan has been teaching in South London for eighteen years. She has taught across the primary, secondary, and further education sectors. She has been teaching in further education since 1978 and is at present Head of English and Communication at Brixton College.

Crispin Jones is a Lecturer in Comparative Education and a member of the Centre for Multicultural Education in the Institute of Education, London University. He previously taught English in secondary schools and also worked in the Centre for Urban Educational Studies.

Rosalind Street-Porter is a Principal Lecturer in education at Thames Polytechnic, where she is the Course Director for the primary PGCE. Prior to that she taught in primary schools and worked in the race and education field as curriculum developer, researcher, and adviser.

ACKNOWLEDGEMENTS

I would like to thank Nick Lewis, production editor of Interlink, for permission to republish part of an article which appeared in the June 1988 edition of that journal. It appears here as the appendix to chapter 1.

Once again, special thanks to Catherine Tyler for excellent secretarial support.

Mike Cole
Brighton Polytechnic

The authors would like to thank the following for permission to use copyright material:

The publishers of Interlink, no. 8, June 1988 for permission to repeat extracts from A Socialist Education Policy, written by the Socialist Teachers' Alliance and Caroline Benn; the NFER and Nelson for permission to use 'The Hidden Messages of Schoolbooks' which appeared in The Journal of Moral Education 15, no 1; and Free Association Books for permission to use material from Marilyn Frankenstein's Relearning Mathematics.

Chapter One

CLASS, GENDER AND 'RACE': FROM THEORY TO PRACTICE

Mike Cole

INTRODUCTION

Those who believe that a primary aim of education should be the promotion of equality are often frustrated by the lack of <u>practical</u> guidelines. Such people include student teachers, teachers, headteachers, and other workers in nurseries, playgroups, and schools, lecturers in further and higher education, advisers and administrators in education authorities and social services departments, as well as youth and community workers. Vocational courses which deal with 'equality' often consider it mainly at a <u>theoretical</u> level.

This is the case, for example, with the bachelor of education (BEd) degree in Britain, which, being an <u>honours</u> degree, inevitably has a <u>theoretical</u> content within its 'educational' component. This is also true of the post-graduate Certificate in Education (PGCE), a one-year course for students who (unlike BEd students) already have a first degree. As far as education for the under fives is concerned, courses leading to nursery nurse or playgroup qualifications are less likely to have this theoretical input. This may in part be based on the myth, highlighted by Jane Lane in chapter 5 of this volume, that caring for and educating the very young is easy - that it is a natural process and that young children are uninfluenced by societal forces and that therefore workers in nurseries and playgroups need no theoretical awareness.

Where theoretical input into the sort of vocational qualifications described above exists, it often encompasses a course or courses which deal(s) with the issue of equality by considering the fundamental concepts of social class, gender, and 'race'. (1) The aim of this book is <u>not</u> to deal with these central forms of inequality primarily at a <u>theoretical</u> level (2) but rather to meet the need for some guidelines for good <u>practice</u>. The need for such guidelines is urgent in the sense that there is no book which deals with all three identities over the wide spectrum that this volume attempts (3) and whose focus is on the practitioner. It is also crucial in the light of

1

the ongoing Thatcherite revolution in education. The book is aimed at all those concerned with education who believe in and advocate equality; at those who, in Kenneth Baker's words, 'simply refuse to believe that the pursuit of egalitarianism is over'. (4) No blueprint is of course possible. However, as Muriel Robinson argues in chapter 7, concrete examples may help the reader to take on the principles that all the contributors to this book believe in. A large part of promoting equality will entail convincing others and, as Pauline Lyseight-Jones reminds us in chapter 3, the crucial area to be aware of is that of 'process'. Individuals begin the process of change at different starting points. They may need time to digest philosophy and information but they need more than the language of awareness. They must also be assisted to develop practical ways of demonstrating awareness. It is hoped that this book will be of use to all those working in education as well as in the narrower context of teacher education, where it might complement, but certainly not replace, the essential theoretical component. In the last chapter Crispin Jones and Rosalind Street-Porter put the case for what they describe as an interactive approach to theory and practice in teacher education, which stresses the need for these two aspects to intermesh constantly, and go on to describe attempts to achieve this in the introductory unit of a primary PGCE course at Thames Polytechnic.

CLASS

For most of this century the only inequality which received serious attention was that stemming from social class. In traditional sociology of education, the central concern was with accounting for the selection and allocation of social classes to their future roles in British society. Its underlying assumption was a broad acceptance of, and commitment to, the values of capitalist society. Social-class differentials in educational achievement were attributed to an unequal distribution of resources rather than to structural inequalities in the system. (5) Hence its assumptions were that dysfunctional elements in the system could be planned away and working-class pupils and students could succeed given the right set of circumstances and a certain amount of affirmative action - 'comprehensivization', extra money for inner city schools, mixed ability teaching, and so on.

A serious challenge to this reformist solution was made in the mid 1970s by Bowles and Gintis (6) and others. As Michael Apple has pointed out, although Bowles and Gintis did not start left criticisms of schooling, their achievement was to focus attention directly, in a structural fashion, on the capitalist economy per se. 'In so doing, they provided a more coherent lens with which to view the schooling process'. (7) The failure of working-class pupils and students was not due to dysfunctional elements in the social structure, to aberrations in the system; rather working-class failure is endemic to schooling in capitalist countries. Schooling's very raison d'être is the reproduction of class inequality. Capitalism needs a vast number of workers and few capitalists and managers, and schooling is functional to this requirement. Schooling is geared to the needs of capitalism, argue Bowles and Gintis, by way of a structural correspondence between schools and the capitalist economy. As they put it:

> The educational system helps integrate youth into the economic system, we believe, through a structural correspondence between its social relations and those of production. The structure of social relations in education not only inures the student to the discipline of the work place, but develops the types of personal demeanor, modes of self-presentation, self-image, and social-class identifications which are the crucial ingredients of job adequacy. Specifically, the social relationships of education – the relationships between administrators and teachers, teachers and students, students and students, and students and their work - replicate the hierarchical division of labor. Hierarchical relations are reflected in the vertical authority lines from administrators to teachers to students. Alienated labor is reflected in the student's lack of control over his or her education, the alienation of the student from the curriculum content, and the motivation of school work through a system of grades and other external rewards rather than the student's integration with either the process (learning) or the outcome (knowledge) of the educational 'production process'. Fragmentation in work is reflected in the institutionalized and often destructive competition among students through continual and ostensibly meritocratic ranking and evaluation. By attuning young people to a set of social relationships similar to those of the work place, schooling attempts to gear the development of personal needs to its requirements. (8)

To the Bowles and Gintis of 1976, the only solution to the emancipation of working-class potential was the establishment of a socialist society. (9) Leaving aside the complex arguments over whether this is possible and if so how it can be achieved and what form it should take, (10) socialism, in the opinion of the contributors to this volume, is a fundamental prerequisite for an egalitarian society. This book does not attempt to argue why this is the case (11) nor does it discuss ways of achieving such a society. Its aims are more modest: namely to inform in a practical way current practice here and now in the present circumstances. Barry Troyna has argued, following the arguments of McFadden, Weiner, and Yates on feminism, that the relationship between conceptions of 'equality' and 'equality of opportunity' should not be seen as incompatible but

3

as points on a continuum designated in terms of the rate and extent
of change. There is a need for short-term goals which are based on
what Weiner labels 'egalitarian' principles even if such goals can
achieve no more than to create easier access to an inadequate
system. At the other end of the continuum are more long-term goals
which seek to transform or abandon systems. (12) Although Troyna is
specifically attempting to relate feminist arguments to issues to do
with racism in education, I believe the arguments are equally
applicable to good practice by egalitarians with respect to gender,
'race', and social class.

Clearly, this book is open to allegations of reformism. However,
for those who believe in longer-term structural change, there is
nevertheless a role now for teachers to play as teachers in
mitigating inequalities, as the contributors to this volume bear
witness. For teachers to do nothing but wait for fundamental change
represents ultra-left idealism. There is work to be done now. This is
something that Bowles and Gintis were well aware of. As they put
it:

> Socialist educators should take seriously the need to combine a
> long-range vision with winning victories here and now. In the
> long march through the institutions, reforms must be sought
> which satisfy the immediate needs of students, teachers and
> parents. (13)

Is this viable however, given the ramifications of Bowles and Gintis's
arguments about the structural correspondence between the social
relations of the educational system and those of production ('the
correspondence principle')? It is a commonplace criticism of the
principle that it represents economic determinism where the
economic base (the capitalist economy) determines in a simplistic
way what happens at the superstructural levels of society - in our
case the education system. (14) Critics have argued that such an
analysis implies uncontested domination in which pupils/students
submit placidly to their socialization into compliant workers, and
teachers and other workers are merely servants of the state,
facilitating this socialization. Clearly this is not the case. (15) In
fact, Bowles and Gintis have recently argued that they have never
remotely entertained such a notion:

> If the capitalist division of labor were itself a system of
> uncontested domination, then the correspondence principle
> would, by default, imply the same of the educational system.
> But we have not treated capitalism in this manner ... . Our ...
> framework (stressed) that the organization of production was,
> and is, the product not of class domination, but rather of class
> struggle. (16)

In Schooling in Capitalist America they argued that the

correspondence principle asserts a long-run accommodation of educational structure to the economic division of labour and that in the shorter term the school system reveals not a smooth adjustment of educational structure to the economy 'but rather a jarring and conflict-ridden course of struggle and accommodation'. (17) It is in the context of this struggle and accommodation that egalitarians can be effective. In the course of the uneven development of capitalism, it may be that at times racism and/or sexism may be functional to capital. At other times it/they may be quite dysfunctional. Consequently comprehensivization or antiracism or antisexism may be more easily won at some times than at others. Once won, such achievements become more difficult to eradicate - though of course, by no means impossible - as we can see by the Conservative abolition of the Inner London Education Authority (ILEA), for example.

GENDER

In chapter 2 Chris Gaine points out that in terms of current education policy, gender gets less attention than 'race' and 'class'. While we do have an Equal Opportunities Commission and while the Sex Discrimination Act did mention education, and its clauses have enabled the removal of explicit subject barriers for girls and boys, the silence from the Department of Education and Science (DES) has been most noticeable. Moreover, gender is neither covered by many local education authority (LEA) policies, nor explicitly an interest of the Council for National Academic Awards (CNAA) - nor is it on the checklist of visiting Her Majesty's Inspectors (HMIs). Finally, it has never been the subject of a national committee of enquiry. Notwithstanding this alarming state of affairs, the relationship between gender and education has been well documented by a large number of feminist researchers, with suggestions made by many for practical guidelines for equality. As AnnMarie Wolpe has argued, much work on girls and education has focused on the experiential - that is to say, it has been largely confined to girls' reactions to certain aspects of boys' and teachers' behaviour, particularly in the classroom and with respect to girls' oppression and the detrimental effect of boys' and teachers' behaviour on girls' progress. This approach has received popular acceptance because of its ability to raise practitioners' consciousness about the effects that their behaviour may have in the classroom. Further it highlights aspects of behaviour which appear to be amenable to alteration. Following Davies, Wolpe notes that this has led to 'do-able' tactics directed against sexist practices that can be immediately adopted in the schools. (18) Understandably, in this book, whose subtitle is 'Some Guidelines for Good Practice', it is this approach which the contributors have tended to adopt. However the importance of Wolpe's intervention is that she goes on to argue that we must not

5

lose sight of the structural conditions in education - in particular the relationship of schooling to the capitalist economy, the demands of the labour market, and the crucial intervening variables of class and 'race' both inside and outside the education system. 'Do-able' tactics and longer-term structural constraints and possibilities closely mirror the aforementioned continuum between short-term goals (based on 'egalitarian' principles) and longer-term transformative ones. As Wolpe puts it:

> Whilst (do-able) strategies have proved extremely useful, particularly in terms of heightening educators' awareness of sexism, it would be wrong to think that they have or can alter drastically the education system to the benefit of girls ... . It is possible to make a start within the schooling system in order to improve the life chances of girls and boys alike. There is an urgent need for the creation of an environment in which the essential aims of a true education may be effected for girls and boys alike. This, however, requires rethinking of all aspects of the curriculum, modes of teaching, the control of pupils, and a revitalization of all resources, in which particular attention is paid to the teachers who for too long have been undervalued and who are are often unable to work creatively because of the difficult and often fraught situation in which they find themselves. Such a programme suggests a complete overhaul of the education system in concrete terms and goes well beyond the call made by Gintis and Bowles for a reformulation of the philosophy of education. As they point out the education system is just one part of a social formation all of which requires change if socialist principles are to be realized for all irrespective of gender or ethnic differences. (19)

'RACE'

It would not be an exaggeration to claim that 'race' and education is the current central concern with respect to the three forms of inequality under discussion. This is the case both in terms of educational research and 'academic' and practitioner writing, in terms of LEA policy formation, and crucially in terms of educational practice.

As I have argued elsewhere, (20) we can broadly conceive of three main approaches to 'race' and education: monocultural education, multicultural education, and antiracist education. (This categorization closely resembles Robin Richardson's conforming, reforming, and transforming perspectives discussed in chapter 4.) The first is probably still the most common form of 'education' in Britain and is to do with propagating the values of the British middle class and urging black people to regard themselves as socially and culturally British. (21) It is the traditional British approach to education. Multicultural education, on the other hand, is about cultural diversity in the classroom, about learning about other people's cultures and ways of life with a view to increasing tolerance and respect among all pupils/students and enhancing the self-image of black pupils/students. This approach has a major flaw. While no one could object to members of specific cultural groups talking about aspects of their culture which they wish to share with others, the multicultural approach tends to be dominated by the white middle class. As such it is clearly distinguishable from antiracist education which maintains that dangerous assumptions have been made about the ability of white middle-class teachers and teacher educators to teach about other cultures or 'do good' to (young) blacks. As Barry Troyna puts it, whereas

> the multicultural education model, which continues to draw its rationale, inspiration and support from white middle-class, professional understandings of how the education system might best respond to the 'needs' and 'interests' of black students and their parents ... the antiracist approach both informs and reflects the struggle against racism which the members of the black community are engaged in. (22)

And as Beverley Bryan argues in chapter 11, the history of this struggle is marked by campaigns by black parents, teachers, and students to improve the delivery of education to the black community - the bussing protests of the late 1960s against black children being farmed out to white schools, the 1970s campaigns against the wholesale misplacement of black children in schools for the educationally subnormal (ESN schools) and disruptive units ('sin bins'), the pressure groups to improve examination results, and the development over several decades of strong supplementary schools.

An antiracist approach starts from the premise that the society is institutionally racist - that there exists a complex 'race'/sex class hierarchy located within an exploitative white power structure and that part of the role of education in all schools is to attempt to dismantle that structure both through the hidden curriculum and the actual curriculum. With both monocultural and multicultural approaches, it is likely that economic-, political-, and gender-based relations of domination are ignored, possibly also along with racism itself. Antiracists insist that these issues be central and that it is up to the black and other minority communities to define and prioritize their current and future needs with respect to combating racism. This will clearly entail a fair share of resources in educational establishments where there are black and other minority community pupils/students and a major recruitment drive for teachers and other workers from those communities to work in all state educational institutions. It is crucial too that such teachers are not marginalized. As Jackie Granados Johnson and her co-authors point out in chapter 6, even when black teachers are recruited 'they are often peripheral, or the ESL teacher working outside the classroom, or the mother-tongue teacher working as a part-timer in a hut in the playground and, as a consequence, underpaid'.

It is crucial that antiracist initiatives be taken in full consultation with and with the support of the white working-class community. The tragedy of Burnage High School, where an Asian boy was stabbed to death, has reinforced the idea that antiracism cannot be forced on people; rather it must be linked with broader issues of class and gender. (23) This is no easy task. The antiracist struggle is inextricably linked with the class struggle and with the struggle for sex equality. However, the history of white working-class support for antiracism has been contradictory. We need to draw on what Richard Hatcher, in a good analysis marred by its marginalization of gender, has called the minority tradition of class-wide solidarity. As he puts it:

> In Britain, the Anti-Nazi League and Rock Against Racism represented a massive popular movement against racism in the late 1970s, and the 1985 miners' strike demonstrated the mutual solidarity of the black communities and the bastions of the traditional white working class, symbolized by the NUM's support at the 1985 Labour Party conference for the right of black people to organize within the Labour Party.
>
> In other words, the white working class contains two contradictory responses to 'race'. For specific historical reasons the antiracist response has been a minority one, but nevertheless it represents a real current within working class politics and culture, including that of its youth. Its existence today is of crucial importance for antiracist education, for two reasons. First, because it provides the potential basis for alliances with wider forces outside education to press for antiracist reforms within education. Secondly, because it provides the potential basis within the culture of white youth in schools for antiracist teaching. (24)

As with class and gender, both short- and long-term strategies are required. We must rid the classroom and the school of subtle and not so subtle forms of racism while at the same time not losing sight of the structural dimensions of racial inequality in the institutions of the wider society.

EDUCATION FOR EQUALITY - UNDER THATCHER?

All contributors to this volume are, of course, aware of the constraints of Thatcherism in promoting equality in education.

Issues of class, gender, and 'race' in Britain today could not conceivably be adequately addressed without reference to Thatcherism. Since 1979 we have witnessed unprecedented attacks on the working class in general, on black people, female and male, on women, black and white, and on gays and lesbians. The project of the New Right has blatantly and unashamedly been to strengthen international and (to a lesser extent) national capitalism at the expense of working people. It has also been to enhance and increase the institutionalization of racism in this country and to force women as a whole back into the home and into part-time wage labour - partly to compensate for cutbacks in state welfare provision and partly because part-time, low-paid, female labour power meets the current requirements of capital. The ideological justification for this is the Thatcherite adherence to Victorian patriarchal values. Integral to all these endeavours of the Thatcher years is the undermining of the Welfare State. Bearing this in mind, it is nevertheless possible to identify three broad phases of Thatcherism corresponding roughly to the three terms of office. The first was characterized by appeals to all families (25) to 'tighten their belts' and prepare for individual sacrifice, coupled with the beginnings of that sacrifice for the working class and for the steadily increasing army of the unemployed. The beginnings of the attacks on trade union power came in this first term. The second phase was mainly about privatization and so-called 'popular capitalism', increasing repression of black people in the inner cities, and the birth of the Nationality Act designed to restrict black immigration further and the shackling of the unions by brute force and by legislation. The third phase which, at the time of writing, is just beginning, represents a frontal assault on the Welfare State itself. This phase, if allowed to take place, will drastically affect the most vulnerable groups in society in a most obvious and direct way. As I have said, the whole of the Thatcher years has seen an erosion of welfare policies; this of course has led to a growing gulf between poverty and prosperity. (26)

Its successes have made the government feel confident enough in the second half of the decade to reveal more of its true face. The 1986 Social Security Act will particularly affect married working-class women who, because they live longer than men, will suffer curtailment of rights to inherit their spouses' pension as well as cuts in their own entitlement. Basic state pensions will continue to fall behind living standards; severance of the link with wage rather than price indices has already produced a 16 per cent real cut since 1979. Recently the government has been sounding out ideas for an increasingly privatized health service. It is preparing for a deregul-ated private rented sector and for the Poll tax which will particularly hit those in overcrowded accommodation - the black and white inhabitants of the inner cities - while the very rich will gain, some saving several thousand pounds per annum. At the same time, the institutions of the Welfare State continue to be inadequately funded; increasingly hospitals and schools are becoming dependent on raffles, sponsored walks, runs and swims, and telethons.

With particular reference to this volume, the 1986 Education Act and the 1988 Education Reform Act represent the greatest changes in education in this country since 1944. The government is creating a system which will combine the worst features of central control with the inequalities of a market system.

Selection will be increased, and disparity of status, quality, and resources between schools will grow. (27) Many see the proposals as the beginning of the privatization of the education system. The immediate aim is less power and control over resources and decisions by local education authorities (LEAs) and less legitimacy for their activities and initiatives. (28) National testing at the ages of 7, 11, 13, and 15 with possible published results, financial delegation to schools, national control of inservice training (GRIST), and the fact that schools may charge for 'extra-curricular' 'extras' will all contribute to the undermining of LEAs. In addition, since the 1986 Act, school appointments have been made by governing bodies rather than LEAs which themselves have fewer LEA representatives. The relaxation of admissions lists to popular schools will also mean that LEAs cannot regulate school size and maintain quality in less popular schools. The ultimate attack on LEA power and control relates to the fact that, under the 1988 Act, schools may opt out of LEA control and get funding direct from the Department of Education and Science (DES). Such schools could raise their standards at the expense of other schools through selection and then gain extra resources by charging fees. Central control will be further facilitated by a new national curriculum. In addition, new City Technology Colleges directly funded by the DES and outside the control of LEAs will cater for a new inner city elite. At the same time the incorporation of higher education (April 1989) is likely to make 'business' more of a controlling force in polytechnics and other colleges.

The net effect of the changes will mean few, if any, improvements in the educational system and almost certainly a worsening of provision for working-class pupils/students in general and for black and female pupils/students and for those with disabilities and learning difficulties in particular. Less LEA influence will mean less attention to equality and equal opportunities with regard to class, gender, and 'race' both in terms of staff appointments and curriculum. Consequently teachers will be under less pressure to consider these issues. In addition the national curriculum and testing will give them less time to take these issues seriously, since its emphasis is subject based, 'fact' based, and competitive. (29) It is highly likely that teachers will feel pressurized to coach for tests as in the days of the old '11 plus', thus leaving little time for education in its wider sense; more schooling, less education. In addition government directives against teaching about controversial issues will preclude for example antiwar, trade union, feminist, and black perspectives on history and current realities just as clause 28 curtails gay and lesbian rights and freedom of expression. There will also be less pressure for school <u>policies</u> for equality and equal opportunity (see the chapters by Chris Gaine and Pauline Lyseight-Jones in this volume) since there will be less or no possibilities of LEA support and, under the present government, no central government encouragement. Finally, national control of in-service training and the national curriculum will mean fewer guidelines and projects incorporating concerns for equality.

The national curriculum is an attempt to transmit Conservative values throughout the system. At the same time, the public schools (i.e. private, fee-paying schools), their populations swollen over recent years, will continue to enjoy their privileges. (30)

As Rehana Minhas has reminded us, it is no secret that the national curriculum and other proposed educational changes have been the creation of an all-white, middle-class, extreme-right-wing group known as the Hillgate Group, prominent members of which are Roger Scruton and Baroness Cox. (31) It is hardly surprising, therefore, given the political philosophies of such people, that the 1988 Act contains no reference to antiracism or antisexism. There is no acknowledgement either in the Act or the Consultation Document on the National Curriculum 5-16 (1987) (32) of the Swann Report (1985) (33) or the DES-funded Eggleston Report, (34) let alone a recognition of racism (35) or sexism as issues to be considered in education, nor an understanding of the way in which class inequalities in general are reproduced through schooling. Again, this is to be expected given the class allegiances and consequent self-interests of those concerned.

As the Socialist Teachers' Alliance and Caroline Benn (36) explain, to service the new system Conservatives want a different kind of teaching force. Teacher unions are under attack; national negotiating rights have been taken away; and headteachers have been given the responsibility and power to define teachers' conditions of service. Managerial assessment of teachers will soon be in force. 'In short, teachers will be the tightly-disciplined agents of delivery of the Conservative curriculum'. (37) Moreover, cuts and privatization have threatened and continue to threaten the jobs of non-teaching staff. These workers, mostly women, who clean the schools and serve the dinners, face either the loss of their jobs or cuts in wages as local councils are forced by law to put their services out to tender. (38)

This is a pretty depressing scenario. However, this is not to say that Thatcherism has gone unresisted nor that it should be seen as a series of assaults unpunctuated by the manifest Tory failures – continuing resistance of trade unionism despite Thatcher 'reforms', (39) continuing failure to reduce unit wage costs sufficiently to achieve a competitive profit rate for the UK economy, the abandonment of monetarism, and the monopolistic nature of the privatization process. (40) There is in addition the Tories' mammoth headaches over, for example, the contradictions between inflation fighting and tax cutting, economy boosting (via supply) and the management of the balance of payments, and free marketing and controlling the value of the pound. Moreover, there is a public awareness of the inequalities of British society and public opinion continues to support the Welfare State. (41) There has also been major black (and white) resistance in the inner cities (e.g. the uprisings of the 1980s) and a continuing women's movement (e.g. Greenham Common and the campaign against the Corrie Bill on abortion).

One particularly important development of modern times is the way in which socialists are increasingly forced to take on issues of gender and 'race' as well as class.

With particular respect to education, as the contributors of this volume demonstrate, there is commitment to resist government policies despite the aforementioned setback of teachers' negotiating rights and conditions of service. This commitment needs the support of local education authorities. However even those with progressive education policies are limited in what they can achieve, because of economic and ideological factors outside their control and because of the increasing curtailment of their powers by government. Thus, in this respect, the question of government is decisive. (42) The Socialist Teachers' Alliance, together with Caroline Benn, have recently suggested both ways to defend education under Thatcher and a draft outline for an education policy under a future socialist government. (43) The latter is reproduced in the appendix.

Whatever is going on in the wider society, however, teachers and other workers in the education system will continue to strive for education for equality. Thus the issues raised in this volume are current but do not die with the demise of either the Thatcher government or of the present modes of education being pushed through. Thus the book is written with Thatcherism in mind but has relevance beyond Thatcherism.

FROM THEORY TO PRACTICE

What then is the contribution of this book to education for equality?

In chapter 2 Chris Gaine suggests ways of getting equal opportunities and keeping them. This is followed up by Pauline Lyseight-Jones in chapter 3 with more detailed strategic advice on making fundamental changes in educational institutions. Robin Richardson in chapter 4 focuses his attention on the racism (and sexism) inherent in teaching materials and learning resources. He discusses the wider question of bias in teaching generally and how teachers should handle controversial issues. He also considers texts currently being published in Britain and provides a draft checklist of non-racist teaching materials. In addition Richardson notes the customary procedure for producing teaching materials and considers what might and should be done to pressurize publishers to change their ways.

The rest of the book is concerned with specific suggestions for good practice at various levels of the education system and in various curricular areas. Jane Lane in Chapter 5 provides an account of the current national situation vis à vis under-fives' provision and suggests detailed guidelines on how all workers involved - not just teachers - might work towards more egalitarian practice. This is followed up by similar analyses, but applicable specifically to the infant years (Jackie Grandos Johnson et al. in chapter 6) and the junior years (Muriel Robinson in chapter 7). Europe Singh in chapter 8 looks at the myth of the neutrality of mathematics and science both in terms of content and pedagogy and then suggests an alternative approach which can both sharpen students' perceptions and which exemplifies good practice with respect to education for equality. Doug Holly, in chapter 9, suggests that the 1988 Education Reform Act's attempt to trivialize and traditionalize the humanities curriculum should be circumvented by, for example, stressing the history of the ordinary people, white and black, whose children are the students of state comprehensive schools. Ahmed Gurnah, in chapter 10, argues for the need for a new discipline - multilingual studies which will outline the essential mutuality of humankind. The last two chapters deal specifically with further education (Beverley Bryan, chapter 11) and higher education (Crispin Jones and Rosalind Street-Porter, chapter 12) with Bryan undertaking a critical appraisal of CPVE and Access courses, and Jones and Street-Porter examining the context of teacher education, the possibilities for change, and the aforementioned need to integrate theory and practice. All contributors are united in their determination not to have equality taken off the agenda and in the belief that education can be liberating. Education is a meaningless process unless it is concerned with the struggle against all forms of tyranny whether based on ignorance, oppression, inequality, or exploitation. (44) If this book goes some way towards enabling practitioners to engage more effectively with that struggle whatever the structural constraints then it will have achieved its aim.

ACKNOWLEDGEMENTS

I would like to thank Clive Griggs, Ahmed Gurnah, Tom Hickey, Jane Lane, Pauline Lyseight-Jones, and Robin Richardson for their extremely helpful comments on earlier drafts of this chapter. I have benefited greatly from their suggestions. Responsibility for inadequacies in the final version, of course, remains mine.

13

Mike Cole

APPENDIX A
SOCIALIST EDUCATION POLICY

Defence of education

The most favourable context for developing support for socialist education policies is action in defence of the real and immediate concerns of parents, teachers, school students, and the community. These concerns include the following:

- To resist the effects of cuts in spending, ranging from lack of books to worsening pupil-teacher ratios to school closures.
- To defend the school meals, cleaning, and caretaking services against cuts in wages, provisions, conditions, and jobs.
- To defend equal opportunities policies and practices against Tory attacks on them and from retreats by LEAs.
- To defend unstreamed teaching against pressure to increase streaming, at primary as well as secondary levels.
- To defend a broad curriculum, not dictated by vocationalism, by narrow and rigid forms of assessment or by Tory values of nation and 'family'.
- To defend teachers victimized because they do not conform to these new models of education - e.g. as a result of clause 28 of the Local Government Bill, or of the clause in the 1985 Education Act outlawing 'political education'.
- To campaign against any school preparing to opt out.
- To minimize the negative effects of open enrolment, by calling for, among other things, extra resources for schools facing falls in roll as a result of that policy.

The aims of education

We believe that the existing political and economic arrangements of society are such as to reinforce inequalities, to stifle creative potential, and to develop the personality in competitive ways. We believe that the school, even after much reforming effort, still reflects this wider system. Access to advanced education is still disproportionately denied to girls, and to black and working-class students. The content, and the hidden curriculum, of education leaves the majority of students with a deep sense of the unimportance of their own lives and with no conviction that knowledge can, in any broad, social, non-vocational sense, be really useful.

We believe that education, in and out of school, should concern:

- The development of people's creative potential.
- The development of students' understanding of the natural world, of the society in which they live, and of the work

14

processes of that society.
- The development of the capacity to work with others in controlling society's collective life.

Organization

We should stand for a social programme which guarantees employment and standards of housing, welfare, and health provision that would lay the foundation for meaningful access to education. We call for support for a wide range of measures to oppose inequalities, to raise the level of achievement of students, and to create an education that can promote the confidence and understanding to participate in the democratic control of society. These measures should include:

- Introducing a new Pre-School System for young children that combines the learning function of nursery classes (DES based, and disproportionately used by the middle class) with the caring function of day centres (DHSS funded, heavily used by working-class parents). Integrating care and education throughout, the service should be available from the early months of life - for those parents who want it. With flexible hours and varied venues, including care centres, schools, playgroups, and child minders. Local authorities should be empowered to organize, set standards, help fund, equip, and train for the service - using the skills of local parents wherever possible.
- Resourcing the school system so as to increase the educational opportunities available to working-class students; greatly reduced class size, staffing levels adequate to provide a wide range of teaching strategies, with support for special needs, ESL, curriculum development and implementation.
- Transforming the system of assessment, so that exams no longer serve as 'cut-off' points which restrict access to employment and further education. At any time in their post-14 educational career, students should be able to accumulate credits for particular courses, which would build up to certificated qualification.
- Creating a single unified system of fully comprehensive schools under local democratic control, without private or selective enclaves.
- Integrating the education of adults and school students. All workers should have the right to educational sabbaticals, and schools, like other educational institutions, should have the resources to provide for them.

Curriculum

Organizational change is not enough. There must also be changes to the curriculum to make it relevant to the experience of the majority of school students, capable of giving an accurate picture of social reality, and of engaging their interest:

- Wherever appropriate, learning should be activity based and organized around student enquiry. The community should be used as an educational resource, and as material for critical investigation.
- The curriculum should encompass areas of knowledge such as philosophy, psychology, economics, sociology, that are essential to understanding modern society, that the Tories will not tolerate, or will accept only in diluted form.
- The curriculum should be attentive to the real cultures of the people who live in Britain. It should not transmit the versions of the national culture promoted by the dominant class in society. The culture which students bring to the school - including community languages - with them should be neither disregarded or patronized, but should be at the centre of many aspects of the curriculum. At the same time, schools should aim to develop in all students the conceptual and linguistic advantages that the dominant group has long enjoyed.
- Schools should consciously organize to develop an internationalist, not an anglocentric, curriculum, and to discourage the racism, sexism, and heterosexism which affect many students.
- All students should study science and technology, both in their technical aspects, and in terms of their social and ecological effects. Likewise, both the techniques employed in the world of work and the social relations and social consequences of work should be studied.

This would raise the levels of achievement of the majority of the school population and create the basis for a different attitude to learning. Whereas its basic outline would be the outcome of a national process of decision-making, every encouragement would be given to local initiatives to devise curricula and teaching methods that take up the general themes. We need more experimentation, not less.

Democracy

Schools should be centres of initiative, responsive to the communities in which they are placed. Democracy should be fundamental to their ethos and their functioning. We need measures to increase democracy and collective participation in the work of

16

the school and in the planning of education policy:

-   Democracy among teaching staff, with curriculum and associated decisions made through collective discussion not management dictation.
-   Meetings of all who work in a school to discuss matters of common interest and to break down professional barriers.
-   The promotion of trade unionism, through opposition to privatization, the restoration of teachers' negotiating rights, and the establishment of agreements that safeguard conditions of service.
-   Secondary students would have the right to organize and be consulted, and would be represented on a school's governing body.
-   Local democratic control of schools. Decisions about educational planning, resources, and the broad framework of curriculum policy would be taken by education authorities which had been broadened to include representatives of community groups, parents, trade unions, and so on. School governing bodies, which should comprise LEA, parent, teacher, and student representatives, should oversee the implementation of this policy at school level.

Education after sixteen

Our aim should be progressively to extend the comprehensive principle upwards from 14 to 16, making 'education for the whole of life' the new reality.

To this end, local or regional authorities should be empowered to create learning networks in existing schools, further and higher education colleges, adult centres, and workplaces, integrating them into a universal and unified tertiary provision (ending the split between further and higher education and the division between education and training). Each area should have its own network with all adults given rights to use it. There must be education and training allowances for 16 and 17 year olds, grants for unemployed and retired adults, and paid educational leave (PEL) for those at work - giving priority to those whom the education system has failed to serve in the past.

This means a great expansion of the system and the range of venues where learning will take place, plus a dramatic increase in numbers and types of access courses - so that no one is denied the first step on any academic or vocational route. It means ending most of the YTS and JTS and integrating only high-quality training with academic and vocational education - within a nationally reorganized 'building block' system of courses and credits (on the lines pioneered by the Open University). This will vastly increase the choice and flexibility of learning programmes available to adults - and reform

17

the current 'jungle' of post-sixteen qualifications. In time it will end the hierarchy of learning which segregates post-sixteen provision into three tiers: the academic (highly restricted and over selective), the vocational (narrow courses starved of general educational content), and the low-quality mass schemes providing few recognized qualifications and little real skills training.

Increased funding would be reoriented to support courses, units, programmes and research projects - rather than institutions, while institutions themselves would diversify - to serve a larger range of students. All centres of learning would relate more closely to their own communities, including those with national and international intakes and reputations.

There should be reforms of course content, extending the concept of a broad and balanced education upwards from sixteen to the adult years. The commercialization of learning - with its narrowing courses 'bent' to serve short-term business interests at the expense of many other fields of learning - should be restricted, while other types of learning, including the humanities and general education, should be encouraged to expand. Learning related to the world as a whole - and international exchanges - should also expand.

Throughout, the equality of the educational and training experience should be monitored - to eliminate discrimination on the grounds of wealth, class, age, race, religion, sexual orientation, gender, disability, and level of previous attainment - and programmes of positive support encouraged.

Popular appeal

A socialist policy has great appeal: not just because it will devote more resources to education but because it will also ensure their fairer distribution. It will remove the selective barriers that restrict real choice, giving everyone meaningful rights - and community support - to advance themselves personally through education and training. Lastly, it will see that education develops away from a service giving priority to elites, small privileged groups, and short-term commercial interests - and renews itself as a community force designed to advance both individuals and society as a whole.

Source: This is part of an article which appeared in Interlink No. 8, June 1988.

NOTES AND REFERENCES

1. While the term 'racism' clearly has substance, 'race' as a concept is problematic and for this reason is in inverted commas. Robert Miles argues against the notion that there exist distinct 'races' since: (a) the extent of genetic variation

within any population is usually greater than the average difference between populations; (b) although the frequency of occurrence of different alleles (possible forms taken by genes) does vary from one 'race' to another, any particular genetic combination can be found in almost any 'race'; and (c) owing to interbreeding and large-scale migrations, the distinctions between 'races' identified in terms of polymorphic (dominant gene) frequencies are often blurred (Miles, R. (1982) Racism and Migrant Labour, London: Routledge & Kegan Paul, p. 16). A good example of Miles' last point can be demonstrated in the black population of the United States (Herskovits, M. (1958) The Myth of the Negro Past, Boston: Beacon Press).

　　In his comments on this chapter, Ahmed Gurnah suggested that I should take out the term 'race' altogether and substitute the term 'black people', since the issue is not 'race' but racism and black people's needs. While I agree totally with this viewpoint, I have retained 'race' for conceptual reasons, i.e. to coexist semantically with class and gender.

2. However, the book may be read in conjunction with Cole, M. (ed.) (1989) The Social Contexts of Schooling, London: Falmer Press. This is an introductory analysis of the issues of class, 'race', and gender and of their interconnection with schooling. It is more to do with 'how things are' than with 'guidelines for good practice'. The use of the word 'schooling' in the title reflects the narrow processes which go on in schools. 'Education' in the title of this volume refers to a more all-embracing approach which the contributors believe should be apparent in the education system.

3. I realize, of course, that there are substantial chunks missing - but then no such book can cover everything. The volume should be seen as a beginning rather than a one-off attempt. Readers will recognize omissions and possibilities for further development and hopefully find ways to redress the balance, in the light of changing economic and political circumstances and developments in theory and practice amongst egalitarians.

4. Baker, K., Speech to the Conservative Party Conference 1987.

5. Cole, M. (1988a) 'Correspondence theory in education: impact critique and re-evaluation', in M. Cole (ed.) Bowles and Gintis Revisited: Correspondence and Contradiction in Educational Theory, London: Falmer Press.

6. Bowles, S. and Gintis, H. (1976) Schooling in Capitalist America, London: Routledge & Kegan Paul.

7. Apple, M. (1988a) 'Facing the complexity of power: for a parallelist position in critical educational studies', in M. Cole (ed.), op. cit., p. 112.

8. Bowles, S. and Gintis, H. (1988a) 'Prologue: the correspondence principle', in M. Cole (ed.), ibid., pp. 2-3. This is adapted from Bowles, S. and Gintis, H. (1976) op. cit.

9. The extent to which Bowles and Gintis have changed their

philosophy is insufficiently acknowledged. But see for example the other chapters of Cole, M. (ed.) (1988); in particular, Bowles, S. and Gintis, H. 'Schooling in capitalist America: reply to our critics'.

See also Bowles, S. and Gintis, H. (1986) Democracy and Capitalism: Property, Community, and the Contradictions of Modern Social Thought, London: Routledge; and Cole, M. (1988b) 'From reductionist Marxism and revolutionary socialism to post-liberal democracy and ambiguity: some comments on the changing political philosophy of Bowles and Gintis', The British Journal of Sociology, September.

10. But see, for example, Bowles, S. and Gintis, H. (1988b) 'Schooling in capitalist America: reply to our critics', in M. Cole (ed.) (1988) op. cit., and (1986) Democracy & Capitalism, op. cit., on the one hand; and Sharp, R. (1988) 'Old and new orthodoxies: the seductions of liberalism' and Freeman-Moir, J. et al. (1988) 'Reformism or revolution: liberalism and the metaphysics of democracy', both in Cole, M. (ed.), ibid., on the other, for opposing viewpoints.

11. But see, for example, Foot, P. (1977) Why You Should Be a Socialist, London: Socialist Workers' Party.

12. Troyna, B. (1987) 'A conceptual overview of strategies to combat racial inequality in education: introductory essay', in B. Troyna (ed.) Racial Inequality in Education, London: Tavistock, pp. 6-7.

13. Bowles, S. and Gintis, H. (1976) op. cit., pp. 287-8. In some circumstances (e.g. capitalist economic growth) some reforms are possible, and all socialists work for improvements in working-class conditions. However reforming capitalism, I would argue, can never lead to an egalitarian society. Basic structural changes (the replacement of capitalism with socialism, the liberation of women, and the eradication of racism) are required for such a society.

14. See, for example, Hall, S. (1977) Review of the Course, unit 32 of the Open University course, Schooling and Society (E202), Sarup, M. (1978) Marxism and Education, London: Routledge & Kegan Paul, and Cole, M. (1988c) 'Contradictions in the educational theory of Gintis and Bowles', in M. Cole (ed.) op. cit.

15. See, for example, the works of Michael Apple, Henry Giroux, and Dennis Carlson. Any parent, teacher, and reader of newspapers or viewer of television would also testify to this!

16. Bowles, S. and Gintis, H. (1988b) op. cit., p. 237.

17. Ibid., p. 238. Aware that they may have inadequately stressed the potentially liberating aspects of schooling, they invite others to repair the fault (p. 239). This is something which, as we have seen, has already been done and something which the authors of this volume attempt to do in a practical way.

18. Wolpe, A.M. (1988) '"Experience" as analytical framework: does

it account for girls' education?', in M. Cole (ed.), op. cit., pp. 138–9.

19. Ibid., pp. 139 and 154. This clearly is not feasible nationally under Thatcher (see the appendix for a socialist agenda) though such major overhauls have been attempted by some LEAs.

20. Cole, M. (1986a) 'Multicultural education and the politics of racism in Britain', Multicultural Teaching, autumn; and Cole, M. (1989) 'Monocultural, multicultural and antiracist Education', in M. Cole (ed.) op. cit.

21. Laud, D., (1984) 'The law, order and race relations', Monday Club Policy Paper, no. 1, R.3, October.

22. Troyna, B. (1987) op. cit., p. 7. (This is, of course, a struggle in which some whites are also involved.)

23. Whereas sections of the media have used this incident to devalue antiracism itself, the intention of the McDonald Report (not publicly available at the time of writing) was to criticize the way the policies were implemented in that school, particularly the way in which they were imposed from above without substantial input from black and other ethnic minority communities and the fact that they failed to involve and get the support of the white working-class community. The report was certainly in favour of antiracism as a guiding principle, but as something which should be implemented with intelligence and sensitivity.

24. Hatcher, R. (1987) '"Race" and education: two perspectives for change', in B. Troyna (ed.), op. cit., pp. 187-8. As Tom Hickey has commented, there is a distinction between class responses and socialist responses, which is an important conceptual context within which to understand working-class antiracism as a 'minority response'. Working-class culture and ideology is a refracted reflection of that of the wider society, but it is possible to transcend that consciousness in becoming and developing as a socialist. The important thing is to see how socialist consciousness (and its antiracism) can become working-class consciousness; to see, for example, how and why it is objectively in the interests of the working class as a whole to fight racism. (His comments on a draft of this chapter.)

25. Louis Althusser has spoken of the familial interpellation (Althusser, L. (1971) Lenin and Philosophy and Other Essays, London: New Left Books). What I understand by interpellation is the way we act and respond to ideology as if we were the originators of ideas and values within it. In other words, when the Sun or the Daily Mail speaks of what 'the public' 'wants', 'needs', 'is fed up with', 'has had enough of it', this strikes a chord with all the other organs of ruling-class ideology - the rest of the media, the various apparatuses of the state. Because we are largely trapped with one view of the world - capitalism/patriarchy/racism - it all 'makes sense' to us. This is not logical, but as Stuart Hall once said 'ideologies don't work

21

by logic - they have logics of their own' (Hall, S. (1978) 'Racism and reaction', in BBC/CRE Five Views of Multi-Racial Britain).

The interpellation characteristic of Thatcher rhetoric is familial. Althusser stresses that it is individuals rather than classes or groups which are interpellated or hailed. This accords perfectly with the essence of 'the new conservatism' which, it is argued, must have conditions which allow 'natural instincts' to prevail (Barker, M. (1981) The New Racism, London: Junction Books).

Such conditions must ensure that nothing mediates the individual and her/his natural unit (the family) and the nation/state. There is a need, therefore, to talk directly to the people, above the heads of union leaders, for example. The ideal image of the new conservatism, then, is of a society of private families linked in loyalty and conscience to the nation.

'Interpellating subjects', therefore, points the way to a more sophisticated analysis than one which suggests that ideology represents a unitary world view imposed on the dominated classes. Interpellations are successful because they can eliminate contradictions between ideologies in the ultimate interest of the ruling class. The familial interpellation, I would argue, is a particularly successful interpellation in that it can evoke and join contradictory elements like 'individual' and 'state', 'providing' and 'sacrifice'. It can serve to unite large segments of the working (and other) classes around 'the nation'.

The problem with structural marxism, of which Althusser is one of the leading theorists, is that, in informing us how powerful the constraining structures are, it tends to lead to determinism and defeatism. However, this should not detract from its explanatory power. As I have argued elsewhere, structuralist marxism allows us to identify the constraining structures of capitalist society. Humanist marxism tells us how powerful the human will is (so necessary in breaking through the structures and without which our commitment would be hollow). Structuralist marxism also tells us how powerful the constraining structures are (which re-emphasises the importance of the power of the will in breaking through them). We should neither overemphasize structuralism (which, as I have said, tends to lead to determinism and to defeatism) nor overemphasize humanism (as this can lead to idealism). (A Review of Madan Sarup (1984) Marxism, Structuralism, Education, The Sociological Review, November.)

26. As Peter Taylor-Gooby explains, the main thrust in the attack so far has been against the politically weak. Unemployment benefits have been cut, the majority of the jobless transferred from national insurance to means-tested benefits, entitlement rules made tougher, and the goal of full employment abandoned. Council house spending has dropped by two-thirds, the building programme has collapsed, and official homelessness statistics

increased twofold. At the same time between 1978/9 and 1986/7 the real value of reliefs on private pensions grew by over 50 per cent, on mortgages by 114 per cent, fringe benefit medical insurance by 400 per cent, and real incomes for those in work increased by 16 per cent. (Taylor-Gooby, P. (1987) Opting out of the Welfare State', New Socialist, no. 53, pp. 28-9.)

At the time of writing a Commons' Committee Report is about to be published which reveals that poverty has almost doubled since Mrs Thatcher took office. Nearly one family in five lives on or below the official poverty line. At the same time, the number of benefit claimants has risen from 4.4 to 8.2 million, with another 1 million eligible for but not claiming benefits (Daily Mirror, 11 July 1988).

27. Socialist Teachers' Alliance and Benn, C. (1988) 'A socialist education policy', Interlink, no. 8, p. 36. An extract from this article appears as an appendix to this chapter.

28. Richardson, R. (1988) 'Opposition to reform and the need for transformation: some polemical notes', in Multicultural Teaching 6: no. 2, p. 5. The following analysis is based on Richardson's flow diagram on that page.

29. This statement should not be used to give fuel to the 'more equality means less quality' position. On the contrary the aim should be for equality and excellence. As Michael Stoten, (Director of Education, London Borough of Brent, 1987) has put it:

The fundamental aims of educational progress and improvement must always be the same: to raise standards, attainment and life chances. In other words, to promote excellence .... Without equality excellence can only be partial and the divide between those who have success and those who don't will become greater. Without excellence those who suffer from inequality will not be able to play a full part themselves in combating and redressing discrimination and disadvantage .... All learners are of equal value and have unlimited potential for development ....

This, of course, contrasts with Kenneth Baker's recent statement at the Conservative Party Conference (1987) that: 'Our first national priority must be to educate the young of today for the jobs they'll have tomorrow'.

30. Socialist Teachers' Alliance and Benn. C. (1988) op. cit., p. 36. For a discussion of recent developments in political attitudes and practices with respect to fee-paying education. see Griggs, C. (1988) 'Fee-paying education: the favoured sector' in M. Morris and C. Griggs (eds) Education - The Wasted Years? 1973-1986, London: Falmer Press.

31. Minhas, R. (1988) 'The politics behind the national curriculum' in Multicultural Teaching, 6: no. 2, p. 9.

32. Department of Education and Science (1987) <u>The National Curriculum 5-6, A Consultative Document.</u>
33. Department of Education and Science (1985) <u>Education for All</u>, London: HMSO (Swann Report).
34. Eggleston, J., Dunn. D., and Anjali, M. (1986) <u>Education for Some</u>, London: Trentham Books (Eggleston Report).
35. Crozier, G. and Menter, I. (1988) 'Anti-racism and the national curriculum: the gerbil's tail - initial teacher education', in Multicultural Teaching, 6: no. 2, p. 31.
36. Socialist Teachers' Alliance and Benn. C. (1988) op. cit., p. 36.
37. ibid.
38. ibid.
39. It took the whole might of the state to quell the miners' dispute. Moreover, despite 'the new realism' that dominates the movement (i.e. Thatcherism cannot be defeated by full-blooded socialism) there does appear to be a new mood of anti-Toryism surfacing in response to what I have called the 'frontal assault on the Welfare State itself'. The government policy of attacking one group at a time (which developed in the mid 1970s after the Heath government was defeated by the miners) becomes problematic when privatizing. for example, education or health, precisely because it affects the vast majority of the population; hence, the success of the nurses' action which evidenced an unprecedented anger and fighting potential, in forcing a Tory 'U' turn on pay.
40. The main theoretical justification for privatization is to restore competitive efficiency, but in practice it has tended to replace state monopolies with private monopolies.
41. Jowell, R., Witherspoon, S. and Brook, L. (eds) (1987) <u>British Social Attitudes: the 1987 report</u>, Aldershot: Gower, pp. 15, 35, 60-1.
42. Hatcher, R. (1987) op. cit., p. 198.
43. Such a programme would require major structural changes and a massive shift in resources and could only therefore be attempted by a government genuinely committed to the principles of socialism.
44. Mullard. C. Talk given at Brighton Polytechnic on 29 June 1988.

Chapter Two

ON GETTING EQUAL OPPORTUNITIES POLICIES - AND KEEPING
THEM

Chris Gaine

For most of this century the only inequality which received serious
attention from educational researchers, politicians, and policy
makers was that stemming from social class. (1) Considered in terms
of the attitudes of the time that attention produced significant
results, both in terms of legislative changes and other changes
brought about by LEAs. Thus, in its way, the introduction of the
tripartite system in 1944 was an egalitarian measure, replacing as it
did the pre-war system where most secondary education was
unashamedly available only for those who could pay. Later, greater
sophistication about the way class affects educational success, and
less faith in simple 'IQ' testing at eleven, led to the general shift to
comprehensive schools. Whatever the motives or the broader social
and economic context of those changes, they were certainly very
large-scale changes, and between them produced a very loose
political consensus for perhaps 25 years.

By the mid 1970s social scientists were beginning to find an
audience for yet more subtle analyses of the processes of class in
education when a more visible and (in the short term at least) a
more divisive inequality grabbed educational attention - 'race'.
There followed a prolific period of policy making, different from
class in that it was seldom on a national scale (explainable perhaps
by the issues being in some ways concentrated in some LEAs rather
than others). At a school level developments were analogous to
those for class (though seldom simultaneous with them) - antiracist
school policies in the 1980s are, I am suggesting, comparable to the
growth in the late 1960s of mixed ability teaching, integrated
curricula, and coursework CSEs in secondary schools: the intended
beneficiaries then were working-class pupils, and they were never
initiated by central or local government.

Gender is certainly the poor relation. The Sex Discrimination
Act did mention education, and its clauses have enabled the removal
of explicit subject barriers for girls and boys, but the silence from
the DES on the matter has been almost deafening. LEAs whose
educational stance has led them to produce antisexist policies seem

also to be high on the Thatcher government's hit list.

This varying and largely sequential attention to the three major inequalities is also to be found in teacher education. Few courses in the 1960s and 1970s failed to cover the issue of class, the limited extent of mobility, the suggested effects of home background, the apparently different languages, and the development of comprehensives. 'Race' came later, as it did in schools, and its coverage in colleges and universities is still much more patchy, but the inclusion of the issue in teacher education is stimulated by local authority policies in some colleges and/or CNAA (2) policy in others, and by the recommendations of the Swann Report in all. Gender is neither covered by many LEA policies, nor explicitly an interest of the CNAA, nor is it on the checklist of visiting HMIs. It has never been the subject of a national committee of enquiry.

This short history could be summed up by suggesting that concern about these three central inequalities has been sequential and seldom concurrent in the same institution. Class came first and, the Thomas and Hargreaves Reports notwithstanding, has slipped away from centre stage; 'race' came next and after a few years of changes at policy level is increasingly being successfully portrayed as 'loony-leftism'. Gender, although now pressing for space, is not doing so at a favourable time.

My aim in this chapter is to offer some practical guidelines about egalitarian policies in educational institutions: how one should frame them, what they should contain, and how they might be implemented. Having given the above very brief historical account it may be useful to suggest some key questions which any policy development must consider:

> Is the policy to be on a single issue or is it to aim to counter all three major inequalities?
> What is the power base of those pressing for or hoping to maintain change?
> What is the rationale or motive given for change? Are the policy goals to be 'idealistic' or strategic?
> How do the institutional structures normally work? How autonomous is it? How is legitimacy to be secured?
> What should the scope of the policy be?
> How is the policy to be maintained and continued?
> How is a backlash to be avoided?

What actually lies behind all of these is the deceptively simple question 'Why do institutions resist egalitarian changes?' Answers, depending on one's perspectives, can be drawn from management theory, individual psychology, micro or liberal theories of institutional power and inertia, or macro theories of educational institutions as part of the ideological state apparatus and/or simple reproducers of the labour force.

I have tried to summarize the interplay of these factors in the diagram on page 28, after which each one will be discussed individually.

Is the policy to be on a single issue or aim to counter all three major inequalities?

I have argued elsewhere about this (Gaine 1987: 178-92), but still hesitate to be at all dogmatic. In practice, as I have suggested above, most developments combating inequality have been born separately and at different times. This seems to be true at all levels: antidiscrimination law on 'race' and sex; educational concern about class; LEA policies about 'race'; the development of advisory teams, staff, resources centres, and strategies on 'race' and gender; policies of bodies such as NAB and CNAA; the production of reports; the focus of journals; and (with the possible exception of this one) the content of most relevant books. This would seem to argue that there is some practical imperative towards treating the inequalities separately. In the previous discussion already referred to I argued that this is primarily a psychological imperative, both on the part of those pressing for change (there is a limit to the number of fronts they can fight on) and of those who need to change (there is a limit to the amount of change they can deal with.) It may also be an organizational imperative - institutions usually change by evolution not revolution, the evolution may be rapid and forced by environmental changes, but to be effective and lasting it has to be a change in structure. More apparently revolutionary changes stand some risk of being merely changes in ways of doing things.

It is important to separate this practical sort of argument from a more theoretical one which argues that the inequalities are linked as forms of oppression and that therefore opposition to them ought to be linked. Ultimately, it is said, we should understand and therefore combat more effectively several linked struggles. I prefer to see this as an argument about intentions and directions not day-to-day strategies. My argument is simply that all initiatives should not be considered worthless solely because they are not well theoretically grounded in a perspective which links them to others. Most schools and colleges seem to move in a piecemeal way towards policies on inequality. It would be poor history to condemn these as partial or inadequate; they are stages, and probably necessary ones.

What is the rationale or motive given for change? Is it idealistic or strategic?

It is confusing and unhelpful that policies are often criticized by the left for their apparent rationale, when it is obvious that even if the drafters had had more radical motives (and sometimes they do) they could scarcely say so in official documents. Troyna and Williams

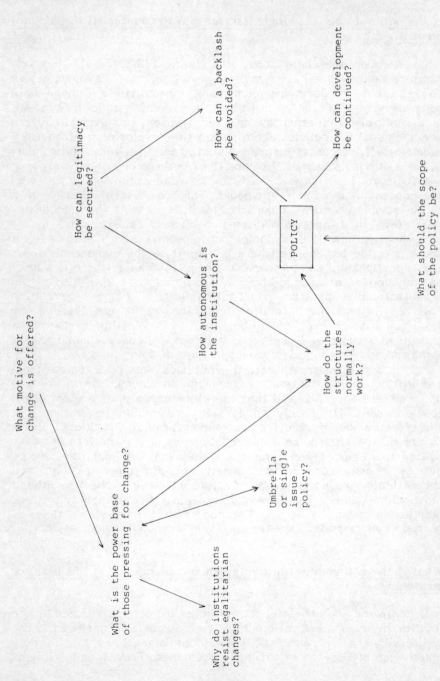

How can legitimacy
be secured?

How can a backlash
be avoided?

How can development
be continued?

What motive for
change is offered?

How autonomous is
the institution?

POLICY

What should the scope
of the policy be?

What is the power base
of those pressing for change?

How do the
structures
normally
work?

Umbrella
or single
issue
policy?

Why do institutions
resist egalitarian
changes?

28

(1986) accurately point to the 'liberal' rationale of all LEA 'race' policies, suggesting that they ignore the argument that racism and sexism may be useful and productively divisive for those already in power, instead couching their persuading arguments in terms of loss, wastage, injustice, and disadvantage which liberal rhetoric is obliged to condemn. The policies would never have been accepted any other way. After all, why should men (or male-run schools and colleges) care about girls and women, and why should white people care what happens to black people? Apart from some appeal to anxiety about social disorder and disaffection on the scale of the 'riots' of the early 1980s, most 'race' policies make an implicit or explicit reference to the values we all apparently share in this so-called liberal democracy.

The question, therefore, for policy drafters is which mast to pin their colours to. Do they espouse socialism? Do they refer to the inherently patriarchial nature of society or the inevitably racist construction of the curriculum, or do they write and argue as if they believe that a just redistribution of existing resources is both possible, concedable, and the limit of their wishes? I have no doubt of the answer in the majority of schools and colleges: distinguish between long-term and probably societal goals and the space for struggle within one's own sphere. That space, in policy terms, consists of using the institution's own professed values against itself, using them as a lever to further change.

If the path in the middle of the road is chosen, however, it has some fundamental implications. The problem of inequality is posited as one of unfair disadvantage, a game of snakes and ladders where the working class, females, and black people have their hands tied behind their backs. The aim is ostensibly to untie everyone's hands so they can climb the ladders; the existence of the ladders and the structure they lean upon is not in question. More radical approaches say the structure scaled by the ladders is a social structure, which has been built to the advantage of those currently at the top of it, and it can be dismantled (or torn down). Beliefs such as 'ability' are merely devices to legitimate the structure. Untying hands will, at best, simply ensure that those who reach the top look and act exactly like those already there; even more apparently radical changes would do no more than provide escalators. A more profound analysis would consider the routes taken by the ladders and the shape or even the existence of the structure.

Policies couched in terms of the 'possible', in terms of current structures, in terms of the problem being access to inequality rather than inequality itself are inevitably self-limiting, but probably necessary. I would argue only that policy drafters recognize this and are clear where they stand in relation to it, not that they seek some kind of total purity in any policy or abandon it. The goal is to develop policies which will come to seem less and less radical because they are promoting change and deepening people's understanding rather than ending up in some ameliorative wilderness. Prevailing definitions have to be pushed and pushed to expose their contradictions, not ignored.

How is legitimacy won? What is the power base of those pressing for or trying to maintain change? How do the institutional structures normally work?

Policies have been initiated by school or college managements, small pressure groups, a large group (like black students) in an institution's make-up, exterior forces (LEA, CNAA), a particular incident, unions, and individuals. Institutions vary so much it would not be very productive to try to suggest a single pathway to change, but there are several, perhaps obvious points which need to be made.

Those pressing for change must try to win legitimacy in terms of the values of the institution. (They may well start out without legitimacy in terms of informal values, whatever is stated officially.) Thus schools and colleges may have some prospectus statement about everyone being treated equally but still accept condescension, implicit barriers, and harassment of women staff and students. While pressing for equality does pose a serious challenge it also takes seriously principles held by those who simply value good education (or at least one version of it), many who call themselves Christians, and many who believe Britain ought to be a just society. Claiming legitimacy in these terms also requires the real opposition to come clean about their version of good education, Christianity, and justice. (3)

Legitimacy can also be derived from documents. Within LEAs which have policies there is an obvious source of authority over an individual school or college, and this can sometimes be effective on comparable LEAs without policies. HMI are (against considerable political pressure) trying to keep progress going, and we may soon see, for instance, reports on all-white schools pointing out the lack of 'multicultural' education. Key phrases from, for instance, Better Schools, are hard to argue with, as are policy statements of the three big teachers' unions and the National Association of Headteachers (NAHT).

If legitimacy is not at first obviously achievable then the 'activists' must be perceived as having some kind of power. It may be that they represent a group large enough to be feared in terms of disaffection at least, or that they have powerful practical or ideological support from outside the institution (a wider policy perhaps, or governors) which limits the autonomy of the institution in resisting change. (Reactionary outside forces can also, of course, limit autonomy.)

An alternative to legitimacy or power is expediency. An institution short of recruits may look to equal opportunities to swell its numbers.

The point is, therefore, that a policy which has any real

implications will not be accepted unless those with the power to reject it are persuaded not to either in terms of values, or because they recognize the power of those proposing it, or because they see some advantage in it.

What should the scope of the policy be?

This is the practical expression of the earlier debate those seeking change will have had about the professed or persuading motive which is to be employed. This question also ought to make us consider the amount of persuasion and debate necessary before pressing for a policy's adoption. Rushing a policy through either democratic, bureaucratic, or authoritarian adoption is a strategy that has been tried and which has failed. One cannot wait for everyone's support, but some is needed, so it may be necessary to build in a period of consciousness-raising. Any policy is helped by having an analysis which is clear to its readers, and this itself can function to clarify key concepts and keep them under discussion. But the problem encountered by many policy drafters is the gap between their own consciousness and that of their colleagues, and it is all too easy in the supportive atmosphere of an action group to lose sight of this. The effect can be that specific disciplinary sanctions for racist or sexist or classist abuse (which are unlikely to be opposed in principle) may be proposed alongside measures about subtle stereotyping in teaching materials. The latter, it seems to me, calls for a greater level of awareness of the issues and is therefore much more likely to be ill-understood and resisted.

This is further complicated by the sense of threat or of accusation felt by many people when asked (or forced) to look at inequalities, despite the fact that most analyses stress that we are all part of networks and structures for which we are not always personally responsible, and that inequitable outcomes are not always the result of someone's conscious discriminatory intention. Thus racism is commonly believed by white people to consist solely of personal racial prejudice, and the processes of cultural, institutional, and structural racism are invisible to those who benefit from them. To continue with this example may be useful, untangling the range of practices and assumptions involved in racism and relating them to policy.

Personal racism is no more than racial prejudice on the part of individuals in the dominant group. It could be conscious and deliberate: 'Get out of here you wog; I don't serve your kind here'; or unconscious and patronising: 'I do admire the natural sense of rhythm of the Africans'. It can also be conscious and 'benign', like not giving someone a jog to protect them from hostility. In the latter two examples it is the consequences which matter, not the intention.

Institutional racism is altogether more subtle. It happens when procedures and practices perhaps date from a time when most of the population were white and Anglo-Saxon, so they operate in such a way as to exclude minorities. For instance, if a school provides all its information about uniform grants in English only, the effect is to keep that information from parents literate in other languages. If a school in Dorset recruits new staff from existing Dorset teachers, their associates, and students from local colleges, black people would not even hear of vacancies let alone get a chance to apply for them. Neither of these are deliberate acts with the intention of disadvantaging a particular group. They are simply the continuation of routine procedures originally devised in different circumstances. Nevertheless, their effect is to disadvantage a particular group.

Cultural racism is something anyone brought up in an ex-colonial society can scarcely avoid, hence many would argue that all white British people are racist. Four hundred years of conquest and rule of other peoples, although now over, leaves a scarcely conscious sense of superiority in many of us. Examples of cultural racism would be the assumption that music has reached its highest forms in Europe, that English is somehow a 'better' language than say, Hindi, that 'great art' means European art, that non-Christian religions are primitive, that 'we' have a more highly developed sense of justice, that other peoples wear 'costumes' while 'we' wear clothes. Cultural racism not only assumes peoples are different, but that 'we' are better than 'them'.

Structural racism exists when it is part of the fabric of a society, when black people are disadvantaged not just in unexamined practices (institutional racism) but in laws and in social structures. Black people in Britain are experiencing structural racism since some laws operate against them in particular (the Nationality Act) or if it is known that odds are stacked against them in some way (e.g. employment) and nothing effective is done to remedy it. Another way of putting this is that structural racism exists when the other three forms permeate the key institutions of the state.

The table on page 34 attempts to continue these distinctions with regard to gender and class, the intention being to focus policy measures carefully. In very general terms institutions can do little about structural factors except be aware of their power over people's lives, and possibly equip students better to deal with them. Institutional factors are in principle more responsive to change, and if identified as such do not, perhaps, make people feel so accused. Cultural factors tend to be much more deeply rooted in people's images of themselves and in their values about education, so tackling them meets with less rationality and more anger. Cultural factors often find their expression in personal racism, sexism, or classism, so confronting them meets with the same anger. However, the policy provisions one makes for dealing with personal behaviour which perpetuates inequality are different from those working against cultural racism.

The table is only intended to provide examples to which others could be added, and they imply a school or college context. Many examples could be duplicated across all three columns.

How is the policy to be maintained and continued?

This has become a sine qua non for 'race' policies in the last few years, it having become conventional wisdom that the first policies like Berkshire's and ILEA's have not delivered what was hoped, despite the years of effort by activists and (sometimes) sincere officials to get them formally accepted.

The question also links closely with others in the above flow diagram, particularly 'what is the power base?' and 'how do the structures normally work?'. A third key consideration is a timetable, a programme with dates attached to realizable targets.

In practical terms this means firstly building the policy implications into processes which are going to happen anyway: curriculum reviews, inspections, evaluations, consultations, job redefinitions. Second, it means extending the existing structure or modifying it so that identifiable people are responsible for implementing and monitoring the policy in specific ways, and answerable for its progress. The policy must be handed over to the institution as its responsibility; if it is seen as 'belonging' to a particular initiator it will be too easily ignored, key people are less likely to feel accountable to it, and it may wither when a particular person leaves. Third, it means giving an institutional voice to a person or preferably a group who care about the policy. On the one hand the policy must become the responsibility of the institution; on the other they cannot always be trusted, so someone must be empowered to watch them.

How is a backlash to be avoided?

In the early 1980s there was a period of optimism amongst many of us working in education and antiracism, fuelled mostly by the adoption of policies in several LEAs. In the late 1980s there is more pessimism, fuelled in turn by a sense of goals being unrealized and the political high ground being captured by someone else. There is also some accumulated experience, mostly to do with antiracism but a good deal from antisexism too.

I am doubtful that the present situation could possibly have been avoided. The language in which educational debate is carried out in the late 1980s is the language of the 'market-place' and of 'individual freedom', dishonest though many of us believe that

33

	"Race"	Gender	Class
PERSONAL (conscious/ unconscious)	insults jokes derogatory stereotypes physical attack	patronising behaviour sexual exploitation options advice fear of effeminacy lower or different expectations	active use of stereotypes lower expectations demeaning language
CULTURAL (often expressed by above)	shared derogatory stereotypes partial/biased depiction in materials Eurocentric science, artistic values ignoring "other" languages	partial/biased depiction in materials (housewives, bikinis) male model of discipline man made language	assumed superiority of Standard English and Received Pronunciation disapproval of particular clothing
INSTITUTIONAL	"Christian" names required on documents non-recognition of qualifications inability to provide for dietary needs word of mouth recruitment information only available in English	segregation in registers & dinner queues structure of staff option structure parents' evenings at young children's bedtime	letters to parents in formal Standard English recruitment routes for staff catchment areas
STRUCTURAL	residential zoning providing information for immigration investigations	male structure of education hierarchy pattern of wider employment media imagery	determination of curriculum power of local business control gatekeeping function opting out clause of 1988 Act catchment areas

language to be. To aid them in purposes which go far beyond education the Thatcher government has assiduously constructed folk devils out of certain LEAs. For those who need to believe it there now exists a demonology of bogey Brent, harpie Haringey, evil ILEA, and of course the ghoul of gay rights. 'Opting out' is justified by the self-evident need of schools to free themselves from these tormenting LEAs; laws are enacted to stop them 'promoting' homosexuality; Thatcher says in a major speech that instead of learning to add up children are learning antiracist maths, 'whatever that may be'. (4) Everyone 'knows' that children have to sing 'Baa Baa Green Sheep' and teachers must not ask for black coffee. (5)

We are now rather more on the defensive and subject to what I shall argue is a nationally orchestrated backlash. This is, in fact, a conspiracy; it is not just bad luck or inadequate public relations. There is not the space here for the series of case studies which would demonstrate how these myths are generated, but no one working in the fields of 'race' or gender inequality doubts that they are manufactured systematically and deliberately. The press have performed their part of the task eagerly, certain newspaper editors being contacted by their friends to turn on the clichés and lies and quarter-truths like a tap. But it has insidiously become part of received wisdom, so that (normally) unhysterical BBC specialists and <u>Guardian</u> readers who are <u>quite</u> above being misled by the tabloids seem to take it for granted that there are 'extremist' councils who do all sorts of odd things. That is why I am not sure it could have been avoided. The opposition, while being by no means monolithic, was certain to get organized sooner or later. It is now not only organized but senses a sympathetic climate for the dormant ideals of systematic inequality to bloom again.

So much for the backlash; how do we avoid it? Part of the answer lies in recognizing it for what it is, and I have suggested it is part of something much larger. Like it or not - and I fully accept many educationalists do not - we have to be good strategists, good politicians. This primarily entails predicting resistance and planning for it, constantly seeking allies, being prepared to deal with the media on our terms, endless patient explanations, advertising success, and not seeing education in isolation. We have to make sure that individuals, individual schools, or even individual LEAs do not become isolated and picked off one by one. It means actually being more respectful of democracy than some of us might have been when we felt we were winning. An absolute insistence on true consultation and debate, whatever the time involved, is part of the process of cementing policies in place.

It may be this which saved Berkshire. Between September 1987 and April 1988 a group of Tories on the County Council planned to do away with the LEA 'race' policy which preceded all the others, which has acted as a model for many, and which was strongly commended by Swann. They were stopped from doing so by a vigorous and unprecedented letter campaign. But people do not write in support of a policy just because they are asked to by its supporters - the campaign to a large extent mobilized support which was already there (not least from black and Asian people: 300 of the letters were written in Asian heritage languages).

The details of how one cements policies in place vary, though they also relate to some of the other considerations I have suggested, especially the policy's power base, its perceived legitimacy, and the motive it provides for change. This latter consideration returns us to the minefield of principles and compromises discussed earlier. Some would argue that the less we aim for, the more modest our demands, the more likely we are to win and to maintain the gains. The trouble is that what we win by this method may be scarcely worth having and fall into the trap of being minor concessions which keep us quiet and change nothing substantial. One alternative (but is it the only one?) is to be clear and explicit about all the ramifications of a policy and risk it being resented and overturned because it is too 'radical' and hence very difficult to cement in place.

Increasingly, however, this cementing must be done or other Berkshires will happen and will not be averted. Small powerful groups like senior managers, governors, or Education Committee members can be useful allies but (quite aside from democratic reasons!) should not be one's sole support - if they change their mind or their political complexion nothing is left.

CONCLUSION

I have tried to outline some considerations which are important in policy formation. They may seem remote from the issues of 'race', gender, and class inequality which initially spur many of us on, but I would want to argue that they actually underlie and structure the inequalities themselves. We all know it is not enough simply to have policies, even policies which are partly effective; they have to be secure, developing, and capable of changing the way people think as well as how they act.

NOTES AND REFERENCES

1. Before the 1970s there were policies about race and gender, but they were not egalitarian ones.
2. The CNAA awards degrees in non-university higher education.
3. Increasingly they are beginning to do so, and it is not a pretty sight. See R. Honeyford's original (1984) Salisbury Review article, (Winter), parts of (1987) The Wayward Curriculum, Dennis O'Keeffe (ed.) London: Social Affairs, Unit, and (1986) Anti-Racism, an Assault on Education and Value, Frank Palmer (ed.), London: Sherwood Press. Also, of course, almost any

edition of the Daily Mail.
4. Opening speech to the Conservative Party Conference, October 1987.
5. The 1987 report from the Media Research Group chronicles the growth of these myths.

BIBLIOGRAPHY

Department of Education and Science (1985) Better Schools, London: HMSO, Cmnd 9469.

Gaine, C. (1987) No Problem Here, London: Hutchinson.

The Hargreaves Report (1985) Improving Secondary Schools, London: ILEA.

Honeyford, R. (1984) 'Education and race - an alternative view', Salisbury Review, Winter.

Media Research Group (1987) Media Coverage of London Councils, Goldsmiths' College, University of London.

O'Keefe, D. (ed.) (1987) The Wayward Curriculum, London: Social Affairs Unit.

Palmer, F. (ed.) (1986) Anti-Racism, an Assault on Freedom and Value, London: Sherwood Press.

The Swann Report (1985) Education for All, London: HMSO, Cmnd 9453.

The Thomas Report (1985) Improving Primary Schools, London: ILEA.

Troyna, B. and Williams, J. (1986) Education, Racism and The State, London: Croom Helm.

Chapter Three

A MANAGEMENT OF CHANGE PERSPECTIVE: TURNING THE
WHOLE SCHOOL AROUND

Pauline Lyseight-Jones

'I want to make change but I don't know how'.
'This is how'.
'I know how but it'll take a long time and a lot of work'.
'I didn't say it would be easy'.

That is probably as good a place to start as any. Making a
major, permanent change happen is a difficult enterprise. Within
educational institutions the enormity of the task will often deter all
but the brave or foolhardy.

In an area such as education for equality, the change which we
are attempting to bring about is not merely cosmetic or practical. It
is also moral and political. Consequently, our quest for change is
going to bring us into arenas which are seldom entered in school life.
No, it will not be easy.

A school is not a static organization. Pressures from outside
and within affect events and practice throughout the school. A
range of stimuli which relate to education for equality may similarly
act upon the school as an institution and the school population as
individuals.

Major education reports, LEA policy, and important external
events are external pressures for change. Specific pupil-related
incidents or a change in the composition of the pupil body are
internal pressures for change. Past teaching or life experience or
course attendance are individual pressures for change. These
pressures indicate differing motives for change. The only uniting
factor is a broad aim to do something towards educating for
equality.

INITIATIVES

Pressures for change - are they internal or external?

Internal factors include staff members attending in-service
courses, pupil-related incidents, or a change in the composition of
the pupil or staff body. A characteristic of such pressures for

38

change is that they are likely to be championed by an individual member of staff in the first instance. The staff member is not necessarily going to be someone with high ascribed status in the school.

External factors include major national educational reports and bills and national and local government education policies. Such pressure for change is likely to be introduced to the school formally, through the LEA administrative processes. The headteacher and the senior management team will be involved at the outset with the contemplated area of change.

DEFINING THE ISSUE

Given that initiatives exist for change it is worth spending some time defining the issue. It may be that a practical, departmental outcome is required or a process-led, whole-school change. Let us take an example: two pupils are caught fighting or arguing in the school grounds. One pupil maintains that a racist and/or sexist and/or classist taunt was used. Both pupils are angry, hurt, and upset.

The school could use this as an opportunity to reinforce its rules about 'the way in which we treat each other in this school' as well as to prompt staffroom discussion on how that kind of incident would be handled in the future. Action would be small scale and relatively easy to implement.

But the school could go further and could define the issue as follows: this is an issue which relates to school discipline, pupil supervision at breaktime, racism and/or sexism and/or classism in our school, and the effectiveness of the pastoral system.

To take action in all of these areas would require detailed planning with long-, medium- and short-term objectives. Most members of staff would be affected by the changes which would be made.

Incorrect or inadequate definition of the issue will lead to inappropriate outcomes. At best such an outcome could be called tokenism.

It may be that the best way of defining the issue is, paradoxically, to define the need. Ideally, the school or department should conduct a needs analysis exercise in relation to the specific areas of concern. From that investigation the first steps in planning a programme for change could be charted. Such a programme should be incorporated into the school development plans and not isolated and turned into a side issue.

INITIATOR

The initiator is the prime mover for change. In the externally generated change the initiator will be the headteacher, senior staff, or an adviser. In other instances a junior member of staff may be the individual who wishes to turn the whole school around. It is worth noting that lasting change in a school cannot come about if the focus for that change and the perpetual initiator is one person - be that person the head or a classroom teacher - as when that teacher leaves the school the project falls. It is equally true that if there is not some measure of high-level legitimization then a project is unlikely to succeed. If a headteacher gives little actual support but is prepared to 'rubber-stamp' or be a figure-head for the initiative then it can succeed - but only just. For whole-school change high-level legitimization should come through LEA support, i.e. advisers being visible in the school and extra resources being given to fund planned appropriate change.

So far we have the impetus for change, we have identified the areas which need to be changed and the prime mover or the catalyst for change. Now we need support.

ALLIES

Allies constitute the support for change. I have already referred to high-level legitimization. That factor is crucial. On an individual level the initiator needs to work towards a position where they do not stand alone, where they can rely on other individuals on the staff to support the proposed initiatives. In an area such as education for equality I find that support or hostility cannot be presumed. It is a wondrous area where things and people are rarely what they seem.

External support is probably the easiest, least painful to develop. Talk to your friends about your ideas and nurture links with support or advisory service personnel. Visit relevant voluntary or community groups. Eschew the High Street bookseller or the independent bookshop. Build up a knowledge, through contact, that you are not alone. This will help immeasurably on the days when you feel you have gone four steps backward in school and your closest colleague makes an ill-considered comment about your motives.

Internal support is tricky in this field. I believe that this is because within school we do not often talk about education and its philosophies. Instead we manage the curriculum, implement the policy, or rewrite the syllabus. There is a corporate complicity which suggests that we all know what education is about and, as fundamentally good people, that that is what we are all working towards. Within school we follow the tenet that religion, politics, and sex should not be talked about or you lose friends. The problem is that education for equality requires us to look at what we believe and then to have the courage of our convictions in attempting to make changes. Our committment may be inexplicable to colleagues as we seem to be rejecting that which we were supporting last week or actually helped to develop last year. When we understand what collusion means a whole range of staffroom conversations and staff-meeting decisions become triggers for our intervention. The racist joke or the sexist or classist assumption are challenged by us and we can find ourselves isolated. It is evident that a school cannot be turned around by isolated initiators.

The initiator has to look at the staff group as a series of groupings of individuals. Those groups may then be acted upon or worked with. In some schools two groups may exist: senior management and the rest. In many more schools the groups would include heads of department, heads of year, heads of house, holders of posts of responsibility, faculties, form tutors, and year teams. It is valuable to recognize the existence of these groups and, at various times, to target the development of elements of the initiative on them. Equally, we must remember that power/authority/status and influence are not synonymous terms. It could be that the senior management team has authority but that the headteacher actually listens to views put forward by a particular deputy headteacher or to the post holder from a particular curriculum area. While an aim is to ensure that the head has respect for your views, it makes sense for as many people as possible to carry the initiative towards that high-level legitimization.

Classifying staff members as supporters, blockers, opinion leaders, and don't knows is a good if cold-blooded exercise to do when planning to develop support for action. Further classifying staff members as laggards (they will do it, but it will take a disproportionate amount of your time and effort to spur them to action) and band-wagoners (those with an eye on their CVs - this may be the most hard-working though uncommitted group) will clarify some matters of strategy and power relationships.

When this exercise was done on an in-service course it led some course members to realize that there were some members of staff who were unknown to them by name and staff with whom they had never had a conversation; that suporters were not in discrete curriculum areas; and that support could be spread across the range of teaching staff, it being no respecter of status. The old adage requires us to know our enemy. In educating for equality we must know our supporters. If we have not spoken with all staff members it is difficult to see how we can plan a successful strategy involving them. Therefore, while our initiative may start on a small scale - with all of those initially involved knowing each other - high-level interpersonal skills are required to achieve whole-school change involving the whole staff. The prerequisite to achieving lasting support is to meet the individual.

Exasperation
Consternation
Inspiration
We've been through the whole range.
We now look forward to doing some application and implementation
(A senior secondary school teacher)

INITIATIVE DEVELOPMENT

The methods of developing initiatives for education for equality depend on the prevailing systems and practices in a school.

Staff curriculum meetings, where the initiative is an agenda item, on a regular basis are essential in keeping up a mainstream, high profile. Education for equality is part of educational good practice. Discussion of developments relating to it has a rightful place in staff meetings.

Departmental or faculty meetings are useful for floating an initiative attempting small-scale change which affects a single subject area. Department-generated change is to be encouraged in a secondary school. Each department comes into contact with the entire student body so changes to teaching style and method, in the provision of course texts, and in supporting stances in relation to education for equality are quickly noticed by pupils. If care has been taken to ensure high quality in such change then colleagues from the other departments will become interested.

Forming a working party may either be a very effective way of bringing together committed hard-working individuals or an even more effective exercise in marginalization. (1) Let us take a little time to look at working parties.

While it is necessary for them to contain individuals who believe in the issues for which they were convened, if whole-school change is aimed for, then membership of the working party should also include the influential. Ideally, the committed and the influential will be found in the same people - but real life is not like that. Some schools hand-pick working party members so that they are representative of all areas of school life. Others choose working party members on the basis of seniority. Braver souls have open membership. In all cases, membership could include powerful blockers. A potentially successful format is to have the headteacher as a member of the group but not to chair it, to inform the head and staff of all meetings, to invite special staff members to be members of the working party (remember the need for strategical choices), and to have some meetings as open discussion meetings to which any staff member could come.

The working party may find that its first problem is not what to do or how to do it, but how much do we know about the issues? Until that question is asked and the answer correctly given then confusion and misguided planning will occur. The working party's first task is to educate itself. This may take the form of making links with relevant groups, exploring specialist bookshops, viewing training videos, and enrolling on in-service courses.

Thought I had my eyes open before I arrived only to find they could open even further. As I talk to colleagues back at school my eyes grow wider all the time and I wish they were here.

It is hard to remember back at work that other colleagues have not been through the same experience and it's hard to know what and how to tell them.

(Senior secondary school teachers)

The working party's self-education process may show the aware that they have further to go and the complacent that they have touched only the tip of the iceberg. It is important to remember that education has something to do with learning. The working party will have learned things which other colleagues have yet to grasp or encounter. Excessive zeal will alienate as will being a benevolent oppressor.

The working party now has to do something. If you believe that behaviour changes attitudes then instituting small-scale change is a first step to whole-school change. Everything which the working party does has to be very good in its early days - mediocrity has no place in its functions either. It is better to do a whole series of small, high-profile, specialized projects than a huge, badly researched, whole-school project. Start with reviewing the texts of a subject area, having open discussions on education for equality based on training videos, or invite LEA staff or members of the community in to speak to staff. Keep all staff members informed of the activities of the working party.

OPPOSITION

Opposition takes many forms, but if you wish to implement any initiative which questions the status quo then you have to expect it and deal with it.

An amount of opposition will come from the usually powerful or influential. Their basis for opposition, however well cloaked, is that they are not in the limelight and not the prime movers. Deliberate strategies to involve them in parts of the initiative can be successful. Equally, creating a climate in which they would find it untenable to oppose is also effective - for example, relating the initiative to good education practice or combining the initiative with a curriculum review or the implementation of a revised examination course. Rewarding sectors of the school who have responded to the initiative with higher priority for equipment funds, access to in-service provision, or additional staff are effective ways in which the head with the LEA on the advice of the working party can raise the profile of the initiative while making it less easy for the opposition to oppose.

If the opposition takes the form of continual blocking, be it overt or not, then action may be taken, but it depends on how powerful the individuals working on the initiative are, how effective the head is, and who is doing the blocking. Then there are several choices to make. First, to go around the blocker - to use methods which neutralize the need for that person in relation to the continuance of the project (e.g. if a keyholder is making it difficult for audio-visual material to be used for in-service training meetings in school then the working party should request its own key). Second, go over the blocker - there may be enough of you to render the opposition of little consequence. You accept the blocking presence but you know its timescale - short and ineffective. Third, you can try to make an accommodation with the blocker. This is only worth attempting if the blocker is being difficult because they have misinterpreted the aims of the initiative and therefore, are misguidedly feeling threatened. Otherwise, you feel, quite rightly, that you are colluding with that which you wish to change. Fourth, you remain blocked. It is possible. It means that you have to abandon that part of the initiative which is being blocked and move on to another area in which the blocker has less influence. If the blocker is the head then you have to institute a personal, parochial autonomy over that which affects you within the school, or you leave the job.

Oppositional statements include not just the blatant, offensive epithet but also the measured discussion point: 'Asian children can't swim - it's their ankles.' - meaning - 'You tell me otherwise.' This is also an example of the self-fulfilling prophecy. 'What about sexism and working-class kids?' - meaning - 'I didn't do anything about improving the educational opportunity for women or working-class kids so I don't see why I should help to improve the lot of black kids.' This is a diversionary tactic. 'Well, they are Pakis aren't they'? - meaning - 'There is a status quo and you're asking us to change it. I call a spade a spade.' This requires everyone to know their place and to accept it. 'We're all God's children' - meaning - 'I am playing my trump card. To deny this statement means that you are rejecting the established spiritual basis of this country and are not fit to be in contact with people's children.' This person is not likely to change as in doing so they will believe that they are imposing a discrimination which they fundamentally reject.

ISOLATION

If you get opposition then you will, at times, feel isolated. As I said earlier, education for equality is a moral and political area, as well as a practical and philosophical one. Consequently, the discussions which ensue in relation to it are not the usual fare of the staff meeting. Staff members will be at different stages of awareness. Your point about the terminology used by staff when talking about black pupils or the tasks given by staff to girls or stereotypical assumptions about working-class and middle-class parental aspirations may not be tacitly and passively accepted by the staff group in total. You may feel that you have misjudged colleagues or they you. You may realize that colleagues are guarding their words in front of you or, on the other hand, mischieviously baiting you. You may find that the headteacher suddenly finds the initiative too hot to handle, as in 'I didn't expect all of this upset' or, 'I didn't expect it to cost money/time/effort'; this makes it difficult for you to discuss plans for the initiative with her or him.

This is where outside supporters are invaluable. It is also where your tactic of doing a series of small, high-quality projects comes into its own - as you will be able to look back on success and to understand that, as a setback, it will be a temporary one. Remember to talk to the other people who are committed to the initiative about your feelings - they may be feeling isolated too.

> My confidence grows every second that I'm here but it takes a bashing every time I go into the big, bad outside world.
> (A senior secondary school teacher)

DISSEMINATION OF INFORMATION

One of the ways in which an initiative fails to gain or keep support in a school is if it is seen to be a private or a partisan concern. It is important to keep up the profile of the initiative as well as detailing progress. To ensure that information is circulated it has, initially, to be collected.

During meetings which are relevant to the initiative notes should be kept to be disseminated as a report, guidelines, points for discussion, or minutes. When guest speakers come to the school for staff in-service training then it may be possible to video the session in progress so that a detailed review can be done. It has to be someone's understood responsibility to collect information or to organize its collection. The designated person might find it valuable to complete a personal diary related to the development of the initiative. The diary and other materials collected should show the course which the school chose to take, where it was successful, and where amended after review.

Secretarial support in school is usually overstretched. It is important that the typing, etc., of papers which are generated from the initiative are seen as part of the general task of the secretarial support. In some instances those involved in the initiative may choose not to put work through a school secretary because of worries about confidentiality. This can be overcome by choosing a method of reporting back which does not identify individuals directly unless they have previously given their consent. In one instance a school secretary was refusing to type reports of education for racial equality meetings because she disagreed with the sentiments expressed within them. The headteacher had to insist that they formed part of the general task of providing secretarial services for the school. The incident alerted the school to the necessity for informing non-teaching staff of the fundamental school policy developments and including them in the in-service programme for the initiative. Depending on which style of developing the initiative was chosen, dissemination of information may take the form of all or some of the following:

> working party reports to whole staff;
> working party members orally report to faculty or departmental groups;
> reports from individual staff members to a working party on their areas of concern;
> reports to governors by the headteacher or other staff members;
> accounts of developments placed on staff notice boards;
> notes of meetings related to the initiative being available for all staff members;
> advance notice of meetings related to the initiative plus its agenda being circulated in good time for interested parties to respond;
> informal staffroom discussions;
> incorporation of the initiative's plans or outcomes in the school brochure;
> an item in PTA discussions;
> a focus for parent/teacher curriculum evenings;
> exhibitions of new materials selected in response to the initiative plus teaching demonstrations with them;
> let the pupils know that the school will be taking a special focus on education for equality throughout the coming year, two years, etc. and that they will be actively involved in the initiative.

SERVICING THE INITIATIVE

'If I gave these books out they'd only read them.' So said a deputy primary headteacher. It may be that having thought about our initiative, set up working groups, and begun an amount of self-examination we are reticent to go the whole way and develop in-school, in-service training. We may be scared because we are not sure what to expect or we may be wary of sharing expertise - some people like being the school expert on issues such as educating for equality.

In-school, in-service training (Inset) is an area of great challenge. It brings with it the danger of status indicators such as seniority, age, and subject specialism being diminished. New expertise for developing and implementing initiatives arises without regard for such indicators. Change is not a respector of status. It may be that the young teachers, fresh from college and fresh from having their teaching observed, analysed, and graded, may well be able to lead or develop in-school, in-service training. It is worth compiling a list of all those outsiders to the school who could or should be useful in developing the initiative. These will include advisers or inspectors, advisory teachers, librarians, careers service personnel, education welfare officers, community members with an interest in the education service, higher education and further education institutions, as well as voluntary or independent and other bodies concerned with education. Remember advisory and support services need good schools to work in.

The scope given to schools to organize their own in-service training has been broadened by the grant-aided Inset fund arrangements (LEATGS) and the five, annual, compulsory, staff development days. When we need to do so much work in relation to education for equality we must ensure that we make it a priority for whole-school Inset and that the Inset takes place when people are alert. In my experience, 4.00 to 6.00 on a Thursday evening is not a good time for new insights to be taken on and new knowledge to be shared.

It has long been said that women have to be twice as good as male colleagues to be appointed to posts of similar status. The same has been said regarding black people in relation to white people. As an assumption, it has some relevance in the delivery of Inset on education for equality. All the sessions have to be good, not satisfactory. All the speakers/facilitators have to be highly skilled. As trainers in education for equality frequently come from the groups which are at present disadvantaged in our system their presence can unconsciously or otherwise set off in the course members an operation of a double standard, i.e. 'they've got to be twice as good as other trainers to convince me that they're as good'.

It is worth learning to deal with colleagues whose complaints about Inset are largely that it is not perfect and did not answer their unspoken needs, thus far transmitted telepathically, if at all. If a system for evaluating all Inset offered is in place then the job will be made easier. Ask colleagues to put into writing what they expect from the Inset, transmit that to the Inset provider, and use those expectations plus the expectations of those leading the initiative as success indicators. This method allows Inset organizers to let colleagues know beforehand which of their expectations are inappropriate in relation to the particular Inset planned.

Pauline Lyseight-Jones

TRAINING THE TRAINERS

Education for equality will require Inset for staff members if only to ensure that the same vocabulary is being used for concepts. In dealing with areas which are rarely discussed in any depth in the staffroom there is always the possibility of misunderstanding, conflict, or alienation. The staff members who are spearheading the initiative may be surprised by the above reactions and may be new to training adults. The task is not made easier because the adults are colleagues. It may be that before in-school, in-service training is attempted some staff members are enabled to join either a training the trainers course or a course dealing with the particular initiative which is being considered for the school. Where this is possible I would strongly recommend at least two staff members attending the course at the same time.

> I found the course informative, provocative and mind boggling at times. It has raised my awareness and made me question my views and opinions on issues which I realised I hadn't really given enough thought and time to before.
>
> (A senior secondary school teacher)

FACILITIES FOR INSET

In the past there has been a tendency to expect a surfeit of goodwill from teaching staffs. All the goodwill in the world will not succeed if what are wanted are:

> non-teaching time to observe the school in action;
> non-teaching time to observe other teachers teaching;
> non-teaching time to visit other educational institutions;
> funds for external course membership;
> funds for books, materials, and speakers to support the initiative;
> secretarial and administrative support for the initiative.

The mobility of teachers seems to be lessening. If that is the case then seeing other teachers in action, in one's own school as well as elsewhere, is important. Equally important is the need to see other whole-school systems in action. Developing links with schools who are working along similar lines is invaluable. A caveat here is that schools may find themselves identified as good-practice schools before they are ready for any such exposure. This is a difficult issue to handle. A staff has to decide how many visitors or enquiries they will accommodate as well as which areas they feel are sufficiently well developed to warrant the title 'good practice'.

REVIEW AND AMEND

In any programme of change due regard must be given to the necessity for revision of the original plan and its amendment. If we conscientiously document and evaluate the work which is being done within the school to bring about education for equality we will realize that our chosen way of meeting a perceived need or tackling an issue may be misguided, inappropriate, or poorly executed. Such a mishap many change the direction of the initiative, if only temporarily. Be prepared for this - expect to be flexible in order to advance. I am not interpreting flexible as compliant, I am recognizing that individuals respond to a range of approaches - there is not just one way.

A newly appointed primary headteacher wanted to implement his LEA's policy on educating for racial equality. He thought that providing new, exciting, high-quality, non-racist, non-sexist resources would be a non-threatening first step. He was right. The staff were pleased that a new headteacher had arrived, seemingly bearing gifts. Unfortunately, when he tried to get the staff to examine the existing bookstock he was faced with hostility. He had presumed that they would see selection and evaluation of books as a professional task; they saw it as an insult to their professionalism. He has had to review the way in which he seeks to make change happen.

NOW - WHERE IS THE HEADTEACHER IN ALL THIS?

The headteacher is central to the development of education for equality. I have stated that there is a necessity for high-level legitimization; high-level enthusiasm and capability are also important. Earlier I referred to change in the context of the school, that is, the internal and external pressures which are being exerted on it. School reorganization, the implementation of a new examination system, or an unexpectedly high turnover of staff are factors which will make the management of a new initiative more difficult. So too may the headteacher. Recent reports have re-emphasized the different styles of headship and their effectiveness in supporting change. (2) It may be that you recognize 'the Administrator' for whom 'change was a source of annoyance' or 'the Systematic problem solver' who had 'high expectations of all pupils ... they were receptive to changes which might achieve these goals'. (3) Add to this the information that a headteacher is most likely to be an innovator and initiator in the early days of headship. With such high activity in the first year or two of headship a consolidation period usually follows the implementation period: a head may feel that the school is where it should be - for the moment - and that the staff have taken on enough change to last them for some time. This transition from initiator to consolidator typically takes four or five years. While a headteacher can remain effective as an overseer of a school which is ticking over, it is difficult for a new initiative to emerge when this stage has been reached unless the headteacher manages a self-remotivation and/or the staff press for a particular change in response to an identified need.

SOME THOUGHTS ON IN-SERVICE TRAINING AND THE MANAGEMENT OF CHANGE

The issues which relate to the management of change in education for equality are similar in many respects to making change in education of any type or magnitude.

The crucial area to be aware of is that of process. The individuals within a school are taking part in a process of change. They began that process at differing starting points. Their opinions and attitudes as well as their teaching style were formed over time. While I am in no way suggesting that we can afford to let our children suffer a substandard education for an unlimited period, it may be that some aspects of change will not occur in any lasting way without staff being given the time to digest philosophy and information. If behaviour changes attitude then the changes which we would wish to focus on will comprise elements which require behavioural change and, implicit within that, an attitudinal change. It is not enough to give teachers the language of awareness; they must also be assisted to develop practical ways of demonstrating awareness. I may not have the time or the will to wait for someone to change their racist or sexist or classist views, but I can insist that they evaluate all materials which they use according to previously agreed, non-racist, non-sexist, non-classist guidelines or that there is an agreed process for dealing with offensive graffiti or name calling.

Given the above, what follows is a checklist for Inset providers or in-school curriculum developers and innovators:

(a) Access to expertise by personal contact, phone, or letter.
(b) Group support in school, a need for at least one other person to be highly committed to the initiative.
(c) Headteachers' support. This should ensure high-level legitimization of the initiative.
(d) External support. The availability of outside specialists to assist with planning, staff-meeting presentations, negotiations, and so on.
(e) Access to papers. Short, authoritative, definitive papers and articles are useful when one considers the very tight time constraints on teaching staff.
(f) Access to appropriate resources at a time when it is becoming easier to say to teaching staff, 'the resources are there, they're being produced'; it is a duty of the Inset provider to provide

some.

(g) <u>Flexibility</u>. The people who undertake Inset out of school and more particularly, in-school, are not of a kind. The more flexible the teaching approaches, the ways of giving information, the location, time, and duration of sessions, the more likely that interest and attendance will be sustained and commitment given.

(h) <u>All promises kept</u>. This is the most important item, I think. If an Inset provider undertakes to provide the article, the time, the support - even the coffee - then those promises must be kept. While in-service training continues to be carried out when people are at their most tired and under pressure, even the smallest hiccough in arrangements can attain vast dimensions.

One last point. It is possible that those people whom you seek to advantage and empower through your initiatives to develop an education for equality will not necessarily be supportive to you. They may suspect your motives (examine them) and they may be weak, weary, and tired as a result of continuous, insidious oppression. You may feel cheated. Once I overheard someone say: 'People who have been degraded are not loveable'. The challenge is to uplift, develop self-esteem, and broaden, not to criticize the powerless for not being grateful to you for your efforts - it has been a long time coming.

Exhilarated, excited but exhausted.

Now worried - wondering - adequacy? Time and energy, involvement, management of time - anxious.

It's the constant realisation that the job is so huge - that we are part of an experience which is not common.

This is a whole new world full of emotions, ideas, controversy.

A wider horizon - a more varied landscape, a richer experience.

<u>I must not forget</u> curriculum change, administration, community development, class teaching, in-service, individual work, pastoral work, reports, appraisal, evaluation, etc.

You're not listening to me! I'm listening, I'm listening but you want me to do something and I want to do something but I can't while I'm listening.

(Primary school staff)

Pauline Lyseight-Jones

Acknowledgements

I have been fortunate to work with many people whose views inform this chapter. Principally, the teachers who participated in the 1986-7 DES course on 'The Curriculum and Ethnic Diversity', the 1987-8 National Priority Course on 'The Curriculum and Ethnic Diversity', and the Good Practice Project 1986-8 on 'Education for Racial Equality - Policy into Practice' all of which took place in Berkshire LEA.

NOTES AND REFERENCES

1. An article written by Massey, I. (1987) in Multicultural Teaching 5: no. 2, spring, would be useful additional reading.
2. Weindling, D. and Earley, P. (1987) Secondary Headship - The First Years, Walton on Thames: NFER-Nelson.
3. Leithwood, K.A. and Montgomery, D.J. (1985) 'The role of the Principal in school improvement', in G. Austin et al. (eds) Research on Effective Schools, New York: Academic Press, cited in Weindling and Earley above.

Chapter Four

MATERIALS, RESOURCES AND METHODS

Robin Richardson

I hadn't realised I was so ignorant, Celie. The little I knew about my own self wouldn't have filled a thimble! And to think Miss Beasley always said I was the smartest child she ever taught! But one thing I do thank her for, for teaching me to learn for myself, by reading and studying and writing a clear hand. And for keeping alive in me somehow the desire to know. (1)

Two cheers for Miss Beasley. And two cheers also for all teaching materials and learning resources which assist her. An essential core mission in education is to teach people to speak and learn for themselves, to form in them minds which will 'stroll about hungry and fearless and thirsty and supple'. (2) It is, yes, crucial and it is praiseworthy to keep alive in children and in the populace the desire to know.

But to know what? It is because Miss Beasley has apparently not asked and handled this question adequately ('I was so ignorant. The little I knew about my own self wouldn't have filled a thimble!') that we can cheer her only twice. Her creator and author Alice Walker, however, does care, and passionately and precisely: worthwhile knowledge is about identity, your political, racial, sexual, and metaphysical identity; it is about oppression, all that stifles you, keeps you down; and about justice, equality, freedom, uplift; and about love. 'We are working', says Miss Beasley's former pupil Nettie, 'for a common goal: the uplift of black people everywhere'. Nettie has not only an enquiring mind, formed by Miss Beasley, but also a committed heart, formed elsewhere. Her commitment is against, in particular, racism and patriarchy. What kinds of teaching materials nurture such minds and commitments, and how do we ensure that they get written and published? How do we prevent materials being published which dull, distract, and deaden such minds and commitments? These are the questions of this chapter.

The chapter has three main parts. First, it recalls that bias in textbooks cannot be considered independently of the wider question of bias in teaching generally, and of how teachers should handle

53

controversial issues. Second, the article considers the textbooks currently being published in Britain, and measures their messages against a draft checklist. The survey is sombre and caustic in its conclusions, though admittedly sketchy and cavalier in its conduct. Third, the chapter notes the customary procedure for producing textbooks of a three-cornered partnership of private capital, dilettante editors, and prima donna authors and suggests that this is a formula which recalls the ancient dictum that 'as you sow, you are like to reap', or, in the less agricultural and less patient parlance of our own dear times, 'garbage in, garbage out'. The third part of the chapter also considers what might and should be done to pressure publishers to change their ways. The chapter closes eventually with a brief epilogue, in the form of a further quotation from the novel with which it also began, The Color Purple by Alice Walker.

TEACHING ABOUT CONTROVERSIAL ISSUES

'I'm not controversial', said someone, 'it's just that ignorant, ill-informed idiots disagree with me'. In a way, that person was right: controversy is not to do with different levels of knowledge and information, but with different opinions, values, and priorities, and, basically and essentially, with different material interests. A controversial issue, in brief, is one on which society is divided. The difference of opinion may be about the very definition and naming of the problem to be solved; and/or about its causes in history, in society, in human nature; and/or about the actions which should be taken, both in the short term and in the long, to remove or to manage the problem; and/or about the structure and contours of the ideal situation, state, or society towards which action is taken, and in the utopian light of which the problem was first perceived and labelled. In medical terms, controversies may be about symptoms, diagnosis, prescription, the concept of good health.

This kind of account of controversy is not unproblematic, however. It envisages that the definition of an issue as controversial, as distinct from one arising only from differences of knowledge and information, is a straightforward empirical question - 'people agree or they don't, society is divided or it isn't'. The reality, however, is that certain interests are served by maintaining that there is no controversy, no difference of opinion, no protest or discontent, that we are all one happy family; conversely certain other interests are served simply through the recognition that such and such an issue should be debated, should be on the agenda. In other words, whether or not an issue is controversial is itself sometimes a controversial issue.

Another problem with the definition of a controversial issue as being one which divides society is that the meaning of the term society is left wholly unclear. The national society or world society? The tendency is to assume that national society should be the focus.

Those of us who assert against the majority view that world society should be the context for the definition and study of controversial issues must acknowledge that such an assertion is itself controversial, since it is bound to question and threaten certain vested interests within national society.

It is often not straightforward to summarize, to agree whether or not an issue is controversial, or to agree what precisely the contours of a disagreement are. Consider, for example, the table on page 56. This attempts to map some of the main differences of opinion to be found in current British society about race relations and multicultural education. The left-hand column in the table evokes the assimilationist perspective which is reflected every day in the British press and on television, and which is reflected also in the vast majority of teaching materials in current use: in most school textbooks, as in most of the media, black British people are invisible, their existence is wholly ignored. The central column in the table evokes - to adapt a phrase of E.M. Forster's, and to make the point unkindly - 'poor little talkative multiculturalism'. The central column also evokes the view that modern Britain is in all important respects a decent and democratic society. The twin emphases have been well expressed by a recent Secretary of State for Education:

> We may be English, Scottish, Irish or Welsh; or our parents or grandparents may have come from other parts of Europe or from the West Indies, Africa or the Indian subcontinent; we may be Protestant or Catholic, Jew or Gentile, Hindu, Sikh or Muslim. It is right to uphold family traditions and values and to have pride in our ancestry ... (We should) start from the premise of a fair and tolerant British society, whose institutions welcome within them people of very different origins ... (3)

The right-hand column evokes antiracism, as distinct from multiculturalism. It does not start from the Secretary of State's 'fair and tolerant British society' but from several centuries of black experience of white oppression. It does not see racism as merely a matter of ignorance, to be removed through the provision of information, nor as merely a matter of political extremism. It sees racism rather as part and parcel of British culture, history, and political economy. The dismantling of racism is a political act in the first instance, and has to take place in each separate institution or organization; in the curricula of schools such dismantling includes, but certainly is not co-extensive with or dependent on, learning about other cultures: 'just to learn about other people's cultures is not to learn about the racism of one's own. To learn about the racism of one's own culture, on the other hand, is to approach other cultures objectively'. (4)

The table is imperfect in all sorts of ways. But it helpfully raises a fundamental question for every publisher of school

Controversies in 'race' and education – three perspectives

A – 'conforming'	B – 'reforming'	C – 'transforming'
Immigrants came to Britain in the 1950s and 1960s because the laws on immigration were not strict enough.	Ethnic minorities came to Britain because they had a right to and because they wanted a better life.	Black people came to Britian, as to other countries, because their labour was required by the economy.
Immigrants should integrate as quickly as possible with the British way of life.	Ethnic minorities should be able to maintain their language and cultural heritage.	Black people have to defend themselves against racist laws and practices, and to struggle for racial justice.
There is some racial prejudice in Britain but it is only human nature, and Britain is a much more tolerant place than most other countries.	There are some misguided individuals and extremist groups in Britain, but basically our society is just and democratic, and provides equality.	Britain is a racist society, and has been for several centuries. Racism is to do with power structures more than with the attitudes of individuals.
It is counter-productive to try to remove prejudice – you cannot force people to like each other by bringing in laws and regulations.	Prejudice is based on ignorance and misunderstanding. It can be removed by personal contacts and the provision of information.	'Prejudice' is caused by, it is not the cause of, unjust structures and procedures. It can be removed only by dismantling these.
There should be provision of English as a Second Language in schools, but otherwise 'children are all children, we should treat all children exactly the same' – it is wrong to notice or emphasize cultural or racial differences. Low achievement in immigrant pupils is caused by factors within immigrant families and cultures.	Schools should recognize and affirm ethnic minority children's background, culture, and language ... celebrate festivals, organize international evenings, use and teach mother tongues, community languages, teach about ethnic minority history, art, music, religion, literature.	Priorities in education are for there to be more black people in positions of power and influence – as heads, senior teachers, governors, education officers, elected members; and to remove discrimination in the curriculum, classroom methods and school organization; and to teach directly about equality and justice and against racism.

textbooks, and for every teacher: how is one to handle these controversies? It also, incidentally, recalls that broadly similar charts could be drawn up in relation to other aspects of equality and justice - for example to do with sexism and women's rights, to do with class, or to do with world development, or with international peace and conflict. Whatever the issues a table can be drawn showing at least three broad approaches: (a) a conforming approach, which accepts the current status quo and dominant ideologies; (b) a reforming approach, which seeks improvements and modifications but accepts the current overall structure as sound; and (c) a transforming approach, which seeks very profound and far-reaching changes away from the present status quo. What should be the stance of a publisher of school textbooks or of a teacher - conforming, reforming, or transforming? Or is there some other possible stance outside the chart altogether?

At first sight there seem to be five different approaches for a publisher or teacher. One, you could reckon to avoid reference to controversies altogether. Two, you could present the views of the majority of the population. Three, you could be neutral - mention the differences of opinion which exist, but avoid taking sides yourself. Four, you could present your own views, whatever those happen to be. Five, you could aim to help pupils develop the basic concepts they need to understand the controversy, and basic skills of enquiry and debate. Each of these five possibilities will be considered here briefly in turn.

The first is the avoidance of controversy. Now in certain countries or situations, at certain times, on certain topics, this is not ignoble - but a matter of simple prudence and self-interest, and of straightforward respect and concern for one's pupils. A teacher in a school near a military base, for example, may understandably and legitimately prefer not to put NATO's defence policy, or direct action and civil disobedience, on the agenda of the school curriculum. Similar examples can be drawn from parts of Britain, including in particular of course Northern Ireland, and from all other countries. Nevertheless we must always be clear that possibility one, the avoidance of controversy, is in practice the same as possibility two, the presentation of majority opinion: they are the passive and the active sides of the same coin. In the terms of the table, for example, the avoidance of those issues is precisely the same as presenting the views summarized in the left-hand column. We must also be clear that certain other reasons sometimes given for avoiding controversy are ludicrous in their naivety. Opponents of peace studies, for example, have claimed that there is no room on the school timetable for studying controversial issues unless you leave out mathematics, history, English and French. They have claimed also that the great advantage of traditional subjects is that in each 'there is an accepted body of communicable knowledge'. 'The truly educational subject', they say, 'forces the pupil to understand something which has no immediate bearing on his (sic) experience. It teaches him (sic) intellectual discipline, by presenting him (sic) with problems too remote or too abstract to be comprehended within his (sic) own limited world. ...' (5) The practical consequences of this educational ideology are that conforming perspectives on society, such as the one summarized in the left-hand column of the table, are presented and celebrated, and that certain large groups of pupils - most black pupils, most girls, most working-class pupils - are ruthlessly ignored and rejected.

The third possibility, neutrality, is the stance of television programmes such as 'Panorama', and indeed of television news programmes generally. It is also advocated quite often in educational circles - 'we should give pupils a variety of views, and leave them to make up their own minds'. In practice this third possibility means either that moderation and anti-extremism are being presented as virtues in themselves, to the material electoral advantage of the political centre or that, in an overall situation of inequality, the majority view prevails. With regard to the table, for example, neutrality would either mean that the perspective in the centre column would be presented, with the other two columns labelled as extremist, or else that pupils would in practice receive very considerably more messages expressing the conforming approach, since these are already widespread in the mass media and the curriculum as a whole.

The fourth possibility, that of presenting your own views, is seldom advocated in as many words. It is, however, quite possibly the only honest and realistic possibility. We will consider this point further in a moment. First it will be useful and relevant to consider the fifth possibility, that of developing relevant concepts and skills.

Teachers should, say the authors of a valuable book on teaching controversial issues, 'provide students with a conceptual framework, skills in discussion, and a critical, analytical approach to events and public disagreements, in order that they can transfer these to issues and situations which they will encounter in their adult lives'. (6) The same authors go on to emphasize and commend the importance of 'critically diagnosing information and evidence', 'asking awkward questions', 'recognizing rhetoric', and 'cultivating tentativeness'.

At first sight this fifth possibility, to be summarized here with the term 'liberal pedagogy', is unexceptionable and indeed attractive. But if you actually adopt it - if, that is, you start asking some awkward questions about it, and wondering whether it might itself be nothing more than mere rhetoric - you are immediately confronted with a whole range of theoretical and practical problems. For a start, you have to note that very few school textbooks do in fact aim to help pupils to 'critically diagnose information and evidence', least of all the information and evidence between their own covers. So you immediately find yourself in politics with a small 'p' - opposition and resistance to commercial publishers, and a great many other, consequent, consonant, and parallel disputes and struggles also. Then, second, there is the problem of choice. Look yet again, for example, at the table. In relation to which of those conflicting judgements and beliefs do you propose developing the skills of critical diagnosis, recognizing rhetoric, asking awkward questions, and so on? All of them?

In an ideal world - a world in which every viewpoint can be stated with equal articulacy, and heard with equal attention - the answer to that question, 'All of them?', would be 'Yes'. Do we, however, live in (more or less) an ideal world? If you say 'Yes' also to this question then you are situating yourself somewhere in the central column of the chart, along with (incidentally) the Secretary of State. If you answer 'No', thinking as you do so of the enormous inequalities between white people and black in their political and economic power to get a hearing for their concerns and beliefs, then you are at the same time situating yourself in the right-hand column. Liberal pedagogy, in other words, has either to combine with liberal politics or else to combine with radical politics: it is not an option existing somewhere outside the table altogether.

The educational system as a whole, and each classroom within it, is a political forum in which individuals and groups advocate their own views and argue against the views of others; and in which, therefore, certain material interests are being advanced, and others being threatened and damaged. This, it is being argued, is the reality.

Every writer and every publisher of school textbooks has political beliefs and advocates these in their work. This is the reality - though it may be obscured from themselves as much as from their readers and customers. Similarly every teacher has political beliefs and advocates these: this is the reality. The questions for each of us are (a) how to engage in our advocacy as skilfully and effectively as possible; (b) how to diminish or remove the influence of our opponents as fully as possible - this includes defending ourselves against them as well as attacking them; (c) what ground rules to negotiate with our opponents.

This notion of ground rules is fundamental. 'If you stop telling lies about us', Harold Wilson is reputed to have said once to Edward Heath, 'we'll stop telling the truth about you'. That evokes the essence of ground rules - they are simultaneously an attempt to diminish the baneful influence of your opponents and to maximize the freedom and space enjoyed by yourself. What ground rules are negotiable with regard to teaching about controversial issues in schools?

We can interestingly follow John Rawls here. (7) He imagines people behind 'a veil of ignorance' about themselves - they do not know whether they are rich or poor, powerful or powerless, young or old, men or women, talented or relatively ordinary - and speculates at length about the ground rules of the society they would rationally plan for themselves to live in. Similarly we can imagine teachers, publishers, and school textbook authors behind a veil of ignorance - that is, not knowing what their own political views are, and whether these are inside or outside the broad consensus of their society - and planning together some ground rules for all to abide by.

The rules they would come up with would surely be very similar to those which have been described here as the fifth possibility, or as liberal pedagogy. It follows that someone may say something such as this: I desire very considerable changes in modern society, in the direction of greater equality and justice. In the terms of the table, for example, my commitment is the one outlined in the right-hand column. As publisher, writer, lecturer, or teacher (or local government adviser, inspector, or officer) I intend advocating and fighting for my views, and against other views. But I shall abide by certain ground rules, the rules and procedures of liberal pedagogy. I shall adopt these on the one hand because I believe they will lead to pupils and students understanding and internalizing the radical beliefs which I shall be advocating; and on the other hand because I wish my 'conforming' and 'reforming' opponents to abide by these ground rules as well.

I deplore, it may be continued, the fact that many school textbooks present conforming or reforming messages, not transforming ones. Further, I deplore the fact that these messages are very frequently hidden, therefore not complying with the ground rules which I am prepared to accept and honour myself. I wish to contact and join allies who have views similar to my own, in order that we may the more effectively oppose the many bad or inadequate books currently being published, and may ensure the publication of good or better books.

Someone may say, to repeat, something like that. To be more precise and less coy, that is what this chapter is saying. We turn now to the second main part of the chapter, concerned with surveys of current school textbooks.

SURVEYS OF CURRENT SCHOOL TEXTBOOKS

A school textbook has two defining features: it is written for pupils or students, and it is read in schools. Well, yes and no. These two defining features are commonsensical, but misleading. In the first regard it is always crucial to remember that textbooks are purchased by, and therefore marketed to, teachers, and that the messages which teachers receive from textbooks are even more significant and formative than those which are received by pupils. What we adults tell the children does affect and mould them to an extent, no doubt, but it affects and moulds us adults even more. In the beginning is the word: it is the speaking of words which is constructive and reconstructive, not the hearing of them.

In a letter to the press in August 1914, Bertrand Russell enumerated, with characteristic eloquence, some causes of the war which had just started:

... vast forces of national greed and national hatred - atavistic instincts, harmful to mankind (sic) at its present level, but transmitted from savage and half-animal ancestors, concentrated and directed by governments and the press, fostered by the upper class as a distraction from social discontent, artificially nourished by the sinister influence of the makers of armaments, encouraged by a whole foul literature of 'glory', and by every textbook of history with which the minds of children are polluted. (8)

Partly, Russell saw that textbooks had polluted the minds of children in the twenty years before 1914, such that adults were now eager to go out and take part in a pointless war. But partly also he was seeing teaching materials as part of society's total culture, affecting and reflecting - and affecting <u>because</u> reflecting - adults in the here and now, not just in the future. It is entirely reasonable and right to see textbooks as communications and currency between adults, as part of adult culture. No textbook can ever be adequately defended with claims that it is intended for children, and that therefore simplifications and distortions are inevitable.

To state that school textbooks are read in schools is to obscure or forget the fundamental fact that there are schools and schools: there are different contexts in which books may be used, and it is often the contexts of books, not the contents of books, which determine the messages which are communicated. This point can be emphasized with a well known optical illusion:

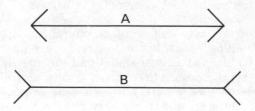

The two horizontal lines, A and B, are precisely the same length. But because they appear in different contexts (the oblique lines at their ends) they seem quite different from each other - that is, the one appears longer. Similarly, a school textbook in one context (a particular school, a particular classroom, a particular teacher) may be excellent, but in a different context may be pernicious. The message actually received by pupils and teachers from a book, as distinct from the message intended by the author, depends on the ethos and relationships in which the book is used: for example, and most obviously, on whether there is an authoritarian pedagogy or a liberal pedagogy. (9) This point cannot be overemphasized.

Nevertheless we shall be in danger of forgetting it throughout the rest of this chapter.

Over the last twenty years or so there has by and large been much more interest in school textbook bias in the United States and on the continent of Europe than there has been in Britain. In the United States there have been excellent and effective campaigns against racism and various forms of enthnocentrism, particularly in accounts of internal American history and society, and against sexism. (10) On the continent there have been thorough attempts to remove nationalist bias from history books, particularly, of course, books about intra-European relationships. In Britain there have been a number of fine analyses, but there has been little or no significant attempt so far by commercial publishers to produce books which attempt to combat class, 'race', and gender inequalities. The fine analyses include the output of two very lively and readable magazines, Dragons Teeth and Children's Book Bulletin; a number of detailed critiques of racism in geography textbooks; (11) papers produced from the Centre for Urban Educational Studies in London; and several articles and papers agianst sexism, of which the best is the excellent Pour out the Cocoa, Janet by Rosemary Stones. (12) Yet little of this sound conceptual work is known in school staffrooms, other perhaps than in London, and even less seems to have had any impact on publishers.

Two small-scale studies can be cited to summarize the overall concern. In London a study was made of the ten most popular reading schemes in primary schools. (13) It was found that even in London, an authority whose teachers are by and large far more aware of these issues than anywhere else in Britian,

> over half the schemes had no black characters appearing at all. Of the remaining books the majority have only the occasional black character appearing tokenistically in the illustrations but not in the text. Books where black characters play a positive and central role are a rarity indeed. The impact of this is to deny black children and their community a voice, and ... to reinforce those post-colonial and supremacist ideas about the Third World that are a part of mainstream British culture.

The other study to be cited here was of two geography textbooks for secondary schools, Man and His World, first published by Nelson in 1975 and reprinted six times by 1982, and Elements of Human Geography, published by Allen & Unwin in 1979. (13) It was noted that both books present the false view that human beings can be divided up into separate races, and that through their unconscious choice of words both present white people as superior and more 'normal':

> Where familiar words are used, the words used for white have positive connnotations (fine, straight, fair), and the words for

non-whites have negative connotations (coarse, woolly, flat, drooping, thick). Where unfamiliar words are used (epicanthic, everted, prognathism, steatopygy) it is the non-whites who have these odd and unfamiliar words applied to them: the whites appear 'normal'. (14)

The appendix is a checklist which outlines such points and criticisms in greater detail. Each separate item in the checklist could be readily illustrated with negative examples from textbooks which have been published in Britain in the 1980s and which are likely to be used uncritically by hundreds of thousands of children and teenagers, and their teachers, over the next eight to ten years. Three examples will have to suffice here. Each relates directly to Britain's relationships with Third World countries and therefore indirectly, at least, also to 'race relations' issues within Britain.

The Beans series, published by Adam & Charles Black, is extremely popular in British primary schools. The series is very attractively illustrated, very clearly written, and very efficiently marketed. Each separate book is about a child aged about 10 to 12 years old. Here are the opening sentences of two of the books, about children in Jamaica and Zambia respectively:

This is Dorothy Samuels. She lives in Cascade, a village near Montego Bay, on the north coast of Jamaica. Jamaica is one of the group of islands in the Caribbean Sea. The islands were discovered by Christopher Columbus in 1492 ... (15)

Jelita lives in a small village in Zambia, a country in Africa. Her village has hot weather for most of the year and she and her brother Milenga don't need shoes when they go to school. (16)

Descriptions such as these emphasize difference rather than similarity, and are Anglocentric or Eurocentric in their outlook. Also the emphasis on arcane geographical detail in the very first sentence of the one book ('Cascade, a village near Montego Bay, on the north coast of ...') gives a sense of distance and irrelevance, and lack of humanity and personality. More recent books in the Beans series have avoided the weaknesses of the first few, and have strikingly switched from descriptions in the third person to descriptions in the first person - the recurring pronouns in later books have been I, me, we, us, not he, she, they, them, etc. This may seem a very small improvement but is in fact surely very significant. The simple grammatical switch means that children in other countries and cultures are now presented as subjects not objects - people who can be addressed, people with whom one can interact, people from whom one can learn. It is important and relevant to note that very many textbooks present people in other countries as objects not subjects. Similarly on British television, incidentally, black people typically appear in long telephoto shots, if they appear at all - across the other side of some street, or behind some window or other: objects in a snapshot album, not makers and picturers themselves.

Messages about personality and impersonality, to repeat and summarize, may sometimes be communicated through grammatical form. But often also they are considerably more overt. Here, for example, is a quotation from a book published by Oxford University Press:

> The countries with coloured inhabitants are backward, so we British govern them, for their own good. After all, it is better for an African to take orders from a Christian Englishman than from one of his own witch doctors. We help these people improve their farming, and we build roads, railways and harbours. We keep law and order and stop tribes fighting each other. We stamp out any evil we find ... (17)

Amongst the evils stamped out by the British, the book expains, was 'a flourishing slave trade' in Africa. Now to be fair, the piece quoted appears in inverted commas, and purports to have been spoken in 1898 by the then Colonial Secretary in Britain, Joseph Chamberlain. And also to be fair, nearly the whole book consists interestingly of statements about events in inverted commas, so that in principle, at least, pupils can be aware of and study bias. But there is no explicit critique in the book, either inside or outside of inverted commas, of the views and vocabulary attributed to Joseph Chamberlain. On the contrary the authors themselves frequently use the offensive word 'coloured'; they say that 'unhappily' foreigners did not see the British Empire as Chamberlain did, and they refer in the same breath to foreigners 'sneering' at Britain rather than, for example, 'criticising'. The reference to Africa, in the piece quoted above, ('it is better for an African to take orders from a Christian Englishman than from one of his own witchdoctors') is the only reference to Africa in this book of over 130 large format pages entitled The Twentieth Century World. Later, incidentally, there is a description of a 'typical' Indian village with phrases in it such as 'there is no proper road ... the houses are one-room hovels ... the villagers have no proper furniture ... while an English housewife just turns on a tap, the Indian village housewife must visit the pond twice a day'. The account closes with a statement that soon there will be a Biogas plant in the village, which 'seems like a miracle to these simple folk'.

One last specific example, this time from a book entitled Peacemaker of Calabar, published by the Religious and Moral Education Press, a subsidiary of Pergamon; it is part of a series which is used in religious education classes in probably every single secondary school in Britain. Each book in the series describes a good Christian doing good works - in most instances a good, white

Christian carrying the white man's, or occasionally the white woman's, burden in the Third World. This particular book is about a white woman, Mary Slessor, who was a missionary in West Africa in the nineteenth century. (18) 'The first Europeans brave enough to explore West Africa', the book tells us in its opening pages,

> felt as though they were on a distant, primitive planet ... . Many explorers died of fevers. The few who did return to Europe told stories of black people who worshipped many gods, made human sacrifices and believed that they were surrounded by good and evil spirits. The West Africans lived according to very harsh laws ... . It was only because West Africa had been cut off from new ideas for thousands of years that no progress had been made there.

Later in the book Mary Slessor meets some Africans described as 'a group of sinister masked officials'. They 'were jabbering with excitement', says the author. One of them approaches Mary and threatens her, but he is 'overcome by the power of Mary's piercing blue eyes'.

Now certainly it is important that pupils in our schools should know about people like Mary Slessor and Joseph Chamberlain, and should know about the world view, the racist and racialist world view, which they and their contemporaries held. That is not the issue. The issue is how to prevent the world view of nineteenth century Britain being presented uncritically, casually, matter-of-factly, in the textbooks and classrooms of the 1980s. To this question we now turn, for the third and final part of the chapter.

WHAT CAN BE DONE?

By and large the worst teaching materials have in common that they are produced by commercial publishers in partnership with individual authors. This structure results in racist books for the same reason that BBC and ITV produce racist programmes: all the people involved in the decision-making are white. It has been observed that:

> The media is almost exclusively controlled by white people, and television programmes are made by white middle-class men on the whole. Therefore there is no opportunity for any different perspective to come through, because all the people making the decisions are part of nothing but a very narrow group. (19)

A television producer has argued:

> White people need to be involved in a constant process of examining all our assumptions, ideas and feelings. We must mistrust most of our judgements, and unlearn many of our ideas ... .

> Most white TV executives and producers simply aren't capable of making the right judgements when it comes to programmes about black people. (20)

So this is the first thing that is required: positive action to recruit far more black publishing executives, commissioning editors, marketing managers, sub-editors, graphic designers, picture researchers, photographers, illustrators, manuscript consultants, specialist readers, and - of course - authors. This will involve a thorough overhaul of current recruiting procedures. These sometimes depend on old boy (sic) nets which certainly contravene the spirit, and probably also contravene the letter, of the Race Relations Act.

Second, there need to be changes in the structure of school textbook publishing itself, not just different people staffing the structure. In this connection the essential need is to get away from the very notion of individual authors for textbooks, as if these books depend primarily on some sort of private artistry. Rather, the role of school textbook writer is analogous to that of screenplay writer for a film: it is a routine, workaday craft, not a mysterious art, and it needs to be complemented, corrected, and completed by the work of many others.

The best teaching materials currently being produced have most or all of the following six characteristics: (21)

(a) they arise directly out of very specific teaching and learning;
(b) they are written by teams, groups, committees, projects, collectives, not individuals;
(c) the people involved in these teams include lay people as well as specialists, and children and teenagers as well as adults;
(d) the books are generous not possessive about copyright, and warmly invite teachers to photocopy and to plagiarize;
(e) profits and royalties are invested in further curriculum development, they do not go into the pockets or purses of individual authors;
(f) there is a local concern and context in the first instance.

It is entirely feasible, incidentally, both in principle and in practice, for the capital investment for such books to be provided by commercial publishers.

Third, we need some decent checklists. At the present, so far as racism and non-racism in textbooks are concerned, all we have got is various indecent lists - tatty photocopies of tatty photocopies of tatty photocopies of papers produced in New York in the 1960s, or in Geneva a little later; the latter are written in that bizarre dialect known as worldcouncilofchurchesese. It is hopefully not merely Anglocentric or nationalistic to ask for some lists made in Britain, and not merely pedadantic to insist on conventional English usage.

The best checklist on textbooks so far produced in Britain is to do with sexism, and was compiled by Rosemary Stones. (12) This has four main excellent qualities. One, it is clearly written, with clear logical distinctions. Two, each item in it is strikingly illustrated with a negative or positive example from a book in current use. Three, is has high legitimacy, being published in association with the Schools Council. Four, it is broad based and non-sectarian - it can therefore be used as a campaigning instrument by people with a wide variety of perspectives. Its only weakness, perhaps, is that it may for organizational reasons, not conceptual reasons, fail to have an adequate impact. (Also, for typographical reasons: Rosemary Stones' list is presented in typewriting. It takes up a lot of space, and is therefore tiresome to photocopy, and also its appearance makes it look private, casual, slight, not something which need be attended to really seriously.)

We need checklists on racism, nationalism, and ethnocentrism as fine as Rosemary Stones' list on sexism in the four respects mentioned, and therefore capable of acting as a manifesto in a weighty, but flexible and nimble, campaign. To organize such a campaign is a fourth urgent priority.

The purpose of the campaign would be straightforward: to demonstrate to commercial publishers that it is in their own material interests to stop producing racist books. We have to be able to demonstrate that we could prevent such and such a book being bought. Consider Peacemaker of Calabar, for example: it would not be organizationally impossible, or even particularly difficult, to get a letter sent to every secondary school RE Department in Britain warning them not to buy this book. The letter would be drafted by a central co-ordinating committee, but would be signed and delivered by each of the country's 104 chief education officers, through their inspectors and advisers with responsibility for RE. Also it would be sent to their local schools by parents' groups and community pressure groups. If we were to get together the capability to mobilize that kind of campaign, and if the capability were clearly credible, we would not often need to use it.

Fifth, some new kinds of material need to be developed. 'Books are not made to be believed', says a character in Umberto Eco's The Name of the Rose, 'but to be subjected to enquiry. When we consider a book, we mustn't ask ourselves what it says but what it means.' (22) We need to produce materials which embody this point - which equip pupils with skills to subject books to enquiry. A brief prototype has been prepared on sexism in textbooks by some teachers of history in London:

Look at the books available in the classroom or school library for information about women in the Middle Ages:

1   How often are women mentioned in the text?
2   How often are women included in chapter headings?
3   How often are women shown in illustrations?

4   How many references are there to women in relation to home/domestic life?

5   How many times are women involved outside the home?

Draw a bar graph to show your findings. (22)

We need very many exercises such as these, carefully structured and focused to equip pupils with skills in analysing the textbooks in use in their own, and in other, classrooms. Amongst other things, such exercises should quote from textbooks produced in other countries, and from textbooks of earlier generations.

To summarize, we need a five-point plan of action. One, positive action to recruit more black people into all aspects of school textbook publishing; two, new kinds of partnership between teachers, their employers, local communities, and private capital in the production of school textbooks; three, some checklists to act as convenient summaries of our concerns; four, some skilful campaigns to boycott certain titles or types of book; and five, some wholly new kinds of educational material, which reflect on the problematic nature of educational material itself.

CONCLUDING NOTE

This chapter began with a brief quotation from The Color Purple by Alice Walker, and with an echo of the title of a famous book by E M Forster, Two Cheers for Democracy. It closes with further reference to these two sources.

'The people I admire most', wrote Forster, 'are those who are sensitive and want to create something or discover something, and don't see life in terms of power, and such people get more of a chance under democracy than elsewhere'. And he went on to discuss Parliament: 'Whether Parliament is either a representative body or an efficient one is very doubtful, but I value it because it criticises and talks, and because its chatter gets widely reported. So two cheers for democracy: one because it admits variety and two because it permits criticism. Two cheers are quite enough: there is no occasion to give three. Only Love ... deserves that'. (23)

There is a certain kind of book, though it is not usually a school textbook in the sense of having been specifically intended for schools, which can raise all three of Forster's cheers. That certain kind of book is the novel: 'the development of the novel', said Forster, 'implies the development of humanity'. (24) The Color Purple is an exploration, as are all great narratives, of the meanings and loves of humanity. May children and young people have the good teaching and good fortune to respond with recognition and insight when they hear, in the text and texture of any story, the messages of someone talking like this, in The Color Purple:

Why us suffer. Why us black. Why us men and women. Where do children really come from ... I think us here to wonder, myself. To wonder. The more I wonder, the more I love. (25)

Yes, may the young have the good fortune and the good teaching to say Amen to that, to give three cheers to that.

APPENDIX: NON-RACIST TEACHING MATERIALS: A CHECKLIST OF POSITIVE MESSAGES

Introduction

A school textbook is non-racist if it has both these characteristics:

(a) It reflects, supports, and affirms, as distinct from ignores or rejects, the identity, experience, and concerns of ethnic minority pupils or students.

(b) It criticizes and challenges, as distinct from reflects and reinforces, false beliefs about white (or European, or Western) superiority in white pupils or students.

The following list explains and illustrates these two main points in greater detail. The list is in principle relevant to pupils and students of all ages, including the very youngest. It summarizes the main positive messages about 'race' and international affairs which textbooks should be presenting.

'Race' and race relations

1   'Race'
     It is not stated or implied that human beings can be divided into biological 'races', and words reflecting this false belief ('Caucasian', 'Asiatic', 'Negro', 'coloured', etc.) are not used.

2   Opposition to racialism
     Racialism - the twin false beliefs that (a) races exist and (b) whites are superior - is opposed and criticized, both as personal belief and as political doctrine.

3   Opposition to racism
     Racism - the combination of (a) unequal power structures, (b) discriminatory procedures, and (c) prejudices - is opposed and criticized.

4   Migration
     It is emphasized that black people came to Britain in the 1950s

and 1960s primarily because their labour was needed by the economy. Many were explicitly invited or recruited.

References to Black People

(The term 'black' is a political term, not a biological term. Its use implies that racism is the basic phenomenon to be named, not cultural differences, and that opposition to racism is a basic political struggle. In contemporary Britain it refers both to Asian people and to Afro-Caribbean.)

5   Control and decision-making
     Black people are shown as in control of their lives and environments, and with intentions, desires, and ideals, not merely as passive victims.

6   Their own words
     The views and perspectives of black people are presented or quoted in their own terms - literally, in their own words, and in their own categories and definitions.

7   Everyday life and values
     There are examples of warmth, care, love, laughter, kindness, in the descriptions of family life and everyday relationships of black people.

References to 'Other' countries and cultures

(The term 'other' here means in principle other than the main culture of the school; in practice in Britain it means non-British, and non-European or non-Western.)

8   Multicultural, multiracial 'West'
     Britain and the United States, and also most West European countries, are shown as multicultural, multiracial, multilingual, multifaith societies. They are not all-white, not all-Christian, not all monolingual.

9   Meanings
     Customs, lifestyles, traditions, and beliefs in other cultures are shown as having value and meaning for the people concerned, not as exotic, peculiar, or bizarre.

10   Generalizations
     Generalizations about all or most people in another country or culture are not made or implied. On the contrary there is emphasis on diversity within other groups.

11 One world
It is clear that many apparently localized, smallish-scale events in the modern world are in fact influenced by, and may themselves influence, events and trends elsewhere.

12 Religion
Christianity is not shown as the only true religion, the only source of valid religious insight and experience. Religions other than Christianity are described in their own terms and categories, not with Christian or Western terms.

13 Interaction and learning
People in other countries and cultures are portrayed as people from whom 'we' can learn - their values, their experience of life, their insights, their politics.

References to the Third World

14 Poverty and politics
It is not implied that poverty is merely the absence of Western goods, nor that poverty is mainly a consequence of climate and environment, or of ignorance.

15 Science and technology
Scientific and technological achievements are not shown as exclusively Western or European, neither in the past nor in the present.

16 History
Third World countries and cultures are shown as having a long history and tradition - they were not merely 'discovered' by Europeans.

17 Liberation and struggle
Struggles by black and Third World people against oppression are shown and evaluated from their own points of view, not merely dismissed as disorders, riots, revolts, insurrections etc.

18 Language
The language avoids insulting or patronizing terms - for example, 'coloured', 'tribe', 'native', 'primitive', 'hut', 'superstitious', 'witch-doctor', 'chief', 'jabber'.

19 Heroes and heroines
People who are considered and admired in Third World countries as heroes and heroines are described in these terms, and their influence and inspiration are clear.

References to Particular Issues

20   Islam
     Islam is shown as a religious tradition of great depth and insight, and as a major cultural influence and civilization. It is not implied that Muslims are typically 'fundamentalists' or 'fanatics', and terms such as 'the rise of Islam', implying threat, are not used.

21   South Africa
     It is not implied that apartheid is merely a matter of segregation - separation in housing, cinemas, parks, railways, etc. The inequalities and injustices of a political and economic nature are emphasized, and there is reference to South Africa's economic links with Western countries.

General References

(These last points are not directly related to racism and non-racism. It is probable, however, that a non-racist curriculum will have these features also, at least.)

22   The role of women
     In all countries and cultures, and at all times in history, women are shown as half of the human race, and their work and actions as essential. The word 'man' is not used to refer to all human beings. Traditional gender roles are shown as man-made (sic), not immutable.

23   Conflict and its resolution
     Human beings frequently, even typically, disagree and dispute with each other; they are in constant conflict. This reality is not glossed over, but resolutions of conflict which are (a) non-violent and (b) just, are emphasized also.

24   The media
     There are frequent reminders that newspapers and television oversimplify and distort - for example by ignoring long-term underlying causes of events, by concentrating on personalities and trivialities, by seeking to entertain rather than to explain, and by flattering and reinforcing the prejudices of the audience.

25   'Ordinary' people
     The vast majority of human beings are 'ordinary' and always have been - not monarchs, rulers, politicians, aristocracy, etc. Their experience and outlook are attended to and respected, both in the past and in the present.

26 Bias
Everything is biased. Every book, talk, lesson, course, syllabus, and topic in schools is biased, and so is every list such as this.

NOTES AND REFERENCES

1. Walker, A. (1983) The Colour Purple, London: The Women's Press, pp. 111-12.
2. Cummings, E.E. (1960) Selected Poems, London: Faber, p. 39.
3. Keith Joseph, speech at Reading on 21 March 1984, Department of Education and Science press release.
4. Sivanandan, A., (1982) Patterns of Racism, London: Institute of Race Relations, quoted in introduction.
5. Cox, C. and Scruton, R. (1984) Peace Studies: A Critical Survey, London: Institute for European and Strategic Studies, p. 24.
6. Stradling, R., Noctor, M. and Baines, B. (1984) Teaching Controversial Issues, London: Edward Arnold. See also the very clear and eloquent account of liberal pedagogy in Bridges, D. (1982) 'So truth be in the field', in D. Hicks and P. Townley, (eds) Teaching World Studies, Harlow: Longman.
7. Rawls, J. (1971) A Theory of Justice, Cambridge, MA: Harvard University Press. For a simplified but excellent account of Rawls's 'original position' and 'veil of ignorance', see Wren, B. (1977) Education for Justice, London: SCM Press, pp. 34-42.
8. Russell, B. letter to the Nation 15 August 1914, quoted in his Autobiography, London: Allen & Unwin, 1968, and in Humphrey, N. and Lifton, R.J. (eds) (1984) In a Dark Time, London: Faber.
9. The traditional classroom context is well described in, for example, Hargreaves, D. (1982) The Challenge for the Comprehensive School, London: Routledge & Kegan Paul, ch. 7.
10. For example, the work of the Council on Inter-racial Books for Children, New York.
11. For example, Wright, D. (1983) 'A portrait of racism in geography', Education Journal 5: 2, May, Commission for Racial Equality; Gill, D. (1983) 'Anti-racist education: of what relevance in the geography curriculum?' Contemporary Issues in Geography and Education 1: Autumn; Hicks, D. (1984) 'Geography', in A. Craft and G. Bardell (eds) Curriculum Opportunities in a Multicultural Society, London: Harper & Row; Naidoo, B. (1984) 'Books that censor reality', Watford Community Relations Council, reprinted in extended form as Censoring Reality, ILEA Centre for Anti-Racist Education, 1985.
12. Stones, R. (1983) Pour Out the Cocoa Janet, Harlow: Longman, for the Schools Council.
13. Reported in Longmore, T. and Burgess, C. (1984) 'Racism in early reading', Childright 11: October. See also Spencer, D.

'Reading schemes accused of racism', Times Educational Supplement, 22 April 1988.

14. Wright, D. (1984) 'What do pupils learn about race?' Education Journal, 6: 1, April, Commission for Racial Equality.
15. Hubley, J. and Hubley, P. (1982) Jamaican Village, London: A&C Black.
16. Peterson, P. (1979) Zambia, London: A&C Black.
17. Speed, P. and Speed, M. (1982) The Twentieth Century World, Oxford: Oxford University Press, p. 19.
18. Buchan, J. (1984) Peacemaker of Calabar, Exeter: Wheaton.
19. Sue Woodford, Commissioning Editor for Channel 4 Multicultural Programmes, quoted in Cohen, P. and Gardner, C. (1982) It Aint Half Racist, Mum, London: Comedia Publishing Group.
20. Freeth, T. (1982) 'Racism on television', in P. Cohen, and C. Gardner (eds) op. cit., p. 31. See also, for an extensive discussion of racism in the media, and of practical implications for teachers, Twitchin, J. (1987) The Black and White Media Book, Stoke-on-Trent: Trentham Books.
21. For example, materials developed by the Afro-Caribbean Education Resources (ACER) project; the Institute for Race Relations; the ILEA English Centre; All Faiths for One Race (AFFOR) in Birmingham; the Development Education Centre in Birmingham.
22. Adams, C. 'Off the record: women's omission from classroom historical evidence', in D. Simkin and J. Simkin (eds) (1984) Curriculum Development in Action, Brighton: Tressell Publications. Excellent American materials relevant to this theme include Robinson, D. (ed.) (1969) As Others See Us, and (1974) Verdict on America, Boston: Houghton Miffin. Geography teachers at Quintin Kynaston School, London, have developed materials to help pupils study bias in commercial textbooks, as described in Contemporary Issues in Geography and Education, 1: 2. There is a theoretical rationale for pedagogy based on examination of bias in curriculum materials in Aoki, T. 'Towards a reconceptualization of curriculum implementation', in D. Hopkins and M. Wideen, (eds) (1984) Alternative Perspectives on School Improvement, London: Falmer Press.
23. Forster, E.M. (1951) Two Cheers for Democracy. The pivotal essay entitled 'I believe' was reprinted in Auden, W.H. et al. (1962) Nineteen Personal Philosophies, London: Allen & Unwin.
24. Forster, E.M. (1962) Aspects of the Novel, Harmondsworth: Penguin Books, p. 173.
25. Walker, A. (1983) The Color Purple, London: The Women's Press, p. 239.

Chapter Five

THE PLAYGROUP/NURSERY

Jane Lane

INTRODUCTION

Most people recognize the importance of the early years of a child's life for the development of intellectual, emotional, physical, and social skills. But the resources allocated to these years and the status accorded to those who educate and care for young children (either at home or in some form of pre-school provision) are not commensurate with this recognition. The needs of young children and of those who care for them usually come low on the priority lists of politicians and policy makers. A recent report (1) provides evidence that childcare provision in the United Kingdom is seriously underfunded, fails to meet the needs of parents and children, and is provided by some of the lowest paid workers in the country. Because the traditional role of women is to be responsible for the care of babies and young children, and because women are accorded less status than men, this leads to a devaluing of childcare, whether done by families or by professional childcare/education workers. This situation is further compounded in that, historically and now, upper- and middle-class white women have often passed the day-to-day care of their young children to working-class women. This reaches its ultimate irony in countries like South Africa where the care of young white children is often given to black women. Under the apartheid system their crucial care is taken over by people who have no formal status in the society.

Possibly because every adult was once a child, and therefore has some knowledge of childhood, there is a common assumption that caring for and educating the very young is easy - that it is a 'natural' process requiring no specific skills. It is bound up with the myths about childhood being 'a period of innocence' where the influences of society are minimal. So it causes particular outrage, in the media and elsewhere, when it is suggested that those influences on young children should be examined to assess if they are in any way damaging. It is generally recognized that children learn about and reflect their own environment from the day they are born and that the values and beliefs around them will be the framework, the context, for learning. What is not generally recognized is that the widespread values and beliefs about women, and about the various racial and social groups that make up our society, also have a powerful influence on young children.

British society today provides an environment where white middle-class men hold most of the positions of power in politics, industry, the judiciary, the media, education, and elsewhere. Children see this 'picture' around them, a picture which is in sharp conflict with whom they see at home or in nurseries and playgroups - women. (For ease of terminology in this chapter, unless otherwise stated nurseries should be taken to include nursery schools and classes, day nurseries, private registered and community nurseries, playgroups, childminders working in their own homes, childminder groups, and crèches.) This reinforces the message that only women are really good at looking after children and that they, and the caring professions generally, do not do the really 'important' jobs in society. So boys and girls learn their 'place' from their earliest years. At the same time the political and social climate of those in positions of power indicates that 'good' mothers look after their children themselves, with some experience of formal peer group activities (playgroup or nursery) between 3 and 5 years of age. Working parents often have difficulty in finding care for their young children, care for which they have to pay and which is much more widely available in almost every other European country. (2)

In largely white areas young children hardly see African/Caribbean, South Asian, and other ethnic minority group people in the neighbourhood and only in particular roles on television. In addition, children's views of the world outside Britain are likely to be limited to information about European or 'Western' society intermingled with vignettes of Africa and Asia that are only partial information, reinforcing a deficit model.

So all children learn who is acknowledged as important - they learn from what they see (and do not see), from what they hear (and do not hear) and from what they do (and do not do) - and adults define what this shall be. Most nurseries reflect society - they provide an environment where white middle-class values, beliefs, and practices are the norm - an environment which is far from being neutral and caring of every child, whether or not they are actually present in the nursery. They are, rather, a framework of conformity where there are powerful pressures to be the same as the dominant group or majority. Children, too, bring into the nursery the attitudes and beliefs they hold - they are not the innocents that adults might fondly imagine or wish them to be.

If these attitudes and beliefs are negative towards particular racial and social groups or accept the sex stereotyped roles of women then, unless they are identified, discussed, and countered, they will develop and flourish into the formal school years. Children are not born racially prejudiced or having notions of social or gender superiority. Although it may be common to hold these beliefs, it is not natural. Any such attitudes or beliefs are learnt - they are not innate. They are learnt from all the influences around them, in their homes, in their nurseries, and elsewhere - the media, posters, toys, books, catalogues, packaging, storytelling tapes, from adults (including nursery staff, parents, neighbours, and shopkeepers), from siblings, peers and from friends. And they are learnt wherever they grow up - in multiracial, largely white, urban and rural areas.

Negative attitudes based on 'race', gender, and social class are pervasive. Children cannot be emotionally fulfilled if they develop such non-caring attitudes to others. When they grow up they may be manifested in oppressive or discriminatory behaviour and treatment of others, reinforcing the existing inequalities of society. The overlapping of groups, where one is more highly regarded than another (for example white people comprise men and women, women include black and white women, and all social classes include men and women, black and white) complicates the power hierarchy and means that some children may be both oppressors and victims subjected to oppression. Does this pecking order mean that children experiencing oppression are encouraged to be oppressors because of their relatively powerless position in society? And are the children of travellers right at the bottom of the pile because of their almost totally powerless position in society?

All children should be equally valued and respected, and it is important that all children feel positive about themselves, their cultures, their languages, and their religions. Pride in one's culture is not the same as believing one's culture is superior to others. Believing one is 'better' because one belongs to a particular racial, cultural, or social group, or because one is male or female, is dehumanizing. It prevents children developing their full potential because their view of the world is limited and it denies them the experiences of understanding, sharing, and learning from others. Children also need to know that no culture is static and that there are many different cultures and social groups within white, African/Caribbean, South Asian, and other ethnic minority groups.

Every under-fives worker and parent would almost certainly agree that the concept of equality encompasses a value and respect for every child and would support this objective. What is not so likely to be agreed is that the definition has consequences for the organization, management, and practice in nurseries. Every child is unique and the way she or he is treated depends on her or his unique needs, but, because the wider society places lesser value on some groups, under-fives workers have to take account of this. For example, because in the fairy story 'Beauty and the Beast' the beast is often portrayed as grotesque and black, and this feeds into the common word and visual association of black and ugly or dirty, such portrayal reinforces negative messages. Imagine if the beast was white or Beauty was black in order to realize just how deep are the assumptions of many white people as to what is beautiful or ugly. It is not the story itself which is dangerous; it is the use of the story in a society that is inherently racist, both presently and historically, and which already reinforces racist and sexist attitudes. So, unless other stories portray white 'beasts' and black 'Beautys' and are readily available for young children to see, this book should not be used. This is not censorship. It is using book-selection criteria that include the need for positive images and take account of societal attitudes.

Similarly, providing a range of multicultural resources that includes positive role models for girls as well as boys, for example, in the home corner, is still only a part of nursery activities and the wider society and, as such, is important but not sufficient. If nothing is done to counter and rectify the way cultures and social groups are ranked in a hierarchy, where some are more valued than others (both in Britain and elsewhere), and if nothing is done to ensure that girls are valued as much as boys everywhere outside the home corner, then existing negative attitudes may merely be reinforced.

Adults have the power to intervene in this process of learning. It is not enough only to be passive because the learning process extends outside parental or nursery staff influence. And it cannot be left to chance. The struggle for equality starts in the earliest years and is about breaking down practices, customs, and procedures that result in some people having poorer life chances, poorer job opportunities, poorer housing, and poorer education than others and having little influence on the political and economic decisions that affect their lives.

Their young children are the most vulnerable. To have a well resourced nursery where any new child arriving tomorrow morning will feel valued, respected, and welcomed by children and staff, be positively reflected (in terms of physical appearance, culture, language, and religion) in the environment, and be expected to learn the skills necessary to achieve academic success later on is a professional objective all under-fives workers can share. Ensuring equality and justice in nurseries is not easy. There are no experts and no simple, quick solutions. But everything that goes on needs to be questioned: What does every child make of this? What are the messages given out? And what are the consequences?

THE PRESENT UNDER-FIVES MUDDLE – THE EXTERNAL HIDDEN AGENDA

Local Education Authority and Social Services nursery provision caters for a minority of the under-fives, the voluntary sector providing the majority of 'places'. This 'muddle' does not facilitate an overall strategy for equality or indeed even make possible a recognition of the dimension and diversity of the need for change. Teachers, 'carers', childminders, nursery nurses, assistants, and playgroup and support staff, who in their various ways are responsible for educating and caring for young children, may not see themselves as part of the same group of people. They are often split in philosophy, in training and qualifications, in individual remuneration, in conditions of service, in materials available, in premises conditions, and are often seen in conflict with each other in the struggle for limited finance and resources. The issue of equality is too important for under-fives workers to be divided in this way. (To counter this division the terms 'under-fives workers' or 'workers' are used to encompass nursery teachers, childminders, carers, nursery nurses/assistants, and all other staff working with under-fives). A co-ordinated, interdepartmental strategy is necessary if existing inequalities are to be broken down.

There are, however, some opportunities to be taken from this 'muddle' and apparent range of choices of provision. Facilities may be flexible and more receptive to new ideas than post-five education where bureaucracy may hinder change. They can develop links with families, forging equal and complementary roles that do not give higher status to one at the expense of the other. Under-fives workers genuinely believe they care for all children, and this is a good foundation for considering the issue of equality. But the variety of provision and their admission arrangements do have consequences in terms of who goes where. Some recruitment methods and admission criteria may, in practice, be discriminatory. Nursery schools and classes are free but everything else has to be paid for, except in specific cases in Social Services day nurseries. Also the hours of opening range from 2 to 3 hours in most playgroups to full-day care all the year round in most day nurseries. For working parents the choice is usually limited to childminders or private and community nurseries, especially in the years before a child is 2 years old. Thus, in reality, economic and social factors largely determine who goes where and therefore the type of pre-school experience received.

Although there is little hard evidence, it is widely alleged that most playgroup places are taken up by white middle-class children and that nursery schools and classes, on the whole, reflect the racial and social composition of the local community but do not generally cater for children when both parents are in full-time employment. Because the criteria for admission to Social Services day nurseries are usually based on 'social and physical' need, children who attend may be stigmatized as having (or being) a 'problem' - by those in the nursery and by those outside. This has negative consequences for all the children and their families. It is known that children of African/Caribbean origin are overrepresented in these nurseries. (3) If, in addition to stigmatization or 'labelling', such children are stereotyped because they are African/Caribbean, this may lead to their families (and indeed the African/Caribbean community) being seen as a 'problem'. This has often led to the pathologizing of such families, where they are stereotyped as inadequate in terms of bringing up their children. Numerically, Social Services day nursery places are very few indeed, but the overrepresentation of children of African/Caribbean origin in them feeds the myth that their families are inadequate rather than having an overall lack of choice.

However, in nearly all provision, with the exception of a few inner city nurseries and some community nurseries, it is likely that the workers are white and female and that where there are African/Caribbean or South Asian workers they are not employed as teachers, officers-in-charge, or as playgroup leaders. So young children rarely see either African/Caribbean or South Asian staff as role models in authority or men in a caring role. In addition, most professionals visiting nurseries, for example speech therapists, educational psychologists, and social workers, are likely to be middle class and white. In stark contrast support staff, for example meals supervisors and cleaners, are likely to be working-class women. If some of them are African/Caribbean or South Asian these may be the only role models the children see. In reality African/Caribbean and South Asian men are totally absent and white men are almost absent from their nursery world. The magnitude of rectifying this imbalance is formidable. For example, a recent survey (4) shows that only 2 per cent of teachers in the eight LEAs selected and 2.6 per cent of student teachers in their final year were from ethnic minorities (defined as 'persons of the New Commonwealth and Pakistani origin and, for example, other minorities such as Chinese and Cypriot'). Until African/Caribbean, South Asian, and other ethnic minority pupils have positive experiences at school they are unlikely to want to be teachers themselves. Similarly, until the status of work with young children is raised, men are unlikely to be involved. And until all people working in and around nurseries are equally valued, whatever their specific roles, there will be some people who appear to be more 'important' than others.

The other factor that is significant in compounding this already diverse situation is that of the differing staff qualifications required in the various forms of provision. As the qualifications are usually attached to specific conditions of service (for example, holidays, rates of pay, hours of work, and status) and some voluntary sector qualifications may not be formally recognized outside their particular form of provision, the difficulty of looking at the under-fives field as a whole in terms of equality is further complicated.

It is with this background of muddle, low status, underfunding of under-fives workers with differing qualifications and hence differing career structures, differential allocation of resources, premises, and staffing, that the consideration of nursery practice in terms of the issue of equality has to take place.

THE ALTERNATIVE AGENDA – THE HIDDEN CURRICULUM

Until recently nursery education* seldom prepared students to work in multiracial urban nurseries let alone provide them with the skills to counter inequalities in both multiracial and largely white areas. Indeed much nursery education has reinforced inequalities by using textbooks and other resources that stereotype some families and devalue particular child-rearing practices. Furthermore the use of visiting speakers about 'race' issues tacked on to a course, while not including the concept of equality throughout the whole course, reinforces the 'exotic' or the 'problems' and allows the issues to be marginalized.

Child development theories, with their norms based largely on white, middle-class, 'Western' concepts, have percolated through to professionals and families both formally in institutions and informally through the media, health clinics, and magazines so that there may appear to be an accepted 'best' way to bring up children. This may result in the child-rearing practices of families who are neither white nor middle-class being seen as less good. It is crucial that this form of thinking and practice is countered at all levels so that the various child-rearing practices and different family structures are not judged negatively from an ethnocentric or culturally superior viewpoint. Rather the many ways of bringing up children successfully should be seen as different, contributing to the richness of our society. More generally, the values and norms of one culture may be different from another. All should be recognized and respected and not some viewed as deficient compared with others.

While lip service is usually paid to making all children feel at ease there is little knowledge about how this should be done in practice. 'Treating all children the same', taking a 'colour-blind approach' (i.e. not acknowledging obvious differences), and 'correcting' children's behaviour and 'manners' from a white middle-class perspective so that they will 'fit in', is not equal treatment. It denies a child's individual needs. A range of languages and dialects, cultures, religions, and dress add to the opportunities for extending the experience of all children and workers.

By not talking about equality and ignoring differences, negative attitudes are reinforced and allowed to develop unchecked. Children who have experienced oppression, for example, by having negative comments made about their appearance, need to know that it is no fault of theirs that this has happened. The cumulative affect of such comments may, for example, lead a child to refuse to wear 'traditional' clothes as a result of 'one-off' remarks. By not taking the original behaviour seriously such children, if not supported, may

---

* This term is used to establish its professionalism as opposed to 'training' and encompasses what is known as teacher education and nursery nurse, playgroup, and childminder courses.

be left hurt, bewildered, and isolated. In these circumstances it would not be surprising if they retreated into timidity or aggression. Indeed this is often the behaviour witnessed by under-fives workers who may wonder what caused it. An ongoing research study, (5) is seeking to identify both whether some existing practices and procedures in the early years operate to the disadvantage of African/Caribbean and South Asian children, and whether there are other practices in operation that promote equal opportunity.

Research (6) also provides evidence of the early age that children learn about racial differences and skin colour and ascribe values to them. It would be surprising, therefore, if most three-year olds were not beginning to distinguish different colours of toys and it would be remarkable if skin colours were not similarly noticed. However there are still many workers who cannot accept that young children notice physical differences or may be learning to hold negative attitudes. By denying this learning process it appears that to tease, to ridicule, and to make negative remarks are somehow normal (if undesirable) and inevitable, i.e. all children behave in this way at some stage.

Furthermore, because of the belief in childhood innocence it is unlikely that young children will be considered capable of rational thinking or expressing their own opinions, when provided with the opportunity. Most young children are quite capable of developing concepts of what is right and wrong in terms of equality and justice. It may be only when multicultural resources are provided or African/Caribbean, South Asian, and children from other ethnic minority groups are present, that ethnocentric attitudes, in certain situations, emerge. Similarly, the presence of children from a social class different from the majority may stimulate discussion that might, in the presence of children only from the same social class, not have arisen. These attitudes may be articulated, perhaps when no adults are around. There are subtle unspoken messages that young children learn - messages that indicate when and where it is acceptable to express ideas based on 'race', culture, gender, or social-class inequality.

The example of a teacher identifying racist attitudes of nursery children (7) demonstrates her powerful, unconscious influence in suppressing the manifestations of attitudes and provides a framework where the existence of those attitudes can be denied by those most close to the children. Workers may never know what children really think, so they do not see the necessity for countering any superior attitudes they may hold. Because girls and boys are nearly always present together in nurseries, and therefore familiar with each other, any sexist attitudes they hold may not be identified or articulated but, rather, may be unconsciously reinforced and supported. However, learning to identify racist attitudes often provides the framework for revealing negative attitudes based on gender or class. But who notices the experience of travellers' children or considers how negative attitudes towards them can be countered?

However, crucially, raising all these issues is more readily considered if families who are close to the child are supportive of the concept of equality and are committed to their complementary role of countering inequality. They, too, may have learnt how various child-rearing practices are ranked in a hierarchy based on 'traditional' norms. They may have learnt to make judgements about such things as bedtimes, sleeping arrangements, diet, cleanliness, punishment, and what makes a 'good mother'. Those who do not 'fit' these criteria may be judged as inadequate. In our present society where stereotyping and inequalities flourish only white middle-class families 'fit'. This often leads to the pathologizing of African/ Caribbean, South Asian, and working-class families, blaming them for their and their children's perceived inadequacies and failings rather than examining the causes. With rare exceptions all families have their own high expectations of their children and want them to succeed and be happy in the nursery. Nursery workers and families both have crucial roles to play in achieving this objective.

The conflict between workers trying to raise the status and practice of childcare/education as a profession and the common assumption that anyone can bring up children may leave families (as non-professionals) inhibited by professional expertise. The ultimate conflict comes between 'How can I do anything with a child who has those parents?' and a belief that professionals are the 'experts'. What is clear is that families are essential and childcare/education must be excellent. So each is complementary to the other. If both families and professionals value their own roles at the same time as valuing each other's role then co-operation on an equal basis becomes possible.

In community nurseries and playgroups with management groups that include family members, this equal sharing of policy and responsibility is really possible, but in nursery schools and classes other ways of involving families apart from school governing bodies and occasional parent or consultative meetings on specific issues need to be considered. The situation is very different with regard to private or Social Services day nurseries where policy decisions are not open to public inspection and are vested elsewhere. Thus the level and degree of parental involvement is dictated by individual perceptions. As Social Services day nurseries are often seen as catering for 'problem' children, their families too may be considered to be 'problems', thus perpetuating the philosophy that people with problems are problem people. Sometimes any problems families may have arise from one source - that of poverty, a poverty which most white middle-class families do not experience. By involving such families in the management of their nurseries, some of their feelings of powerlessness can be broken down. Can families and workers persuade each other to work together to effect change?

There are a few other interlinked issues which need to be emphasized if under-fives workers are to be able to examine their own practice in detail. First the role of stereotyping and expectation of under-fives workers in the socialization process. It is well known that having low expectations of children based on stereotypes is likely to be self-fulfilling. Believing that African/Caribbean boys (or boys in general or working-class boys) are unable to concentrate may lead workers to allow them to ride bicycles and not encourage them to learn the full range of other skills, or to create experiences that will enhance overall development. This is likely to result in their dominating the wheeled toys - the holding of the stereotype has created the behaviour and denied the boys access to cognitive learning skills. Similarly if under-fives workers believe that girls are less demanding and aggressive than boys and that they can pick up skills for themselves, they may give more attention to boys. This means that girls only get attention when they hang around or are near the worker, i.e. they are seen as 'dependent'. This may result in girls having less access to detailed instruction.

Further evidence from research (8) in the classroom shows that nursery teachers reinforce sex role stereotypes in many subtle ways of which they are frequently unaware, including allowing boys and girls to play with gender-determined toys that limit each from learning the skills of the other. And it is well known that factors of culture, 'race', gender, and social class determine academic success at school and impact on adult life later on. It is therefore essential that, in these crucial early years, when cognitive skills are learnt and developed, workers should have high expectations of all children, free of stereotyped blockages.

Another issue that is worth considering is whether, as part of the socialization process, workers may reinforce or determine what they consider are 'good manners'. 'Manners' are aspects of behaviour that are culturally conditioned and learnt responses or actions and, as such, may be different in different cultures and social groups. There is a whole range of 'manners', particularly table manners and expressing appreciation of politeness that, if it is not recognized that they are culturally learnt, may be interpreted in their various manifestations or omissions as being 'bad manners' or as having 'no manners'. Because what is considered good manners in one culture is generally so deeply ingrained in people's thinking, the absence or presence of particular practices or the failure to conform to expectations may lead workers to try to change the situation by instilling what they believe are 'good manners' into young children, rather than accepting that what is really occurring is a different cultural response to the same situation. For example, the words 'please' and 'thank you' may not be the common words in all cultures and social groups that they are in white middle-class culture and practice. There may be other ways of expressing respect and gratitude that, because they are not so obvious, go unnoticed - or such expressions may just be considered unnecessary because people do things for each other with no expectations of any kind of 'reward'. Particular ways of eating food may lead to workers correcting children to conform to what is assumed to be universal 'good manners', rather than just one form. It is precisely because such concepts are so deeply ingrained that it may be difficult to stand back and question whether workers are, in fact, forcing children to change to fit into their ideas rather than trying to understand that their families may do things in different ways, but with just as much caring and respect. Although socialization is important, workers therefore need to ensure that correcting children's behaviour is not based on irrelevant cultural standards of what are 'good manners'.

Another aspect of mealtimes is the terminology used to describe each meal - the words 'dinner', 'tea', 'supper', and 'lunch' may not only refer to different times of meals between cultural and social groups but also to different foods eaten at these times. For example, 'tea' may be a cooked meal after work in one situation and dainty sandwiches and a cup of tea in mid afternoon in another. Apart from the different ways of eating food - with fingers, cutlery, or chopsticks for example - the range of cutlery/implements available and their use varies between social groups. As with manners, no child should be made to feel inadequate because she or he does not conform to a white, middle-class pattern of terminology, behaviour, and ways of eating at mealtimes. A child may not know how to use a knife and fork because she or he uses a spoon at home and another may be bewildered by the various shapes and sizes of cutlery that other families use. Again these are different ways of eating and, as such, none is 'better' than another. Open discussion of mealtime terms and ways of eating in the absence of judgements about them will demonstrate the differences to children so that none feel ashamed or humiliated because they are made to feel that they do not 'know how to do things properly'.

This leads to the last issue - that of assessment (testing). Many tests given to young children, in health clinics and nurseries, are standardized on white, middle-class, 'Western' children. The norms for other children may be different. Cultural bias in tests is well known but such tests continue to be used. Under-fives workers need to consider what such tests are used for and to make sure, wherever possible, that children are not disadvantaged by them, for example by assessing them using unfamiliar objects or an unfamiliar language or dialect. Similarly, forms of assessment that require workers to evaluate children without specific criteria should be avoided. For example, measuring a child on a continuum between 'aggressive' and 'timid', in the absence of criteria, is not only subjective but is open to the influence of stereotyping.

PRACTICE

Before practical methods of working towards equality are considered it may be helpful to take a careful look at what is going on in the nursery. What would a stranger make of it, what are the messages given out, what are the children (as individuals and groups) actually doing, and, if possible, what are their feelings, attitudes, and beliefs? A simple 'survey' will help to reveal the hidden (or not so hidden) curriculum. A properly standardized research survey would require far more time and resources than is available to most under-fives workers (especially those in the voluntary sector) and it is unlikely that an observer will be able to answer more than a few of the questions. Nevertheless the process of observing may indicate and clarify some of what is going on and perhaps reveal what otherwise may not have been noticed.

First, what resources are used?

Looking at the books, toys and other materials including the physical images of people represented (in posters and elsewhere) how many are of white, African/Caribbean, South Asian, and other ethnic minority group people or of working-class people?
How many are of men (boys) and women (girls)? What roles are they playing?
Do they present positive images of all people?
Do they reflect society as it usually is or do they attempt to change ideas by having, for example, a black teacher or a woman mechanic?
Do they caricature people?
Are photographs used to counter this?
Do the images reinforce 'race', class, and gender oppressions?
Does the text say the same thing as the pictures or do the pictures alone give a different message?
Do illustrations reinforce some social-class-determined roles more than others?
Who is pictured on packaging?
Are there male and African/Caribbean, South Asian, and other ethnic minority dolls and puppets? Are they accurate representations?
What is in the dressing-up box?
What is available in the range of domestic equipment?

Second, what is going on between children and between children and workers (or between workers)?

Who is playing with what? Who is playing with whom?
Are there any children who are not playing or playing alone?
Are there patterns (based on 'race', gender, social class, or other grounds) of who plays with whom?
How do workers interact with children? Do they talk to all - in the same way?
Is there any difference of behaviour (or treatment) of girls and boys or of other groups?
Are some reprimanded more than others? If so, why?

What is the location of children to workers in general activities or at storytime?

And what is the reason for the location? For example, is the child near the adult at mealtimes because they have been 'naughty' or because they eat food 'nicely'?

Who dresses up and what clothes are used (or not used)?

Who plays in the home corner/area?

Are other uses made of the home corner/area to reflect children's experiences?

Are any children deliberately encouraged or discouraged from taking part in any activity - by other children or workers?

How do workers respond to aggressive or disruptive behaviour?

Is there a difference between the response to girls or boys or to any other group of children - or to any particular child?

How is conflict between children resolved?

Does any one sex or social group behave differently from another in a conflict situation and is the situation treated in a different way by workers?

Do workers give the same attention to all children whether they are near them or further away?

Are there opportunities for discussion and sharing of ideas?

Do any children experience harassment or abuse? If so, what kind? How is it dealt with?

These questions are just a few of what might be considered. The tentative results are likely to point to some issues that need further thought. Perhaps the results could be shared with families and workers in terms of illustrating what is going on in reality - a basis for working together for change, where necessary. But it is only the beginning of ensuring that the nursery is based on equality and justice. Every facet of resources and all practices and procedures need now to be carefully examined. What becomes immediately obvious is that these are interlocked. For example, the way a black doll is introduced and played with is ultimately more important than the doll itself. This leads to thinking about 'play' with co-workers and families and support for training and discussion. And the way all staff are valued indicates how different children may be valued - so the ethos of the whole nursery is crucial. Because of this complexity and the limited space available only a few of the key concepts can be raised. There are, however, an increasing number of support materials available and groups of people who are considering the implications of equality for under-fives workers.

LOOKING AT RESOURCES

Resources alone cannot change the way people think. Even good multicultural resources can be counter-productive if they are used inappropriately, if they are viewed as exotic, or if they are seen, by children or workers, as inferior. Only by countering the racism and classism themselves that rank cultures in a hierarchy can such resources be used effectively. It is the way they are used in play and learning that is important. Limited, ethnocentric, stereotyped resources may reinforce racism, sexism, and classism. Therefore they need to be evaluated to ensure they are positive about all people, free of stereotypes, accurate, and that they reflect the real and international world. Educational resources on 'race' and gender, (9) a list of background reading referring to materials for under-fives, (10) and a list of some literature relevant to equality of opportunity and antiracist childcare/education organization and practice (11) are available.

Books

Books are important for developing linguistic skills, imagination, and vocabulary. They are also vehicles for reinforcing stereotypes or for challenging them. There are now many good books for young children that positively value all people and a few that are beginning to offer alternative role models, although there are still very few with mixed-'race' (or mixed-parentage) families in the story. Criteria for evaluating books (12) and considering hidden messages (13) from the perspective of equality are available.

Toys

With rare exceptions, (14) (15) compared with books, the issue of equality and the role of toys have seldom been considered. Although space precludes a detailed examination here, all toys need to be discussed in detail before they are bought and used.

Jigsaws: Most of the issues raised around books apply equally to jigsaws. But because there are a limited number of good jigsaws compared with books they need to be particularly carefully selected. There are a few positive examples with people doing a variety of jobs, with multicultural street scenes, mixed-'race' families, African/Caribbean and South Asian women and men, and white women doing work that white men usually do. Although young children like bold images it is not easy to have positive ones that do not become almost caricatures or cartoons. This does not matter so much with white people because there is an abundance of positive physical portrayals of them generally, but in the absence of images of African/Caribbean and South Asian people anyway, such 'caricatures' may reinforce racism. The use of photographs and a range of jigsaws, perhaps using ones of people the children know, avoids this.

Dolls: These are important because they represent people. Again there needs to be a range of male and female dolls (including rag dolls) each with a range of clothes and a range of accurate skin tones, hair textures, and hair colours. The emphasis on 'range' is to try to avoid stereotyping. In a racist, sexist society it is difficult to avoid this. Dolls are like three-dimensional cartoons and, as such, fall into all the traps of caricaturization. Often male and female dolls have the same faces, and African/Caribbean and South Asian dolls have the same features as white dolls but coloured differently. Having only blonde-haired white dolls may reinforce racist and sexist imagery of what is 'beautiful'. Black dolls with lifelike hair that can be braided give opportunities for African/Caribbean children and others to practice what they may see done at home and for all children to learn to value African/Caribbean hair. Many dolls reinforce sexism by the high-fashion clothes and shoes that they wear. So dolls should be chosen that also wear ordinary everyday clothes.

Children often have only one or two dolls at home, so families can learn about the issues by being involved in the 'selection' of nursery dolls. Care must be taken to avoid selecting ones that have the stereotyped hair and features that are typical of a 'golliwog'. Golliwogs are yet another demeaning stereotype, historically created and maintained by white people. White children sometimes equate them with black people and young black children still say they are taunted with golliwogs by white children. Black adults have recounted their painful memories as children when they were likened to golliwogs - feelings that, at the time, they kept to themselves. They have no place in today's nursery (or anywhere else, for that matter).

Dressing-up clothes. It is worth thinking about why children like to dress up. There is often such a variety available including what could be described as everyday (and night) clothes, national costumes, fashion clothes, traditional dress, fancy dress, and uniforms. What does a child make of this variety and what are the messages given by this mixture of categories? In the absence of an internationalist perspective, can they distinguish, for example, celebration and everyday clothes in different cultures? Children need to have positive attitudes to each other and each other's families in order to use dressing-up clothes positively. It is not acceptable for children to dress up in something worn in one culture in order to ridicule it (and the people of that culture).

On the other hand to dress up is to fantasize - to be dressed up like someone who is important to a child. When boys dress up in women's clothes are they being like their mothers or are they laughing at what women wear? The distinction is important. The wearing of skirts by boys is particularly important because men in many parts of the world wear material in a 'skirt-like' way. The

Scottish kilt, the Indian dhoti, and the Nigerian wrappa(er), for example. It demonstrates the need to unpack the attitudes behind these issues and to give the children factual information on how, where, and why particular clothes are worn so that they learn to place positive values both on the clothes and the people who wear them. Photographs can aid this understanding.

Domestic equipment. This needs to reflect a variety of cultures so that children can become accustomed to using it and learn to explore both familiar and unfamiliar objects. Items should be correctly named and workers should know how they are used as everyday objects and not as strange or exotic.

Other toys. A few other toys need to be highlighted. Alphabet games and friezes often include 'I for Indian' portraying a Native American in full ceremonial head-dress. Apart from the stereotyping of the Native American (and the associated myths of being the 'baddie' in 'Cowboys and Indians') the nomenclature is incorrect and such imagery will not encourage a respect for Native American culture. Puppets sometimes portray evil by having black, ugly faces with broad white eyes resembling golliwog features. Because black is often associated with evil this feeds into the myths that black people are evil and, as such, should be avoided. Packaging tends to portray white children only, girls often having blonde hair and blue eyes, thus reinforcing the idea that brown skin, black hair, and non-blue eyes are somewhat less worthy. Paints should include a range of colours so that all children can paint skin colour accurately.

The essential aim is to correct the lack of balance in resources and to take account of the existing inequalities when selecting new ones. This means devising criteria that clearly define what needs to be looked for in the selection process.

LOOKING AT PLAY AND ACTIVITIES

The way resources are used and the way they are played with has already been identified as important. All children play. If a child appears not to be playing, what is inhibiting her or him? There is no 'wrong' way to play except when the play involves the hurting or ridiculing of another child (or group of children) or adult, whether or not they are present at the time. Practice must be the same as the ethos in the nursery. An Indian child is unlikely to play in the home corner if he or she has heard remarks about 'funny food'; a boy is unlikely to express emotion in play-acting if he has heard that 'big boys don't cry'; and a girl is less likely to play with boys if groups are divided up on the basis of gender.

Play and activities practice

Listed below are some brief ideas/suggestions for nursery activities, taking positive account of cultural variety.

Food. Visit local foodshops and buy food. Look at a range of foods and eat them together. Introduce and practice various ways of eating, placing equal weight on the skills needed for each - for example, with chopsticks, fingers, and cutlery. Discuss the various ways of making tea. Encourage children to try a variety of foods and to give their reasoned opinions about them.

Storytelling. Ensure that listening and talking roles are given to all children and that all children have equal access to sitting near workers. Read stories with positive roles of women, working-class people, and African/Caribbean, South Asian, and other ethnic minority groups of people.

Sand play. Because sand is difficult to remove from oiled, curly hair, offer head coverings that are attractive to wear for all children playing with sand.

Counting. Consider the various ways of counting - for example, on fingers, with beads, and on knuckles.

Music. Invite people to play a variety of musical instruments and provide opportunities for listening to recorded music from different cultures. Provide musical instruments from different cultures for the children to learn about and to play correctly and sensitively.

Painting. Encourage children to paint pictures of themselves and others using a range of coloured (including black, brown, and white) paints and paper. Use the opportunity to discuss physical differences positively.

Visits and programmes. Check any television, radio programmes, or outside visits, where appropriate, in advance to ensure that what the children will experience fits the ethos of the nursery.

Photograph book. Take or get photographs of all the children and their families doing what they like doing and make up a group book for each to take home in turn and share with their families.

Sharing cultures. Provide opportunities for children to tell each other about what they do at home and elsewhere and encourage them to question one another informally about social group and cultural differences - not only about their family countries of origin where relevant but about what they do here in Britain. Use resources to discuss cultures, including working-class cultures.

Holidays/festivals. Share and discuss family celebrations and festivals, placing equal value on all.

Posters and exhibitions. Collect and display posters and other materials showing various cultures and the variety within them. Ensure that all the messages are positive for all children, taking particular care to include people in positive situations where they are not normally seen. Discuss the posters with the children, giving them space to ask questions. Ensure that questions are answered correctly or that, if necessary, further information is sought.

Impact of the outside world. Many children will be conscious, directly or indirectly, of issues outside the home and the nursery. Immediate issues, for example, disasters, international events, uprisings, or festivals, whether they occur locally or in another country, affect even young children and their experiences will be brought into the nursery. Opportunities to support children and their families where appropriate or to discuss situations of concern should be provided so that workers and families can share their concern together.

LOOKING AT LANGUAGE (16)

Children's languages and dialects are integral to their identities. To value their languages and dialects (their language variety) is to value them. Languages and dialects are also crucial to cultural maintenance. Standard English has no innate linguistic advantage over any other language or dialect, although it is necessary to speak it in order to achieve success in British schools. Because no language or dialect is deficient it is essential to break down the hierarchy that places a superior value on some at the expense of others, a superiority which is reflected in the racism and classism that some children (and the languages or dialects they speak) experience. Children only have to be laughed at once for the way they speak, to feel their language or dialect and they themselves are not valued.

Multilingualism and bilingualism are skills that few, white, British people have and the learning and speaking of English, as well as speaking a home language, should be seen as having two (or more) first languages. (It sometimes appears that only when bilingualism is associated with an oppressed group is it seen as a disadvantage). Home languages need to be extended in vocabulary, creativity, and understanding at the same time as (or before) English is learnt. Also children learn English better in the presence of English-speaking children. Withdrawal for tuition prevents this and gives messages to English-speaking children that their language/dialect is superior. All nursery activities are extended if bilingual staff are present, not just to help children whose home language is not English but to provide a role model for all children. Ensuring that language variety is valued by all children provides an impetus for learning other languages later on at school.

Language practice

Some brief suggestions for breaking down language and dialect hierarchies and supporting the learning of English are listed below.

Language survey. There is a great number of languages spoken in Britain. Even in a largely white area, there is likely to be a range of languages and dialects spoken by family members. Make a chart of the home languages and dialects of the children and their families and discuss the way they have influenced each other with the children. For example, what 'non-English' origin or regional dialect words do they know? Put notices and words around the room in different languages and dialects.

Written language. Share with the children the way different languages and dialects are written down and read, for example, right to left and top to bottom. Illustrate how characters and letters can be understood by their readers, involving practical examples where possible. Make a chart of welcoming phrases in different languages and dialects to be placed near the entrance.

Nursery rhymes and songs. Use recorded songs or ask local people to sing rhymes and songs in different languages and dialects from different parts of the world. Share rhymes with common themes in different languages and dialects. Encourage all children to listen to others singing in their home languages and dialects, perhaps sharing simple parts together.

Stories. Tell stories where possible in different languages and dialects perhaps using picture books as illustration. Tell stories with dual texts in both languages and dialects so that children hear the sounds. If there is no one fluent in a language or dialect, use recorded stories. Encourage active listening of different languages and dialects by all children. Involve parents, where possible, in writing and illustrating stories in different dialects and languages to share with the children.

Home language. Encourage children to speak their home languages and dialects together, just as English-speakers talk together. Encourage families similarly, perhaps in a family room where possible.

LOOKING AT TERMINOLOGY

There are some words in fairly common usage that are factually incorrect, insensitive, or offensive. Such words as 'coloured' (referring to people), 'half-caste', and 'Red Indian' derive from white people's description of African/Caribbean, South Asian, or Native American people from a superior viewpoint. 'Paki' is not an abbreviation for a person from Pakistan but a derogatory word often used to include both African/Caribbean and South Asian people. These words should not be used.

Other words such as 'primitive', 'uncivilized', and 'backward' are sometimes used to describe people from Third World countries, whether or not anything is known about their cultures. They have negative emotive overtones, viewed from a ethnocentric perspective that reinforces international racism. The use of the word 'immigrant' is extremely unlikely to apply to young children, given the present strict limits on immigration. People who are settled in Britain are no longer immigrants.

Because the word 'black' is often used negatively to denote 'bad', care should be taken in the way it is associated with other words. What would both black and white children think when a black child is asked to 'wash your dirty black hands!'? In this instance the use of the word 'black' is superfluous and only reinforces the equating of 'black' with 'dirty'.

There are many other words that have come to be associated with specific people or things. For example, 'pretty' is often associated with girls having long, blonde hair, blue eyes, and white skin. Those not fitting these criteria may not be considered so desirable. Similarly 'strong' is often associated with boys, and identical behaviour in children might be termed 'aggressive' in girls and 'assertive' in boys. The sexist and racist use of words should be thought about carefully and ways of breaking down the association, by offering alternative models, considered.

The name of a child, like a language and culture, is integral to her or his identity. It is therefore important, in recognizing this, that a child should be given her or his correct name, not shortened or nicknamed because it appears to be long or difficult to say.

COUNTERING INEQUALITY

The provision of good multicultural resources and having positive attitudes to play and language are important in breaking down hierarchies based on class, 'race', and gender. But it is also necessary to develop skills to counter other covert and overt inequalities. Countering inequality is best facilitated when young children are given opportunities to explore their environments, to develop their intellectual curiosities, and where they are encouraged to question and to develop cognitive learning skills. Ultimately it is about having a respect for young children. Are they all valued? Are they asked what they think and for their opinions?

Workers themselves need to show in their actions that they value all children. Personal likes or dislikes play no part in this valuing. Workers also need to demonstrate that they value all kinds of play and activity. So they need to be seen by the children not only at the jigsaw table but also with the bicycles and building blocks. Beginning to break down apparently sex role-determined resources and providing alternative role models, for example by seeing a man playing with dolls, will give children an opportunity to reconsider their play patterns. Workers should praise all children, give instruction to all children, and look at what all of them are doing. Children should be encouraged to play, together, with all toys - to encourage co-operative activity among boys and girls and of children from all minority cultural and social backgrounds. Getting access to all resources and activities gives all children access to all skills. Sharing these concepts with families is important in, together, rectifying inbalance.

Sexism, classism, and racism have some aspects in common but there are also many differences. While boys and girls of different cultures are usually identifiable, the subtleties of disadvantage and discrimination based on class are often less recognized. Although the sections below appear to concentrate on racism and sexism it is important that, wherever possible, workers take account of the particular needs of children from different social groups. In particular, ways of equally valuing and respecting working-class children and staff must be implemented. A few ways that might begin to counter inequality are now considered.

Judgements about child-rearing practices

It is important to assume, in the absence of contradictory evidence, that all families do their best for their children. Making negative judgements about the way children are brought up needs to be very carefully analyzed because child-rearing practices vary both among and between cultures and social groups. For example, if a variety of family members meet an Indian boy from the nursery, rather than think he is insecure because he does not know who is coming to fetch him, there could instead be a positive interpretation - that he has many people who care for him in practical ways. Or a young child may sleep in the same bed as a sibling - rather than make a judgement that children should have their own beds, it may provide an opportunity to take responsibility to care for each other. The following procedure could be adopted by workers when judgements around child-rearing arise. Is the first reaction valid? Could there be another, more positive explanation? What might be the other reasons? What might have been the consequences of any first, negative reaction by a worker on the child and the family? Adopting such procedures may begin to counter deep-seated assumptions of superiority so that various child-rearing practices can be judged on criteria that are not based on racism, sexism, or classism.

Ridicule

Laughing at and taunting someone because of the way she or he dresses, behaves, speaks, or looks is nearly always harmful. But laughing because of racial (or cultural), sex, or class differences feeds the feeling of powerlessness based on belonging to a group that is not ranked highly and that a child cannot (and should not wish to) change. Laughing at a child, a child's language, or dialect or hair or the way she or he eats, for example, means that she or he is likely to internalize messages of not being valued, a feeling that may well extend to the whole family and group not being valued. Similarly the child who is laughing is having her or his sense of superiority reinforced. Laughter, when it is directed at a child (or an adult), should be taken seriously and dealt with immediately - supporting the child who is hurt and encouraging the other child to talk through her or his action.

Graffiti

Care should be taken to ensure that racial or sexual graffiti is removed immediately, especially if it is on nursery premises. Many African/Caribbean and South Asian families and their young children are abused on the way to the nursery and the nursery itself should be a haven of security for them. The presence of graffiti will indicate that workers are not really supportive.

Answering factual questions

When children (or adults) seek information about cultures, religions, languages, or gender, social-class, and racial differences, every attempt should be made to answer such questions correctly. Indeed children should be positively encouraged to ask questions. This means that workers need to inform themselves as much as possible and where they do not know the answer to seek it out, perhaps with the help of the children and their families. It also means knowing, for example, why skin colours and physical features are not all the same and being able to offer explanations of genetic difference that a child can readily understand. Or of saying, 'I don't know but we will find out together.' This provides an opportunity for being positive about difference and diversity.

Dealing with 'subtly' racist or sexist remarks

Some negative remarks are not recognized as such and their impact on children is consequently ignored. For example, making remarks about a African/Caribbean girl's hair as being 'difficult' indicates to her that she has a problem, when the only difficulty is ignorance about hair care. Sensitive awareness will identify words that are culturally and negatively loaded in particular contexts. Such awareness means listening carefully to what is said and then identifying any subtly negative messages. The loaded words can then be unpacked and any damaging consequences rectified.

Dealing with overt, racist, or sexist incidents or remarks

These are almost certainly damaging both to instigator and 'victim'. All such incidents should be taken seriously and followed through. They should not be dealt with by saying 'that is not kind' or 'how would you feel if someone did that to you?' - making light of the matter is ignoring a responsibility for both children, to help them to care for each other. Priority should be given to supporting the child who is hurt and assuring her or him that she or he did not cause the incident personally. What has happened should be clearly identified as wrong and the reasons why it is wrong discussed with both children, involving other children in the discussion where appropriate. This needs to be done in a supportive and caring way, making sure that instigators understand that only what they have done or said is being criticized and that they, themselves, are not being attacked or undermined. It is only when children feel personally supported and cared for that they can reflect on what they may have done and come to terms with it.

Discussing inequalities with children

In order to open up the whole issue of inequality it is important to provide regular opportunities for children and their families to discuss it. This might mean having an informal 'slot' where children, families, and workers (together or separately) discuss any issues of interest or concern to them in a non-threatening way. This could provide a forum where all children can speak, learn to express their ideas and share them in a supportive environment, and where workers can raise issues that may not, so far, have been noticed. This could be an opportunity to correct misinformation or a partial viewpoint that children may have heard about (in however simplistic a way) from the media or elsewhere. For example, they may have learnt vague ideas that poor or unemployed people are lazy or that African/Caribbean and South Asian people are responsible for crime. Although these are relatively sophisticated concepts for young children, they nevertheless play some role in children's thinking and beliefs. This is particularly important in largely white areas. The insidious way that negative attitudes are learnt, but usually remain hidden in the early years, should be recognized. They need to be allowed to come out because, otherwise, their existence may be denied. Only when they are articulated can their extent be measured and specific action taken to counter them and for children to have the opportunity to think and talk them through.

Deeply entrenched classist or sexist attitudes may be even more difficult to reveal than racist attitudes. What is important is to provide an ethos where everyone is valued - nursery workers, support staff, meal supervisors, caretakers, cleaners, families, and children and where differences are viewed positively. Learning to see things from another viewpoint, learning to weigh up conflicting information and making decisions based on correct information (for example, learning that wealth is not equally distributed) is fundamental to learning the skills needed for later study at school. Providing this framework means that it is possible for children to change their minds without criticism. Thus they can learn that there is a good side to admitting being wrong or to altering an opinion in the light of information. Children can begin to consider why (middle- and upper-class) white men are powerful and to learn that working people in general and women and men from minority cultural backgrounds can also have power. Young children can learn to recognize remarks that reflect this power and can learn to take responsibility for opposing them. Learning to be open and honest, instead of pretending that racism, sexism, and classism do not exist, provides young children with a framework where they can make their own decisions and make up their own minds using information that adults have provided for them. Where ignorance prevails, fears and myths also prevail.

Adults are important to young children - their families and under-fives workers. If they respect young children, children are more likely to learn to respect others. The opening up of the issues of racism, sexism, and classism with young children begins to break down the barriers that prevent adults from recognizing their influence on young children.

Mutual staff support

The issue of equality affects all workers - they all have a responsibility to identify and counter inequality. For example, women should not be the only ones expected to deal with sexism and black staff should not be expected to be the only ones to deal with racism. When women or ethnic minority group staff experience sexism or racism (from children, other workers, or families) they should receive support from other staff, a support that extends to action, where necessary. All staff should guard against marginalizing any worker on grounds of 'race', gender, or class or because they challenge inequality.

An overall approach

Guidelines for good practice cannot function in a vacuum. Nurseries need a policy for equality and justice. Policies must be jointly agreed by families and workers because the role of both is complementary in breaking down inequality. Starting from the basis of caring for all children in a multicultural society everyone can take part in the learning process of what that means in practice. A policy should include a strategy for monitoring and evaluating how it is being implemented. This means an ongoing examination of resources and activities, recording negative incidents, a constant evaluation of the way adults counter inequality, and developing strategies for positive and supportive action.

Workers or families who wish to meet together in particular groups should be supported. Support groups are important in giving members confidence to understand and counter oppressive power structures. Workers and families need to consider how any barriers between them can be broken down. Perhaps everyone could occasionally share a meal together in the nursery at the end of a day. Circulars should be translated where necessary and families can teach workers words in languages other than English. Interested adults could examine resources together and develop their own selection criteria.

Under-fives workers who are promoting equality are likely to need support. One way of doing this is to start a group to look at childcare, education, and equality. This can be interprofessional and interdepartmental across statutory and voluntary provision and there may also hopefully be family members who wish to join. Trainers, advisers, administrators, and practitioners all have much to share with each other and much to learn. This group can plan activities, organize and facilitate training, and draw up policies to implement equality in childcare/education. The group can, together, develop an expertise in supporting members and in influencing under-fives policy generally.

CONCLUSION

If children in their earliest years are not given a chance to be equally valued, there is even less hope that they will be accorded equal treatment as they grow up. Providing a framework where young children can think for themselves, evaluate information, and respect and value difference may give them a chance of justice and equality that is the fundamental right of all children. It is a right that adults (under-fives workers and families) must support.

ACKNOWLEDGEMENTS

I would like to thank Reading Council for Racial Equality for the practical support they gave me in producing this chapter. In particular, my gratitude to Beverley Belgrave and Helen Townsend for typing the manuscript so carefully. I would also like to thank those who gave their valuable time so generously to make constructive comments on the contents of this chapter.

NOTES AND REFERENCES

1. Cohen, B. (1988) Caring for Children. Services and Policies for Childcare and Equal Opportunities in the United Kingdom, London: Commission of the European Communities.
2. Moss, P. (1988) Childcare and Equality of Opportunity, Consolidated Report of the European Commission, London.
3. Van der Eyken, W. (1984) Day Nurseries in Action, Department of Child Health Research Unit, University of Bristol/DHSS.
4. Commission for Racial Equality (1988) Ethnic Minority School Teachers: A survey of eight local education authorities.
5. Commission for Racial Equality. Unpublished research into comparative primary school experiences of black and white children.
6. Milner, D. (1983) Children and Race: Ten Years on, London: Ward Lock Educational.
7. Jeffcoate, R. (1980) Positive Image: Towards a Multi-racial Curriculum, London: Writers' and Readers' Publishing Co-operative, pp. 12-15.
8. Serbin, L.A. (1978) 'Teachers, peers, and play preferences: an environmental approach to sex typing in the pre-school', in

Barbara Sprung (ed.) <u>Perspectives on Non-Sexist Early Childhood Education</u>, New York: Teachers College Press, Columbia University, pp. 79-93.

9. Brooking, C., Foster, M. and Smith, S. (1987) <u>Teaching for Equality. Educational resources on 'race' and gender</u>, London: The Runnymede Trust.

10. Smith, S. (1988) <u>Racism in Children's Resources: Background reading with specific references to materials for under-fives</u>, Manchester: Librarians Anti-racist Strategies Group, c/o Stephanie Smith, Library Services, 164 Clapham Park Road, London SW4 7DD.

11. National Children's Bureau. The Under-Fives Unit of the National Children's Bureau will supply references to literature relevant to equality of opportunity and antiracist childcare/education organization and practice.

12. Council on Interracial Books for Children (1980) <u>Ten quick ways to evaluate children's books for racism and sexism</u>, 1841, Broadway, New York, NY 10023.

13. McFarlane, C. (1986) <u>Hidden Messages: Activities for exploring bias</u>, Development Education Centre, Selly Oak College, Bristol Road, Birmingham B29 6LE.

14. Working Group against Racism in Children's Resources (1989) <u>Guidelines for Evaluating Toys</u>, 460 Wandsworth Road, London SW8 3LK.

15. Dixon, B. (1989). <u>Playing Them False: a Study of Children's Toys, Games and Puzzles</u>, Trentham Books.

16. See also chapter 10 which deals exclusively with language.

Chapter Six

THE INFANT YEARS

Jackie Granados Johnson, Jane Helliwell, Joan Nicholson, Diane Reay, Helen Schwarz, and Geraldine Wright for the Anti-Sexist Working Party

We are a group of white, women, primary school teachers from very different backgrounds, working in inner London with children from many different cultures. We all faced similar feelings of isolation and a need for support in our attempts to challenge sexism in the organization and curriculum of our schools. The core of the group made contact in 1981 at the Developing Anti-Sexist Initiatives (DASI) conference for secondary teachers. At that time the concern was for the underachievement of girls at secondary school. There was interest from primary teachers but there was no such initiative at the primary level. Several others joined the group later, basically through personal contacts with members of the group. We wanted to share the problems we faced in our classrooms and school and discuss practical ideas about how to build a curriculum which presents positive views of girls and women and challenges stereotyped images of both sexes. We have since broadened our perspective to try to challenge any form of oppression and exploitation within education. Working in schools in inner London, black working class girls are at the core of our work because of the triple oppression they suffer from 'race', class, and gender.

It is unrealistic for us to try and overcome the inequalities in society and so our main aim in the classroom has been to try to create an atmosphere within which all the children feel safe and where they can talk about themselves and be listened to. Within the infant school age range one's self-image is precarious and attention should be directed at helping each child to feel valued and listened to (see section on strategies).

> There has to be selection because we are beginning to create aspirations which society cannot match... . If we have a highly educated and highly idle population we may possibly anticipate more serious social conflict. People must be educated to know their place.
>
> (DES Official, Guardian, November 1987)

This is the political climate under which any serious consideration of education for equality must be made. What the current government is after is a reinforcement of inequality. They do not want children questioning in an international arena but want to narrow their experience down to reading, writing, and arithmetic. A philosophy of equal access to the 'goodies' within a society where resources and control over these resources are unequally distributed will never be popular with those who have more, as the implication is that they will have to give something up. Therefore we recognize that attempts to counteract inequality in the classroom inevitably bring with them feelings of failure for the teacher.

The self-interest of the educational establishment (HMIs, teacher trainers, administrators, LEAs, even members of the antiracist, antisexist educational industry) ensures the maintenance of hierarchies, perpetuation of stereotypes, desirability of competition, not least between teachers, and a lack of non-judgemental valuation of individuals. Therefore it is only through groups of like-minded teachers who are prepared to tackle the issues, that any teacher can get the support they need to try to tackle inequality within the system, let alone in their own classroom.

THE HIDDEN CURRICULUM IN THE SCHOOL

The hidden curriculum in the school is a reflection of the way society outside the school is structured; just as society is hierarchical, so teachers have to work within an education system which is hierarchical. There is a fundamental contradiction in expecting teachers to work in an egalitarian framework when, all around, the opposite is the case. Tory education plans will result in more power being given to heads and less status and power to the hard-working class teachers. The changes that are taking place have resulted in a longer working week/year; in order to keep up with new ideas, teachers need to have in-service training (Inset) and yet the first people to be considered for this are the headteachers.

Recruitment has not actually resulted in more black teachers coming into the profession. Even where they are recruited, they are often peripheral, the ESL teacher working outside the classroom, or the mother-tongue teacher working as a part-timer in a hut in the playground and, as a consequence, underpaid.

Non-teaching staff are predominantly white working-class women. Their low status is reflected in their low pay. They are an extremely valuable group of people doing a tremendous amount of support work in the classroom. It is interesting to note that recruitment of black employees as non-teaching staff has risen marginally. Their low status is constantly reinforced by such comments as 'you are only a helper' or 'I don't have to do what you say' said by the children. Where have they heard these comments and who has allowed them to get into the habit of saying them?

On the other hand, a much higher status is given to the schoolkeeper with his big bunch of keys. He can play a very important role. He is usually male and white, and is seen as very important by the children. He has a big influence on how the cleaners' job is interpreted and how they are made to feel about their job. It is important that the teachers and the head have a good relationship with the schoolkeeper. Much more notice needs to be taken of how important these relationships are in relation to the smooth running of the school.

The school gives a higher status to men in general and their career prospects are better. At the same time the system seems to judge them far less harshly than women. Men who take an infant class are assumed to have some kind of special quality, whereas 'it just comes naturally to women'. It is an extension of their 'maternal role'. There is a total lack of recognition of the skills involved in being an infant teacher, e.g. 'all you have to do is to tell a few stories, play a few games, and paint a few pictures' are phrases often aimed at infant teachers. The infant teacher is seen as no more than a good enough mother, which totally dismisses the professional content of the job.

The pressure from white middle-class parents in schools where they are actually a minority totally unbalances any coherent dialogue between people. There is a striking imbalance in resourcing between middle-class areas and working-class areas. As a result, the middle-class school often has extra resources and personnel; and reinforcing that are the higher academic expectations of middle-class schools. It would be very illuminating for new teachers to visit a school with a social composition different from their own.

Working-class children are faced with a dilemma as soon as they enter a school; most of the teachers in the school that they attend are middle class with middle-class values, and assumptions are made about these children by the teachers from the very start. Estelle Fuchs, in 'How teachers learn to help children fail', (1) says:

> Thus before these youngsters have completed a full four months of schooling, their educational futures have been tracked ... Some youngsters are selected very early for success, others written off as slow. Because differential teaching occurs and helps to widen the gap between children, the opportunity to move from one category to another is limited. In addition, the children, too, become aware of the labels placed upon them. And their patterns for achievements in later years are influenced by their feelings of success or failure in early school experiences.

The working-class parent has always been <u>told</u> how their children should be educated and never consulted. The whole way the system works renders them powerless.

Relationships between parents and schools need to be strengthened (see section on parents' involvement in schools). The role of parents as natural educators of their children should be recognized. Sending out letters in a multicultural school, without any translations, totally ignores the existence of other cultures. The school does not regard it as its responsibility to communicate adequately. When it does think about it, the parents themselves are expected to do the translating unpaid.

Education authorities have, in the last few years, published pamphlets on racism, sexism, and classism, saying that different cultures are of equal value and that education should not seek to destroy them. Children are seen as having their own cultures, which must be respected, but the aim in school is that every child should learn to function within the mainstream culture. As Martin Hoyles says in 'The politics of literacy': (2) 'It is not suggested that middle-class children be initiated (our emphasis) into working-class culture, or whites into black culture'.

THE HIDDEN CURRICULUM IN THE INFANT CLASSROOM

Inherent in the concept of the hidden curriculum is the implication that teachers are doing something wrong without even being aware of it. However, placed within a wider context than just the classroom the hidden curriculum becomes one of the many ways society covertly transmits its values. The hidden curriculum is informed not just by teachers' attitudes but the attitudes of children, their parents, and, in a less direct but equally powerful way, the whole of society. Teachers are the products of the school's hidden curriculum as well as unwitting agents of it.

Within the classroom context the hidden curriculum is the part of the learning experience that is determined by the teachers' attitudes and behaviour rather than by the formal syllabus. Lobban (3) defined the hidden curriculum as, 'those aspects of learning in a school that are unintentional or the undeclared consequences of the way in which teachers organise and execute teaching and learning'. She was referring to gender but the tendency whenever children are not known individually is to categorize them on the basis of superficial differences and this can apply equally to 'race' and class as well as gender. Professor Carol Jacklin has found in a recent study (Guardian 6 October 1987) that there is a direct correlation between stereotyping and lack of detailed knowledge of an individual. She asserts that the more children in a class, the more teachers stereotype and make assumptions at an unconscious level.

The hidden curriculum operates on two levels: the easier to eradicate organizational procedures, e.g. division of sexes on the register, lining up separately; and the more insidious elements diffused through teacher/pupil interactions, relationships between children, and teacher attitudes.

Awareness of the hidden curriculum is a vital step in challenging discrimination in the classroom. Once it is accepted that stereotyping inevitably goes on then it is easier to discern the pathologizing of black and white working-class families that is the corollary of stereotyping. The black family and the white working-class family are presented as 'the problem' rather than the structural inequalities in society which are the real cause of the tensions. The value of black and working-class children is persistently undermined by the equating of educability with middle-class status or skin colour. The pervasiveness of cultural and racial stereotyping is exemplified by a range of common assertions such as the one 'that boys from Greek or Muslim cultures will not respect female teachers because their culture endorses low opinions of women', or statements that 'boys of West Indian parentage find it very difficult to cope with the relative freedom of school because of rigid discipline patterns at home'.

Working-class children of all 'races' are consistently presented with middle-class values in the classroom and inevitably have difficulty relating to them (see R. King). (4) The primacy of white middle-class values is disseminated through language, books, learning materials, and implied cultural norms and ideals. For example, in writing about expectations around appearance Jackson and Marsden (5) comment:

> Rules about pupils' clothing underpin the orthodoxy and the ethics of the school and also satisfy a desire on the part of both parents and teachers that the child appear respectable, i.e. middle-class rather than working-class. How many infant teachers have at one time or another made a comment on the unsuitability of a little working-class girl's clothing?

Research has actually indicated that the middle-class value system operates more powerfully in working-class schools than in middle-class ones. 'Teachers are not as rigid in the preservation of the social structure in middle-class schools as they are in working-class schools'. (6)

B. Bernstein (7) distinguishes between the invisible pedagogy of the infant school and the visible pedagogy of working-class homes. He argues that the invisible pedagogy of the 'new' middle class has penetrated the infant school effecting continuity between the pedagogy of the 'new' middle-class mother and the teacher, but causing a sharp discontinuity between working-class homes and school. The theory of invisible pedagogy with its elements of implicit social control, play integrated with work, and emphasis on structure, may not be known by working-class mothers, or perfectly understood. Unlike the middle-class child who is socialized by the same invisible pedagogy, the working-class child is faced with different pedagogies in the home and in the school, and their parents mystified by an educational process in which facilitation replaces imposition and accommodation replaces domination. 'The invisible pedagogy contains a different theory of transmission and a new technology which views the mother's own informal teaching where it occurs, or the mother's pedagogical values as irrelevant if not downright harmful'. (7) If the mother is to be helpful she must either be resocialized or kept out of the way. If the former then the teacher has the power as the mother becomes a pupil alongside her child.

Much has been written on the effect of stereotyping in relation to gender. (6) (8) (9) In a number of studies, such as Clarricoates, (6) teachers' expectations deny reality. Pupils are labelled as conforming to gender stereotypes: boys as active, aggressive, and extroverted; girls as passive and dependent, even when research based on objective testing indicate no such differences in girls' and boys' behaviour. Brandis and Bernstein (10) found infant teachers perceived girls in their classes to be cleverer than boys but rated them less highly in terms of innate potential.

A lot of emphasis is placed on boys' relative lack of success in reading and language skills at infant level, but at the same time there is rarely any perceived necessity to offer girls extra help and support in numeracy and spatial skills, both areas of the curriculum where a large proportion of girls underachieve relative to boys. If the bricks, trains, and construction toys, which facilitate the development of visual-spatial skills, are rarely played with by girls they will need specific encouragement to venture out into this less familiar sphere.

The pupil culture within the classroom leads to the formation of hierarchies within the group of which often the teacher is only vaguely aware. Such hierarchies invariably underline the higher status of boys, the middle class, and the white children. At its most apparent the hierarchy can be seen to give boys first rights in the classroom - to materials, equipment, space, and teacher attention. One six-year-old girl in a top infant class refused to be represented on a class graph as a girl 'because I'm a tomboy'. When prompted to explain further she said in a very matter-of-fact way that 'being a tomboy was nearly as good as being a boy'.

One aspect of the hidden curriculum that has received a great deal of attention from teachers and researchers over recent years is the area of learning materials such as books, posters, pictures, games, jigsaw puzzles, and worksheets. In the world of children's books the 'normal' home environment is white 'middle class' - daddy goes to work in a car, mother, dressed in her apron, stays at home. (11) Detailed examinations, such as that carried out by Celia Burgess, (12) have highlighted how books and learning materials present a stereotyped picture of gender roles or virtually ignore girls or women except in passive or domestic roles. As Judith Whyte (13) points out, in order to counter stereotyping in books and learning materials, teachers need to alert children to race, sex, and class bias in books. Teachers can point out that nowadays mothers go out to work, dads bath babies, large numbers of children do not live in the traditional nuclear family; that detached middle-class homes with two cars are not the norm but the product of privilege; that men can be nurses, women can be carpenters or police officers; and that black people can be all of these things. Whyte sees this process as both 'reassuring' and 'educational';

> "reassuring" because the "official" recognition of differences or minorities by the teacher can help all children to appreciate "differentness"; and "educational" because the notion of rapid social change built in at an early stage of children's schooling can promote adaptable and flexible attitudes.

One implication of expanding the curriculum in the way that Judith Whyte (13) suggests may be that 'social studies' or project work on sex roles in society, often considered suitable study for adolescents, would be just as relevant in the infant years. Depriving people of the ability to question the way society is structured is a disturbing aspect of the hidden curriculum. A critical view of relationships both inside the classroom and in the world outside is needed from the pre-school and the infant class upwards. Children know what is 'fair' and 'unfair'. Their grasp of this concept can be built on in order to look at inequalities both inside the classroom and within society on both a national and an international scale.

Because the hidden curriculum is not an articulated, planned part of the school it is difficult to tackle. It is especially difficult to identify gender-, race-, and class-related differences in our expectations of children. However, a much greater emphasis on co-operative learning is one positive strategy for challenging the workings of the hidden curriculum. One of the very first lessons taught by the hidden curriculum is that co-operation between children is a kind of cheating. This attitude is exemplified by comments such as 'let him do it himself', 'let her work it out on her own'. A lack of a co-operative model of any kind leads to less confident children equating school with 'things being done to me and for me'. This is particularly stigmatizing for girls and some working-class boys in whom passivity and learned helplessness are already established.

There is obviously a need for much more research to explain the processes implicit in the hidden curriculum of the infant school. The social interaction in the classroom, both between teachers and pupils and between pupils themselves, remains extremely difficult to analyse because of its constantly changing and shifting nature. However closely observed, interpupil and pupil-teacher interactions do seem to replicate the gender, class, and race power imbalance of the outside world. This mirroring of wider societal inequalities is a cause of extreme concern for all teachers committed to education for equality.

CLASSROOM STRATEGIES

The infant classroom needs to be a place where all children can feel safe in what they think and feel and do. In working towards practice which develops and values the self-esteem of all the children we need to look at the way space is used in our classrooms. It is important to be aware how some activities are dominated, how space is owned, and whether all children have access to all activities, e.g. large construction, lego, home corner.

The home corner is a part of every infant classroom and can also be where stereotyped play is reinforced by the limited materials available, but it is also a place where stereotypes can be challenged. The space can be used more imaginatively by adapting it to become a baby clinic, a post office, a cafe, a spacecraft, a hairdressers, an office. The list is endless but it needs teacher intervention to structure and extend play.

Stories can be designed to encourage home corner play which challenges racist, classist, and sexist stereotypes. We hope that bilingual children will be encouraged to participate using their home language and/or English.

The introduction of utensils from a wide range of cultures and equipment which reflects a whole range of adult roles will also encourage positive use of this area. (A resource list for home corner materials, crafts, food, and books is available from the Centre for Urban Educational Studies). (14)

The images with which we surround children in books, illustrations, and displays give a powerful message about the values we have. It is useful to look around the school and count how many black/white female/male faces are displayed. Do they reflect the different backgrounds (race and class) of the children and do they challenge stereotyped views of women and men, girls and boys?

In school and in the media children who are not white, middle class, and male may find few positive role models to develop their perception of themselves. You can make your own resources. For example, children can draw and paint portraits of each other and then caption them with a positive comment about each person. We can enlist the help of parents and older children to make alphabet, colour, and number charts and audio tapes of comparative number systems, alphabets (as in Anna to Zoulla) (15), etc.

Schools can invite parents to come in and tell folk tales and stories in their own language. A sequence of large pictures to illustrate helps all children understand. Bilingual children could retell the story in English. All bilingual children know songs and rhymes in their mother tongue. These can be put on tape and bilingual books made so all children can enjoy them.

To make stories accessible to all children, cut-out characters, magnet boards, puppets, and models made by children can be used. These can be housed in a 'listening corner' alongside a tape recorder and headphones where the children can go and listen to favourite stories whilst following the text and retell a story or make up a play using these resources.

Board games which require collaboration and discussion develop mathematics and language. Simple models made by the teacher stimulate the children to make their own. We need to be careful in our selection of published materials. Examples of the type of book we want to see in the classroom can be found in Stones (16) and Tuggs (17). Many of the books we use in school fail to recognize that we live in a multiracial society where the roles of women and men are changing. We want children to develop skills to question the images and information that are part of their everyday life. Children can extend this analysis by making graphs and sets, e.g. what people wear, what people do in books, and compare it to their own lives.

They can write to authors and publishers of reading schemes stating what they feel about the contradictions between what is portrayed and their own lives. Rewriting books is an activity that alerts children to bias and has the bonus of producing books for the classroom. Many of the reading schemes have central characters who are male and white, and characters set in very rigid sex roles. Mothers are shown wearing their aprons and holding brooms and fathers are often reclining under a newspaper. Children enjoy talking about how this fits in with their own reality and can rewrite these books so that they reflect more accurately the children's own experience. In many of these books it is the illustrations that are the most oppressive. Children's drawings or photographs can often be used to fit the text, making the book acceptable and providing a challenging activity. For ease, non-stereotyped illustrations in Changing Images (18), available from Sheba Publications, can also be used. In this book we find only one illustration of disabled people and few images are found elsewhere. But this could perhaps be a valid starting point for raising issues and for making links with schools for disabled children and other organizations in the local community. There are, as yet, few materials focused on disabilities but it is important to make use of those available and to produce your own.

Sharing, talking, and listening are part of the way children learn. It often seems to be one group, the boys, who dominate in discussion, and another group, the girls, who listen. A ball of wool passed to each child who speaks, unravelled, and passed on to the next speaker reveals a web of speakers and observers. Infant children come together to share experiences with each other and their teacher several times a day. It is worth looking to see where children sit in this situation. Who is sitting in direct eye contact with the teacher and therefore participating most actively, and who is sitting close to their teacher yet out of eye contact and passive? On some occasions it might be possible to designate certain groups as speakers or listeners. In discussion we try to establish respect for the views of all children so that calling out and interrupting are not allowed to become strategies for gaining the teacher's attention.

The children could sit in a circle and pass round a conch shell or other precious object. Only the person holding the shell may speak. If they have nothing to say they may pass it on to the next person. This gives everyone a chance to speak uninterrupted, encourages the children to listen carefully, and helps to develop linear discussion.

Taping discussions can be useful in several ways. Children can themselves hear who dominates and ask 'is it fair?', 'what do you think?'. But it could also be valuable when starting topics designed to overcome stereotyping. They can be asked what they know and their opinions on the subject can be kept until later and replayed.

We believe that skills of communication, self-confidence, and co-operation are developed when children are working together. We do need to be careful that children are not working as individuals sitting together but that the task given requires real collaboration.

BILINGUALISM

Supporting bilingualism can only benefit the teacher and the whole school community. It increases knowledge of, and improves the relationship with, individual pupils. It recognizes the importance of the pupil's family/community as a resource. It increases teacher awareness of linguistic and cultural diversity and strengthens the school/community links. It is important that bilingual children are not extracted from the class as this can be seen as exclusion from the class.

When the child comes to school we need to find out as much about them as we can, e.g. full name, what the child is to be called in class, other schools both in UK and other countries, father's name, mother's name, family name, and how these names work (see Naming Patterns published by the Minority Group Support Service (19)), language spoken at home, religion, diet, special health needs, mother-tongue classes. This information is needed to counteract stereotyped assumptions about cultural groups.

We also need to look at the strengths of those systems in operation in the community and consult and value them, e.g. women's organizations, childcare groups (see Bryan et al. (20)).

Dual-language texts enable readers with different languages to enjoy the same book. Parents, too, can take an active role in the shared reading process, regardless of whether or not they are familiar with written English. Readers will be able to develop their own mother tongue and English together.

The Children's Language Project (21) produces text-free materials for any language, as well as activity cards and teachers' book, which encourage children to use their own language as well as the language they encounter around them. The School Curriculum Development Committee (22) publishes Bengali and Greek primary readers and workcards (see also Luzac and Co. Ltd (23) and Side by Side (24)).

111

There should be work around the school in the children's home languages, e.g. greetings, please and thank you, and numbers. Interpreters should be available for parents' evenings from your local education authority, and, if not, pressure should be put on them to do so. Letters home must take account of children's home languages.

THE CURRICULUM

A child's home culture, including language, should be valued by the school. By ignoring its importance school devalues the child. Antiracist objectives should not just be tacked on to the curriculum as festivals or a welcome poster in sixteen languages. These objectives must become part of the total ethics of the school and need careful consideration by all workers in the school.

Look at the cultural values of your classroom. Study countries and cultures other than your own and the ways they are similar to and different from yours. For example, in a project about ourselves or food or clothes or homes we can help the children to view the world as a mixture of interacting parts. This can help infant children understand the wider world whilst also learning about themselves and local environment. For example, during a project on homes, time could be spent on children who have lived somewhere different. The children can draw and the teacher can act as scribe. This gives bilingual children an opportunity to talk about the country they have come from and also gives children who have only moved down the road a chance to talk. World Studies 8-13 Projects (25) 'Getting on with Others' and 'Learning about Other People' are also suitable for infants.

Make sure you have clothes and costumes from different cultures, black and male dolls, recipes for cooking, puzzles and games, songs and musical instruments which reflect cultural diversity (see list of shops and projects which supply these (26)).

Our experience has also shown us how often we choose topics, or stories to read, with the boys in mind. Topics can be chosen that will interest and involve all the children and encourage positives images, e.g. myself, my family, work people do, toys, comics. (For more ideas and development of topics see Look Jane Look, ch. 11 (8)). It is important for all children to have an equal opportunity to solve real problems and develop scientific attitudes in the infant classroom. In science, because it is the activity that is all important, observing new things happening will be a motivation for language.

Our own attitude to science, mathematics and problem solving is important in developing confidence and interest in children. The teacher in the infant class is a vital role model. It is essential that we should have our confidence boosted by courses in areas where we feel uncertain and unwittingly conform to the stereotypes we need

to challenge. The way we behave creates the atmosphere in scho
and should be co-operative and sharing rather than competitive and
isolating.

In recognizing that children come to school with very different
experiences and that these can be determined by their gender,
'race', and class, we must be prepared to encourage all children to
become confident with unfamiliar activities. The possibility of being
creative in needlework or knitting, inventive in three-dimensional or
constructional toys, should be there for all our children.

Collaborative learning is the way in which children learn to
value each other. For ideas for co-operative games and sport see
Orlick. (27) The antithesis of collaboration and co-operation is
conflict, and the way the school operates in dealing with conflict is
as important as promoting harmony. Schools need to develop their
own policy. Is there a democratic process for children to follow?
Does school promote a non-violent stance? What rights and
responsibilities do children have? Are they the same for all
children?

Conflict does not just mean violent behaviour. Name-calling is
just as damaging to a child's self-esteem. The issue of name-calling
must be dealt with seriously and time given to discussing policy and
dealing with each incident as it happens.

We ask children what they think the reasons for abuse are.
What do the terms mean? What is the abuser trying to achieve?
What do you do? How do you stop it? What do grown-ups do? What
do you think they should do? How children deal with oppressive
language reflects the ethics of the school. (For more ideas contact
the Centre for Peace Studies. (28))

GIVING GIRLS SPACE

When we first introduce a topic we realize that girls and boys bring
different experiences and have different expectations of
themselves. The enthusiasm and confidence with which we see boys
approach topics like electricity leave girls feeling uncertain and
reluctant. We believe in affirmative action, to give girls the
encouragement to become involved in design-, technology-, and
science-based topics. Giving girls space and time separate from boys
is important for them to learn skills and to feel confident and
assertive. Only then do they have a chance to participate equally.

We try to find a place in the school where girls can go to work
quietly, either alone or collaboratively. We have given girls the
opportunity to explore their feelings about being girls through
drama, art, writing, and also by looking at media images of girls and
women. They have been encouraged to communicate their ideas
through plays shown at assembly, which open the topic for discussion
with a mixed group.

It is useful to invite adults in non-traditional roles to talk to the

113

children. However, we would not label a visitor as a woman carpenter, but would introduce her as a carpenter. Local community groups can be contacted and will often have people willing to come in and talk to children about their experiences.

GIRLS' FUN DAY

We wanted a day for girls to enjoy themselves, learn skills, and be with other girls and women. We chose a Saturday in the summer and chose a local primary school as a venue. A coach was provided to collect girls from their own schools and take them to the fun day. We invited women to run workshops, e.g. bike maintenance, juggling, self-defence, computers, dance and drama. (We have a short video which records Girls' Fun Day '86 and the day is written up in 'Primary Matters', (29) which gives further details of both the planning and the problems.)

On both occasions the days were a huge success and rewarded all the time and hard work put in. On the second time many girls came who remembered with enjoyment the time they had had at the first fun day. Many women accompanied their daughters. They enjoyed meeting girls from other schools and there was a great feeling of co-operation, caring, and friendship.

WORKING WITH PARENTS IN PARTNERSHIP

As we have already demonstrated, schools in this country are white middle-class institutions set up to assist the upwardly mobile. It is not surprising, therefore, that many working-class and black parents feel wary and rather intimidated by schools. Nowadays, when the cry from many teachers is 'why won't more parents get involved with the school?', it is easy to forget that not long ago there were notices requesting parents to leave their children at the gate and parents were only allowed into the classrooms on special occasions, like open evenings. 'Working with parents in partnership' cannot, therefore, be assumed to be the aim of all schools. Many teachers would defend the belief that their aim in part is to teach a whole set of values and morals, many of which are different from those of the parents. Many parents also see this as the job of the school and they want their children to be more upwardly mobile than they were. In this situation parents feel they have little to offer and likewise teachers see their jobs as easier if parents with different values and views do not get involved.

But if you, as a teacher, believe that the values that should be taught within school are tolerance, understanding of differences, valuing people as individuals, then your approach would need to be different from the traditional middle-class educational approach. If parents feel comfortable at the school and have some understanding

114

of what it is trying to do and feel they can support this at home the children will also feel more comfortable, relaxed, and therefore more able to learn.

Teachers must try to accept within themselves that all parents want what they see as the best for their children, whatever their background, and we must avoid quick condemnation or stereotyping when a parent's view seems to conflict with our own. There is no short cut to open and full discussion on issues and changes within the school and this applies equally to the working community in school as to the relationship between parents and teachers.

'Any change in what is traditionally expected of school works better if parents understand the reasons behind the change'. (13) Within this there does seem to be an assumption that it is the parents who would change when faced with reasoned arguments. It is essential that in truly open discussion it could be the view of the teacher or the school which could change. It is up to us, however, to facilitate this kind of decision-making. It must be stated that this is not the general practice in schools and it is therefore very hard for an individual teacher to provide individually what is lacking generally. It is up to the headteacher to facilitate the same kind of open discussion with workers in the school. Open discussion necessitates giving up some control, in fact sharing control, and in the educational hierarchy this is not encouraged. It requires a confident school community to take this on board. But if it is felt important to try to create an atmosphere in which children can feel valued and listened to, it is equally important to try to create an atmosphere in which all workers and parents can feel valued and listened to.

There are ways of generating this atmosphere, but it must be remembered that as infant school teachers many ways are beyond our control. We do not want to discourage class teachers from trying to nurture a warm, open, valuing relationship with parents, but any feelings of personal failure must be seen within the full context of the structure of the school. It is this structure which needs to change. For example, a school should aim to have a workforce that reflects the pupil community and is as little stereotyped as possible. The workforce includes helpers, caretaking and cleaning staff, office staff, and teachers. Directives from above will inhibit this atmosphere. All workers must feel valued and listened to. (We must point out here that, as a group of teachers, we are only too well aware that the current educational political climate is probably more directive than it has ever been.)

If the workforce, to some extent, reflects the pupil community there will probably be informal links between some staff and parents making parents feel more 'at home'. Making a space or room available with a parents' noticeboard, tea, coffee, etc., could make the informal involvement for parents easier.

In setting up and organizing parents' groups staff and parents alike need to be sensitive to how difficult it is socializing across

115

cultural, class, and sex barriers. The traditional PTFA (parents, teachers, and friends) termly meeting may intimidate many parents who find its middle-class structure of officers and agendas and articulate speakers alien. Links need to be built up gradually and the starting points should be as secure and relaxed as possible for parents.

The following are possible starting points:

(a) Parents' gatherings focusing on something to do with the work or the needs of their child's class;
(b) Meetings of different groups of parents who have a particular interest in common, e.g. cultural, own educational development (use of computer, English classes, self-defence, keep-fit), parent and toddler group.

In a school trying to be open we would be aiming towards any initiatives which value the contributions parents make through their own culture and experiences with parents imparting skills and knowledge as part of the curriculum, e.g. parents' and children's bookmaking workshop, carpentry, personal histories. (30)

IN-SERVICE TRAINING (INSET)

If teachers are to develop anti-oppressive education, current policy has to be reversed and money spent on supply cover to release teachers for Inset, and to enable us to work collaboratively. Policy documents (31-33) seem irrelevant and are not effective if no time is made available for overburdened primary teachers to read them, let alone work out strategies to put them into practice.

We need to be constantly learning and developing our own ideas and practice, and Inset is, therefore, vital. We need to plan collectively, share responsibility for development and direction, as well as each participating. Also, meeting with others as a support group is very positive. We need to meet socially to unwind after the pressures of school, as well as to work, e.g. weekend conferences, which bring a group together, are also the basis for the focusing on and planning of future work. We can share information, ideas, new resources, and current experiences as teachers, but also talk about our needs. As well as giving great strength to a group it is a chance to discuss issues at length, without feeling pressed for time, having rushed from school, and before hurrying home to domestic chores, family or other commitments.

There is a need to continue developing strategies and materials, but also together we can act as a pressure group on education authorities and other agencies, to make policy changes, and develop alternatives to the resources still being produced with stereotyped content and images. Also, as a group we can help each other develop relationships with, and overcome conflicts, problems, and misunderstandings amongst, our co-workers and parents.

SOME CONCLUSIONS

We need those in a position of power to take a stand and support us visibly, because no matter what strategies, resources, and support we have, we still come up against racism, classism, and sexism 'hidden' in the curriculum. There seem to be contradictions in 'equal opportunities' programmes which do not include consideration of LEAs' practices as employers, as well as the practical classroom implementation. We need release for practising classroom teachers (not advisers) to work alongside us, and to be involved in daytime Inset. To make a commitment, not a gesture, we need extra staffing. Lack of crèches, or babysitting payments, inadequate maternity leave and paid leave to look after sick children, as well as tokenistic paternity leave, all serve to sustain inequality and show a lack of concern and understanding of equality.

We have been very optimistic, but in today's political climate we have become more realistic in our expectations. We know that the attitudes of society and the system cannot be changed overnight. We have less energy and enthusiasm owing to a lack of commitment and support from our employers as well as cutbacks and steadily worsening conditions in the education system. It is hard not to become demoralized, having put a tremendous amount of time, energy, and money into something to which we feel fully committed. Yet it is necessary to have time to get together to talk and support each other.

Our attempts at anti-oppressive education will not stop. We still feel that by exposing children to a wider range of perspectives, offering them alternative images, and by giving them the tools to examine critically all that is around them, we can at least make these issues visible in schools.

But school hierarchies have to play their part because children, parents (and many teachers) do not read guidelines and reports. They believe the evidence of their eyes which tells them that power and authority still lie with men, who are usually white and middle class.

For education to be accessible to all, the help we give each other is of central importance. We cannot rely on outside agencies whose commitment, priorities, and ways of approaching issues are different from ours. It is through sharing ideas and pooling knowledge, through working collaboratively, raising our consciousness of the issues of 'race', class, and gender, that we can begin to develop equality in our society today.

NOTES AND REFERENCES

1.   Fuchs, E. (1977) 'How teachers learn to help children fail', in M.

    Hoyles (ed.) The Politics of Literacy, London: Writers' and Readers' Publishing Co-operative.

2. Hoyles, M. (ed.), op. cit., p. 178.
3. Lobban, G. (1978) 'The influence of the school on sex-role stereotyping', in J. Chetwynd and D. Harknett (eds) The Sex Role System, London: Routledge & Kegan Paul.
4. King, R. (1978) All Things Bright and Beautiful? A Sociological Study of Infants' Classrooms, Chichester: Wiley, p.147.
5. Jackson, B. and Marsden, D. (1966) Education and the Working Class, Harmondsworth: Penguin Books, p. 47.
6. Clarricoates, K. (1987) 'Dinosaurs in the classroom - a re-examination of some aspects of the "hidden curriculum" in the primary school', in Women's Studies International Quarterly, 4: pp.353-64.
7. Bernstein, B. (1975) Class, Codes and Control, 3:7, p. 139.
8. Weiner, G. (ed.) (1985) Just a Bunch of Girls, Oxford: Oxford University Press.
9. Spender, D. (1982) Invisible Women, the Schooling Scandal, London: Writers' and Readers' Publishing Co-operative.
10. Brandis, W. and Bernstein, B. (1974) Selection and Control: Teachers' Ratings of Children in the Infant School, London: Routledge & Kegan Paul.
11. Stones, R. (1983) Pour out the Cocoa, Janet: Sexism in Children's Books, Harlow: Longman, for the School's Council.
12. Burgess, C. (1981) Breakthrough to Sexism, Teaching London Kids, no. 17.
13. Whyte, J. (1983) Beyond the Wendy House, Harlow: Longman, for the Schools Council, p. 53.
14. CUES (Centre for Urban Educational Studies), Robert Montefiore Building, Vallance Road, London E1 5AD.
15. Chrystie, M. (1983) Anna to Zoulla, London: Centreprise Trust Ltd.
16. Stones, R. (1984) Ms Muffet Fights Back, Harmondsworth: Penguin.
17. Tuggs, P. (1985) Books for Keeps, London: Children's Books for a Multi-Cultural Society.
18. (1984) Changing Images, London: Sheba Publications.
19. Minority Group Support Services (1984) Naming Patterns, Hillfields, Coventry.
20. Bryan, B., Dadzie, S. and Scafe, S. (1985) The Heart of the Race - Black Women's Lives in Britain, London: Virago.
21. The Children's Language Project, Philip and Tacey Ltd, Northway, Andover, Hants.
22. School Curriculum Development Committee, 45 Notting Hill Gate, London W11.
23. Luzac and Co. Ltd, 46 Great Russell Street, London WC1B 3PE (Luzac storytellers - dual-language texts).
24. Side by Side, 90 Palatine Road, London N16 8SY (dual-language texts and tapes).

25. Fisher, S. World Studies Project, 12 Fairfield Road, Bedminster, Bristol B53 1LG.

26. Shops and projects which supply multicultural books and play material:

Afro-Caribbean Educational Project, Wyvil School, Wyvil Road, London SW8 2TJ.

Anti-Sexist Resource Guide, Centre for Learning Resources, 275 Kennington Lane, London SE11 5QZ.

Arawidi Ltd, 10 Dyson Road, Leytonstone, London E11 1LZ.

The Book Place, 13 Peckham High Street, London SE15. Tel.: 01 701 1757.

Children's Rights Workshop, 74 Balfour Street, London SE17.

Harriet Tubman Books, 27/29 Grove Lane, Handsworth, Birmingham B21 9ES.

Letter Box Library, Children's Books Co-operative, First Floor, 5 Bradbury Street, London N16 8JA. Tel.: 01 254 1640.

National Childminding Association, 204/206 High Street, Bromley, Kent BR1 1PP.

New Beacon Books, 76 Stroud Green Road, London N4.

VOLCUF, c/o Thomas Coram Foundation, 40 Brunswick Square, London WC1 1AZ. Tel.: 01 278 2424.

Building Blocks, Castlemead Estate, The Rampway, Camberwell Road, London SE5. Tel.: 01 711 4418.

SOMA Books, 38 Kennington Lane, London SE11. Tel: 01 735 2101.

Headstart Books and Crafts, 25 West Green Road, London N15. Tel.: 01 882 2838.

The Commonwealth Institute, Kensington High Street, London W8. Tel.: 01 603 0754.

Sunpower Books, 83 Blackstock Road, London N4. Tel.: 01 226 1795.

Books from India, 32 Coptic Street, London WC1. Tel.: 01 405 7226.

Centerprise Bookshop, 136/138 Kingsland High Street, London E8. Tel.: 01 254 9532.

Compendium Books, 234 Camden High Street, London NW1. Tel.: 01 485 8944/2267/1525.

Corner House Bookshop, 14 Enden Street, London WC2. Tel.: 01 836 9960.

Housemans Bookshop, 5 Caledonian Road, London N1.

Latin American Books, 16B Low Ousegate, York. Tel.: 0532 755872.

Pams Sikh Bookshop, 7 Abbotshall Road, London SE6. Tel.: 01 698 55010.

Buanghwa (Bookshop), 9 Newport Place, London WC2 and 2 Andre Place, London SW8.

Deptford Book Traders, 55 Deptford High Street, London SE8. Tel.: 01 691 8339.

Books Plus, 23 Lewisham Way, London SE14. Tel.: 01 691 2833.
Bookspread, 58 Tooting Bec Road, London SW17. Tel.: 01 767 6377.
Third World Bookshop, 28 Sackville Street, London N4. Tel.: 01 608 0447.
Zeno Books (Greek), 6 Denmark Street, London WC2. Tel.: 01 836 2522.
Thap Community Bookshop, 178 Whitechapel Road, London E1. Tel.: 01 247 0216.
Third World Publications, 138 Stratford Road, Sparkbrook, Birmingham B11. Tel.: 021 773 6572.
Ujamaa Bookshop, 14 Brixton Road, London SW9. Tel.: 01 582 2068.
Sisterwrite, 190 Upper Street, London N1. Tel.: 01 226 9782.
African Students Publications, 103 Douglas Road, Esher, Surrey.
Reading Matters, 10 Lymington Avenue, Wood Green, London N22. Tel.: 01 881 3187.

27. Orlick, T. (1979) Co-operative Sports and Games Book - Challenge Without Competition, London: Writers' and Readers' Publishing Co-operative.
28. Dr David Hicks, Centre for Peace Studies, St Martin's College, Bowerham, Lancaster LA1 3JD.
29. Adams, C. (ed.) (1986) Primary Matters, London: ILEA.
30. Dodgson, E. (1984) Motherland, London: Heinemann.
31. ILEA Inspectorate, (1982) Equal Opportunities for Boys and Girls.
32. ILEA Inspectorate (1983) Race, Sex and Class 1. Achievement in schools, 2. Multi-ethnic education in schools.
33. ILEA Inspectorate (1985) Race, Sex and Class 6. A policy for equality: sex.

FURTHER SOURCES OF INFORMATION

ACER Project (Afro-Caribbean Educational Resource Project), 275 Kennington Lane, London SE11 5QZ.
AFFOR, 173 Lozells Road, Lozells, Birmingham B19 1RN. Tel: 021 523 8076.
ALTARF (All London Teachers Against Racism and Facism), Unit 216, Panther House, 38 Mount Pleasant, London WC1.
CRE (Commission for Racial Equality), Elliott House, 10-12 Allington Street, London SW1E 5EH.
NAME (National Association for Multi-Racial Education), 86 Station Road, Mickleover, Derby.

FURTHER READING

Adams, C. and Laurikietis, R. (1975, 1976) The Gender Trap, Series:

Education and Work, Sex and Marriage, Messages and Images, London: Quartet.

Arnot, M. and Weiner, G. (1987) Gender and the Politics of Schooling, Oxford: Oxford University Press.

Equal Opportunities Team, (1987) Stop, Look and Listen, London: ILEA.

McFarlane, C. (1986) Hidden Messages - Activities for Exploring Bias, London: Development Education Centre.

Smail, B. (1984) Girl Friendly Science, Avoiding Sex Bias in the Curriculum, Harlow: Longman, for the Schools' Council.

Chapter Seven

THE JUNIOR YEARS

Muriel Robinson

> The doleful litany chanted endlessly is that the children and young people in schools are totally submerged by powerful manipulative forces outside their control which brutalize and stupefy them. If that message strikes home then it is small wonder if teachers who step forward to expose, analyse and demolish, feel in their hearts that they are puny in the face of giants who can spend more on one advertisement than one of them will spend on school books in the whole of a teaching career. (1)

When I began teaching London primary school children in the 1970s, I had a very limited notion of education for equality. If I thought about this at all, I suspect that I saw it as my duty to ensure that the children in my care benefited from the kind of white, middle-class education I had enjoyed. Having learned the hard way how inappropriate this notion is, I hope that by sharing my experiences I can help student teachers and teachers to form a more coherent view of their roles as educators for equality, so that all children in their care, of whatever 'race', sex, or class, will gain as much as possible from their junior education. In this chapter, therefore, I hope to do two things. First, I want to explore the broader issues of teacher attitude and pedagogic style, together with the underlying issue of the hidden curriculum, and second I plan to work through the kinds of activities I believe to be valuable for children in junior school, giving examples from my own experience. I do not offer my own practice as a paradigm; in fact, the more I reflect on my own practice, the more I become aware of its limitations. However, concrete examples may help the reader to take on the principles I hope to establish.

THE ROLE OF THE TEACHER

The role of the teacher in a junior classroom seems to me to be central. If teachers see themselves as the providers and definers of a cultural norm, then there must be the risk that for many children in the class that cultural norm will not match their own experience, which in turn will be denied validity. Equally those children whose cultural background matches closely that assumed by the teacher will tend to see this as the only possible model and will not be encouraged to question their own cultural assumptions.

John Hardcastle has talked about the teacher's need to 'cede the making of meanings' (2) to the children, seeing the classroom as 'a potential site of cultural production'. (3) For this to happen, there must be an openness on the part of the teacher to children's experience, which must be seen both by teacher and children as a valid part of the classroom learning environment. The children's own cultural experiences must be the starting points for the learning that takes place, and so the teacher needs a readiness to enter into the children's concerns, which in turn implies a readiness to enter into the concerns of their parents.

This can only be achieved, in my opinion, by a significant shift in the predominant teacher styles in which the teacher dictates to the children which areas of learning are on the curriculum and which activities a child will undertake at a particular time, whether in the guise of class teaching, group work, or individualized learning programmes set out by the teacher. What is needed instead is a negotiated curriculum, in which children are able to have a say in both the topics to be explored, in the particular aspects of those topics which interest them as individuals and as groups, and the ways in which they wish to organize their learning time. Some people may see this approach as lacking in structure, with an abdication of responsiblity on the teacher's part. This should not be so, since the teacher has a clear responsibility to be an active partner in the negotiations, taking their overall view of the children's learning needs into account to ensure a clear progression and helping the children to see the learning which is taking place. In fact, I found that the only way to operate this system satisfactorily was to keep a very close eye on the children's development and to be sure that I knew what they were learning. It was only when I moved to this approach that I began to understand more fully the need for carefully worked out long-term forecasts, adjusted regularly in the light of the children's responses and my assessment of individual and group needs. Apart from any other considerations, a teacher working in this way will need to be able to explain and justify it to parents and colleagues, which in itself helps one to think much more deeply about the underlying structure in order to be able to articulate it. In my last classroom I tried to achieve a balance between my concern for their learning and the children's own views by working out collectively with the children how we should interpret the theme set out for us by the school, and then at a more immediate level what activities should be on offer over a given period of time (anything from a day in the case of a fairly limited activity to several weeks for more complex ones). It would be pointless to deny the constraints on these negotiations. There were certain activities laid down by the school as timetabled lessons (PE and music for example), and there was my concern that children should be experiencing a balanced curriculum, at least over a week or so. For many teachers there are imposed schemes, and the approaching National Curriculum must also be taken seriously. However, there is always some room for negotiation within the constraints, and I certainly found working in this way to be much more satisfactory. It enabled me to make space for different children's needs and to be open to their experiences out of school, which they in turn gradually realized were a valid part of the cultural pattern of the classroom.

There are difficulties which teachers need to be aware of in changing to this way of working. If children have to articulate their interests and concerns in the classroom, particularly if this is a new experience in their school career, there will be some children with much more confidence to stake their claim than others. Often these confident and articulate children will be those who already have a good chance of success within the system. Tizard and Hughes (4) have suggested that working-class girls are often socialized into a quiet, submissive role in the classroom, rarely taking the initiating role in conversations, for example. The teacher has a responsibility to see that all children are given a chance to contribute. To start with this may mean some careful monitoring. We need to know, for example, whether girls get a fair turn at practical activities, and which children are contributing to discussions. We may need to intervene directly to create space for some children, and to support some children as they learn to articulate their choice. There are also implications to do with the control of the physical environment. If children are to feel that they are genuine partners in learning with the teacher, then they need to be involved in the organization of the environment, displaying their own work as a part of this.

Another crucial element is the role of the teacher as a partner with children's parents and family. We do have a responsibility not just to tell parents what we are doing and why, but to take into account their views of what education is for. It may not be possible, or even desirable, to adjust our approach to match parents' expectations (I am thinking here of the majority group of white parents who resisted our efforts to make the experience of our Asian children a valid part of the culture of the school) but neither can we achieve our aims by riding roughshod over parents. This is a difficult matter, and I do not think there are any easy answers, but by showing our readiness to enter into a dialogue with parents we can start to work towards genuine partnership.

In the last primary school in which I worked, we attempted to foster better relationships with parents in some quite specific ways, believing that possibilities for a broader dialogue would grow out of the particular instances. The school was a voluntary-aided, one-form-entry primary school in South London which also had two part-time nursery classes. Many of the children came to us at the age of three and stayed until they were eleven, although we also had a sizeable minority who were in temporary DHSS accommodation and spent less time with us. Although it was a Church of England school, the admissions policy for most of my time there was one which encouraged all local parents, of whatever ethnic, cultural, or religious origin or persuasion, to see us as their local school. As a result, we had a very mixed intake, including white, Afro-Caribbean, and Asian children from a wide mix of religions and cultures and from different social classes in a proportion which roughly matched that of the local population as a whole. We tried to ensure that prearranged meetings with parents were at times convenient to them, and that parents also felt welcome in the school at any time. We were helped in this by being a primary rather than just a junior school, so that parents were already used to coming into the building with the children. Regular appeals for parental help were sent out and also followed up orally when parents did come into school, and we tried to ensure that those parents who did come in felt comfortable both in the work they were doing and in the environment. Something which helped here was arranging for more than one parent to come in at any one time, particularly for the first few visits, and making sure that there was somewhere comfortable for them to have a cup of coffee and a chat during their time in school. The headteacher held a series of coffee mornings at the beginning of each year, one for each class, and these had some success in bringing in new parents. There were regular meetings for such things as the home-school reading programme, which itself provided a direct line of communication with a lot of parents, and for school journeys. Every Wednesday afternoon there was a parents' social club with a crèche on school premises, and this helped some parents to feel more at ease in the building. Similarly, the PTA held regular meetings, social and otherwise, to which staff tried to go. In this way we managed to make contact with a large proportion of parents from all social classes. However, we did find difficulties. First, the parents of Asian children in the school rarely attended meetings. This seemed to be because the social functions were very monocultural in their format and because of language and cultural barriers between home and school. To try to break these down, we made use of the local authority translation service and also made contact with local community leaders, who then liaised with us to encourage more Asian parents to become involved, initially by enlisting their expertise for a particular project. One very real problem here was the fact that a sizeable minority of our white working-class parents found it hard to accept these moves and a certain amount of racism came to the surface. On this issue we believed it to be important to stand by our strong commitment as a school to antiracist education, while at the same time, making every effort to involve and convince this sizeable minority. Another difficulty was that certain parents, being more confident and articulate than others, came to be seen by other parents as a favoured clique. To some extent we overcame this by direct invitations to other parents to take responsibility for certain activities and events, but again it is a very real problem in many schools and one for which teachers need to be vigilant, particularly in view of the fact that so many teachers themselves come from the same social setting as this clique, as Granados Johnson et al. have discussed in chapter 6. (5)

THE HIDDEN CURRICULUM

The hidden curriculum of the primary school has been discussed in depth in chapter 6, and this section should be seen as complementary to that. Inevitably there will be some overlap but I have tried to limit the extent of this. In order to look more closely at the effect of the hidden curriculum in junior schools, I want to look separately at the issues of 'race', gender, and class. However, before doing so I want to make it clear that this is an artificial division and that many of the points I shall raise transcend these divisions.

'Race'

There are still many teachers in our junior schools who trained before colleges of education began to explore the notion of antiracist education and who have not had the chance to attend in-service courses. It is also still by no means universal for initial teacher training students to be given a thorough introduction to the ideas of ántiracist education. Many schools are still at the assimilatíon level, particularly in areas where the population is still largely white, and many more have a tokenistic approach, introducing isolated topics on 'Festivals' or 'Food'. As a result, many teachers believe that racism is not a problem for them. Racist abuse is frequently dismissed as 'normal' name-calling which needs no special attention. Some local authorities have worked hard to re-educate their employees, but there will be a continuing need for in-service work for many years.

Granados Johnson et al. (6) have discussed the limited effect of measures taken to increase the number of black teachers in primary schools. This is particularly evident outside the big cities, although even in authorities such as Ealing there has been little progress, despite the council's clear commitment to equal opportunities. (7) Departments of Education have made little progress in recruiting more black students to teacher training courses. All of this means that children are unlikely to see positive role models of black teachers and heads, thus reinforcing any notions they have already received from society about who holds authority.

The images which children in many schools will be seeing are those which accompany charity appeals for famine and disaster relief, which reinforce the notion of passivity and helplessness. Even if these are accompanied in school by more positive images and by discussions of the responsibilities of the developed world, children see the same passive images daily on their TV screens.

Teachers can take some positive steps here, both by being vigilant when choosing books and resources for their classrooms and libraries and by taking action as citizens to let the media know how they feel, but without the positive support of central and local government this will be hard going. Even in those authorities where positive action has been taken, there is still a long way to go. The somewhat heavy-handed imposition by the ILEA of antiracist policies alienated many, particularly many non-teaching staff. Changing people's attitudes is a long and difficult business, not best brought about by threats. To me this seems to be an aspect of the hidden curriculum which is most problematic, particularly in monocultural schools.

There are some specific issues here which need addressing. One area of difficulty can be diet. Teachers need to be well aware of the fact that some or all of the children they are teaching may have cultural or religious attitudes to food which can make school dinnertime a stressful experience. A Rastafarian girl who joined my class was initially criticized by teachers and dinner ladies as a fussy eater because they did not expect a black child to have religious objections to eating pork. Teachers in primary schools have considerable influence over the views of children in their care, which should be used positively to encourage an understanding of different values, rather than allowing misinformed prejudice. (In monocultural white clsasrooms it is also of course essential to encourage a more informed attitude.) Similarly, teachers also need to be well informed about different cultural attitudes and beliefs about dress and behaviour, and to examine school expectations in the light of those of the home. As new staff are appointed, part of their introduction to the school could perhaps include some form of information on this, provided where possible by the local black community or alternatively by other relevant black groups, bodies, or individuals (which would in turn provide valuable in-service work for the existing teachers who have to organize it).

Gender

I would like to start by considering the staffing patterns that junior children will see in schools. Although men and women theoretically have equal chances of promotion as junior teachers, in fact this does not happen. Surveys repeatedly find that women teachers make up the bulk of the ordinary teachers, whilst the much smaller number of men entering the teaching profession are appointed to the majority of senior posts. In many schools there will be fewer men teachers, but these men are likely to be the head or deputy head and to teach the older children in the school. They often have a special role as chief discipliners. Since most children see the school structure as even more hierarchical than it is ('Will you be paid more now you're teaching top juniors, Miss?' is a question I have been asked more than once), the relative roles of men and women in the school have great significance for these children's own developing notions of gender roles. Similarly, non-teaching staff in schools are almost exclusively women by virtue of the low rates of pay, so that again women will be seen in a subordinate role. Apart from the male teachers, the only other male is often the schoolkeeper or caretaker, who again is in a dominant position.

Some of these are not issues that we can overcome individually. The problem of recruiting men to the profession can only be resolved with some fairly fundamental societal changes: as long as teaching is a low-paid, low-status job, with primary education seen as intellectually less rigorous than secondary and offering considerably fewer promotion prospects; it will be hard to convince boys that teaching is a feasible career choice. Similarly, non-teaching positions in school would need radical reforms before men would rush to be dinner helpers or school secretaries. If these changes occurred, there would be real hardship caused to those women who rely on jobs which release them to care for their children in school holidays and who find great satisfaction in working in schools, both as teachers and as non-teaching staff. However, within these constraints there are things that we can do collectively or individually. One possibility here would be to discuss with children the ways in which men and women in our society find different careers easily achievable. It is also a responsibility of all staff in a school to see that children do not treat different members of staff, teaching or non-teaching, differently. Again this is something that we could discuss with a class; however, our own attitudes are likely to be very influential, so we should also guard against differential attitudes ourselves.

Children are also directly affected by many school practices which reinforce stereotypical gender images. Registers in many schools are still divided by sex, though some authorities have managed to do away with this without any great resulting confusion. Children are asked to line up in gender groups. If it is necessary to have two lines, there are many other ways of dealing with this - alphabetically, by friendship group, or even at random in two roughly equal lines. (We found that it was necessary to introduce some alternative method as children otherwise automatically still lined up in sex groups, probably as a result of earlier conditioning.) Boys are often asked to do physical jobs, such as moving tables or chairs, whilst many teachers rely on girls to tidy up. It's easy enough to ask for 'four strong children' or 'four children to help move the stage blocks' instead of 'four strong boys'. The tidying up may not be

so effective to start with if boys as well as girls are involv
teachers may need to ensure that the boys are actually doir
fair share, but this is surely something worth perseverance. Again,
this is the kind of issue which could and should be addressed directly
with junior children, so that they become aware of the underlying
issues.

Playtime may need a bit of attention, too. In many schools the
traditional game of football dominates the play area, so that other
activities are crowded out or disrupted. In one school we were lucky
enough to have a ball court, so that at least there was also a quiet
space, but the boys then saw the ball court as their own territory.
Girls who were seen to be good at football were tolerated, but there
was no space for other large ball games or for girls to play football
by themselves. A solution might be to have certain days designated
as girls-only days, though teachers would need to be ready to resist
resentment from the boys on this and to talk about the reasons for
the change. An allied problem could be that games lessons are
timetabled rigidly so that only boys can do football while girls play
netball. To start with, we tried to overcome this simply by letting
children choose, but if netball and football happen at the same time
often very little will change. We eventually overcame this by
offering both sports to both sexes at different times in the week;
other schools might want to reconsider the range of games on offer.
There are still schools where needlework and woodwork create
similar hidden messages for children about appropriate activities for
girls and boys.

Teachers also need to watch to see how certain activities and
pieces of equipment are used by boys and girls. In my experience,
boys tend to dominate such things as computers, cameras, and
construction toys; this can be resolved by setting up girls-only
groups to increase the girls' confidence in handling them. Boys also
tend to dominate class discussions and to engage in attention-
seeking behaviour such as 'ruler-wanging', (8) as Margaret Sandra has
shown, and we need to intervene to give girls a space where
necessary.

Class

The junior school can be seen as a middle-class institution,
perpetuating the cultural and personal values of the middle classes
and imposing them on children from other classes. The Education
Reform Act was presented by Margaret Thatcher as a weapon in her
claimed desire to make everyone middle class (everyone,
presumably, except the upper classes, who will continue to use their
own elitist schools outside state control). This implies that to be
middle class is infinitely desirable, an idea that needs challenging.
Teachers in junior schools are mainly from the middle or upper
working classes, and a sizeable minority of applicants to the primary

education department in which I currently work come from private education, so this situation seems unlikely to change overnight. The only working-class adults that children are likely to encounter in schools are those in less prestigious positions, so that the role models provided for working-class pupils create a vicious circle. Working-class parents often find schools alienating, partly as a result of their own educational experience, and so the pattern goes on.

There needs to be action by teachers on two fronts to deal with this. First, there is a need for a reappraisal of the teacher's role and the cultural environment of the classroom, as I have already suggested. This will need support of a more immediate kind - schools need to think about the implications of demanding that children have PE kit, and of organizing school outings, particularly those which fall outside the scope of the Education Reform Act or of arrangements for free school dinners. Many children also suffer at school because their parents do not conform to middle-class attitudes, to uniforms, absence letters, or dental appointments. If we can make the school a place in which children of all social classes feel at ease and that their experience is valid, perhaps this may help to widen the recruitment pattern for future primary teachers.

THE ACTUAL CURRICULUM

While I would not want to advocate a subject-based approach to the junior curriculum, I would argue that it is the duty of the teacher to ensure that children's learning encompasses the different curriculum areas, even if children themselves are not aware of the divisions. I have accordingly decided to deal with the question of activities that might be on offer in rough subject groupings for convenience.

Language and literacy

Since the Bullock Report we have had a clear directive from the DES that

> no child should be expected to cast off the language and culture of the home as he (sic) crosses the school threshold, nor to live and act as though school and home represent two totally separate and different cultures which have to be kept firmly apart. (9)

However, many teachers are still unaware of the fact that all accents and dialects of English, including Standard English and Received Pronunciation, are linguistically of equal merit. (10) The social advantages of Standard English have led many to view it as 'correct' or 'proper' English, with many children being criticized for using non-standard forms. With juniors it is possible to examine the history and geography of accent and dialect in such a way that they become more open to other varieties and begin to understand the allied questions of prestige and power. (11) Similarly it is crucial that all children's languages should be valued by the school, and that multilingual children should feel at ease speaking a language other than English in school, particularly in view of the value this has for their acquisition of English. (12) It is also important that children in monolingual English classrooms should realize that all other languages are of equal validity, and again this is something which could be done as part of a project on communication generally, as well as being part of the hidden curriculum.

Reading schemes are particularly problematic. Even those recently released tend to be based around middle-class white families in which girls play a passive role, despite publishers' claims to the contrary. (13) In addition, the recent research on reading indicates that programmed approaches to reading have serious drawbacks. (14) Many schools now are moving towards an apprenticeship approach based on real books. (15) I found this generally to be much more satisfactory in terms of children in my class becoming enthusiastic readers; it also makes it much easier to ensure that the range of books provided contains positive images of a variety of cultural situations. I think it is important that the books on offer are truly representative of attitudes to be found in Britain today, including some with which I would disagree, so that children can also learn to look critically at books and begin to be aware of prejudice in society and ways of dealing with it. Junior children can be very perceptive about such matters. (16) It has to be said that there are some books which I would never want to see in a classroom, and I would want to choose particularly carefully those books which I read to the class or recommended to individuals, since I would not want to give the impression that I was giving particular status to books which I found in some way unacceptable. In short, the books in the classroom need to reflect the children's realities, experiences, and desires, and to help extend these through powerful literature. A wide variety, including picture books and dual-language texts, is crucial for all junior classrooms, since it is hard to know which books will speak to particular children.

When children are asked to write, it is important that they should have control over the form and content of their writing, with writing about their own experiences, interests, and opinions a normal part of the routine. The move towards conventions of spelling, grammar, and form needs to be one which develops the child's own confidence as a writer. Many teachers have found that the ideas put forward by Graves (17) are helpful here; I certainly found that his approach, which involves helping children see themselves as writers, proudly publishing their work for an audience they had chosen rather than just writing for the teacher's red pen, valuable.

Drama is invaluable in helping children to explore their prejudices and beliefs in a relatively safe environment. I worked with some third-year juniors on the American pioneers' experiences on the Oregon Trail, which allowed them to think deeply about population movements and the relative rights of different cultural groups. Work with another class of the same age based on a commune in modern China allowed the class to explore ideas about individual and collective responsibility and about gender roles.

Parental involvement in language development can help bring school and the home environment closer together and can broaden children's cultural experiences. Jennie Ingham has shown that storytelling in school is an activity which can involve parents and relatives from many cultural traditions. (18) Some schools have involved adults from the community in working alongside junior children to produce picture books for infants. (19) I found the daily contact with parents created by our home-school reading system helped me to get to know parents as individuals and to communicate much more openly about their children. Some schools extend this to include a school bookshop; this can be valuable, but can put economic pressure on many families and therefore needs sympathetic treatment by teachers.

In many ways, language development can be seen as the central element in the junior curriculum. Hardly any school activities do not involve reading, writing, or talking. As a result, teachers' attitudes to language affect the whole of their teaching. As Hardcastle says, 'the acquisition of literacy is a socially mediated process'; (20) it is up to us as teachers to develop a pedagogy for this which will support our aim of education for equality.

Mathematics

There has recently been much debate as to whether mathematics can be seen as culturally neutral and whether we need antiracist approaches to mathematics teaching, to the point where the 1988 International Conference on Mathematical Education is to spend time considering 'social, philosophical and cultural issues'. (21) In fact, I would claim that even such an apparently culture-free area as the addition and subtraction of numbers has in fact been presented over the years in a misleading way. Few children are brought up to realize that numbers themselves are a construct of society, and fewer still realize that the counting system we use has its origins not in Western Europe but in Indian and Arab cultures. (22) It would be relatively simple to encourage children to find out about great mathematicians of the past and to see the broad range of cultures from which they came. Similarly, it might well be interesting to encourage children to think about ways of improving on our number system and to look at other ways of counting as a way of helping them to see this as a construct. When we look at the mathematics schemes available for the junior school, they seem very remote from reality for many children in terms of the situations in which they set mathematical problems. (23) Walkerdine (24) has shown how children have to take on different discourses in order to operate successfully in the classroom, and this seems particularly true of much traditional mathematics work, which assumes a common cultural approach when attempting to set abstract operations in everyday situations. Many children have found it hard to respond appropriately to questions which ask them to subtract one sum of money from another by suggesting the former sum has been lost, because the social and familial implications of losing money interfere with the numerical operation; losing money is just too threatening to contemplate in the way we expect them to, and this must be appreciated by teachers. Just as children come to school with a great deal of knowledge about language which must be built on by the teacher for them to become literate, so children come to school with some understanding of mathematical principles. If we start from the child's experience and build on this by using the real concerns of the children in our care as a basis for mathematical work then we have a much better chance of helping them to take on abstract mathematical discourses. My children grasped the concept of a metre much more firmly when they were making the paper-chains at Christmas than when asked to measure the classroom for no apparent purpose. Similarly their grasp of the concept of area became firmer when working out how big a piece of paper was needed to make the cover for their handmade books. These examples may seem trivial, but there are already many real applications for mathematics in the life of the junior school. It is up to us as teachers to make these explicit, to match them to the real concerns of our pupils, and to make clear links to the abstract symbolic thought involved.

There has been growing concern about girls and mathematics. The report on 'Girls and Mathematics' sums this up:

> The evidence ... indicates that girls and boys achieve the same overall performance in mathematics at primary level, although specific topics are dominated by sex. Despite this, teachers and pupils regard mathematics as a subject at which boys are likely to achieve a higher overall performance than girls, and teaching styles and expectations are modified, often unconsciously, accordingly. Boys achieve significantly better in applying numbers and measures of length, area, volume and capacity, for example, whereas girls achieve significantly better than boys in only one area: computation of whole numbers and decimals, which figure decreasingly through the secondary years. (25)

Boys tend to dominate practical activities so that girls appear to be taking part but are actually passive members of group. This is another area in which girls-only groups might be necessary on occasions; teachers need to monitor this closely. The report referred to above gives a useful list of suggestions for teachers on ways of changing the present situation, (26) which points out among other things the importance of encouraging women teachers to improve their own mathematical confidence by such means as in-service education.

Topic work (history, geography, science, and RE)

This is too broad an area to be covered comprehensively in a chapter of this nature, and although as a primary teacher I was expected to make provision for these curriculum areas, I have no great amount of specialist knowledge. However, two areas seem to be central. First of all, the choice of topic carries many implications. If the children are genuinely involved in making decisions about their learning, then any topic to be studied needs to be mutually agreed through negotiation between children and teacher. Points which might influence the teacher's contribution to the initial choice and to the routes through the chosen topic might be the dangers of tokenism and Eurocentrism. An excellent example of good use of a topic which is often very Eurocentric is provided in one of the broadsheets published by the Language in the Multicultural Primary Classroom Schools Council Project. (27) Here, a study of Tudor Britain was extended to a study of different aspects of world history in the sixteenth century, including a comparison of the Mughal ruler Akbar the Great with the Tudor ruler Elizabeth I.

A topic which I found particularly helpful on one occasion was one based around the Hindu festival of Divali. At first, this might sound like one of the tokenistic approaches I was criticizing earlier. However, I believe that the ways in which we explored this topic genuinely increased the children's understanding of each other. Although we did explore the story behind Divali and the traditional ways in which it has been celebrated, I also ensured that the Asian children in the class were able to explain to us how their families marked the occasion. This led to much fruitful discussion about the differences within cultures and similarities between them, as the children discovered for example that what to the white children were Christmas decorations were used by some Asian families at Divali. For some of the children in the class it was the first time that they had felt that their experiences outside school were valued as a learning resource within school, and as they grew in confidence we were inundated with other stories about their home lives which the other children were eager to match with their own. There were valuable discoveries made about the nature of language and about the fact that some children in the class were multilingual. The increased confidence of the Asian children began to show right across the curriculum and socially, and I felt they were much more ready to form an open relationship with me as a result of this work.

The second issue which needs consideration here is that of resources. First, teachers need to be alert to the kinds of images presented in books and other sources of information which children may be using for a particular topic. These need to provide a rounded view as far as possible, and children need to be encouraged to question any obvious cultural assumptions. ('Do you think everyone living in South Wales worked in a mine? Would the miners' lives have been the same as the mineowners'? What about miners' wives? What about miners in other areas or other countries?' and so on). Second, if practical resources (science equipment, computers, cameras) are involved, teachers may need to intervene so that all children get a fair chance to use these.

PE and games

This might not at first appear to be a relevant area. However, there have been many different situations where schools have failed to take account of religious scruples in planning PE, or where failure to arrive at school with the proper kit has been punished.

The major concern here must be that parents' and pupils' religious and cultural beliefs are taken on by the school. Many children will find changing for PE unacceptable, especially in mixed groups. Swimming may be especially difficult. If sufficient children are affected, it may be necessary to rethink the whole approach. Sometimes a compromise over required clothing can be reached, and schools need to be ready to ask themselves why they are asking for certain forms of dress and whether there are alternatives.

Teachers also need to be sensitive to the economic realities that parents may not be able to provide specialist clothing and to the fact that for some parents this will not be seen as a priority anyway. Even if parents would somehow manage to buy it, children may not want to ask their parents for money if the family is not well off. I wore hockey boots several sizes too small for years rather than ask my parents to spend more money on an already over-priced school uniform. One solution is for the school to provide equipment and clothing where possible, but this needs to be available for everyone rather than means-tested, or those children not bringing their own things will feel marked out. Teachers need to be more ready to accept excuses about 'forgotten' kit as possibly revealing difficulties of this kind. It will help if children are only asked to wear very simple clothing rather than elaborate uniform requirements of colour and style; the important issue is that clothing should be safe for the activity rather than smart. It is also important that the availability of clothing grants is publicized widely so that all parents can take advantage where possible.

A broader issue here is the nature of games activities on offer. As I have already suggested, the traditional games choices in the primary school can be limiting, not just in terms of denying girls

ess to certain games but also in developing an idea that boys who
not like contact sports are inadequate. Coupled with the
problems that traditional activities can cause culturally and
economically, it may well be that junior schools should broaden their
approach to this area of the curriculum, providing a much wider
range of competitive and non-competitive sports, as suggested by
many PE experts.

Expressive arts

This has great potential as an area in which there can be a genuine
sharing of all children's cultural experiences and an introduction to
art forms from a wider society than that represented in the
classroom. However, this could lead to a tokenistic approach. What
seems important is that this work should be linked to work that
children are engaged in across the curriculum and that it should
where possible arise out of their expressed interests. For example,
work on 'faces', which goes on in many schools, could involve a
consideration of sculpture and pictorial representation from many
cultures, not just the Western European tradition; similarly work on
'sound' could explore different musical traditions. The danger in the
past has been that where particular cultural experiences are
included in the curriculum, they have been marginalized. For
example, in one school in which I worked we had a set of steel pans,
but almost without exception only Afro-Caribbean children were
allowed to play them. The instructor was not a part of the school
staff and no links were made to the everyday experience of the
classroom. In another school, all children automatically began to
learn to play the pans and then decided whether they wanted to
continue; the teacher responsible took the trouble to involve the
class teacher and to build on the rest of the children's experience. In
this way this type of music became a part of school life and a part
of all children's cultural experience.

The role of expressive arts in the junior curriculum has often
been marginalized, but if we are to help all children develop fully,
then the aesthetic experience must be a crucial element of
education for equality.

CONCLUSION

In such a short chapter it is impossible to do more than scratch the
surface of the complex issues raised here. I believe that the
essential element for all primary teachers, particularly in the junior
years, is that children must be helped to become autonomous
learners, responsible for their own actions. If we are to achieve this
we must accept their learning out of school about how the world is
as an important part of their education, and we must help them to

see the validity of that learning as part of the world of school. If our classrooms reflect the best primary practice, then they will also be sites for education for equality. Teachers cannot achieve this, though, in the face of those who control the system. Unless and until central government can be brought to realize the need for education for equality and to finance the necessary improvements in initial and in-service training, it seems inevitable that those teachers dedicated to striving for education for equality will be fighting a losing battle. However, it is such a crucial battle that we must continue to fight it, at the same time doing whatever we can to change governmental constraints in the hope that eventually the struggle will be worthwhile.

REFERENCES

1. Rosen, H. (1977) 'Out there or where the masons went', in M. Hoyles (ed), The Politics of Literacy, London: Writers' and Readers' Publishing Co-operative, p. 204.
2. Hardcastle, J. (1985) 'Classrooms as sites for cultural making', English in Education, 19: no. 3, p. 9.
3. ibid., p. 9.
4. Tizard, B. and Hughes, M. (1984) Young Children Learning, London: Fontana, pp. 220-2.
5. Granados Johnson, J. et al., chapter 6 of this book.
6. ibid.
7. Guardian 16 March 1988.
8. Margaret Sandra (1985) 'Ruler wanging and other noises', English Magazine, no. 14.
9. Department of Education and Science (1975) A Language for Life, (The Bullock Report), London: HMSO, para. 20.5, p. 186.
10. Trudgill, P. (1975) Accent, Dialect and the School, London: Edward Arnold, pp. 27-8 and throughout.
11. Gregory, A. and Woollard, N. (1985) (eds and compilers) Looking into Language: Diversity in the Classroom, 2nd edn, Stoke-on-Trent: Trentham Books.
12. Fitzpatrick, F. cited in Edwards, C., Moorhouse, J., and Widlake, S. (1988) 'Language or English? The needs of bilingual pupils' in M. Jones and A. West (eds) Learning Me Your Language, London: Mary Glasgow Publications, pp. 79-80.
13. Harland, L. (1985) 'Why doesn't Johnny skip? Or a look at female roles in reading schemes', in Language and Gender Working Party Alice in Genderland, Sheffield: National Association for the Teaching of English, pp. 29-34.
14. Smith, F. (1983) 'The choice between teachers and programs', in F. Smith Essays into Literacy, London: Heinemann Educational Books, pp. 107-16.
15. Waterland, L. (1985) Read With Me: An Apprenticeship Approach To Reading, Stroud: Thimble Press, pp. 3-48.

16. Jameson, G. (1986) 'Content analysis with children', Language Matters no. 1.
17. Graves, D. (1983) Writing: Teachers and Children at Work, London: Heinemann Educational Books.
18. Ingham, J. (1986) Telling Tales Together, (video), London: The Cadmean Trust.
19. Wallen, M. (1987) 'The St. Leonard's storybook project', English in Education 21: no. 1, pp. 3-9.
20. Hardcastle, J. (1985) 'Classrooms as sites for cultural making', op. cit., p. 9.
21. Guardian, 3 November 1987.
22. Shuard, H. (1986) Primary Mathematics Today and Tomorrow, Harlow: Longman, for the Schools Council, p. 38.
23. ibid., p. 39.
24. Walkerdine, V. (1982) 'From context to text: a psychosemiotic approach to abstract thought', in M. Beveridge, (ed.) Children Thinking Through Language, London: Edward Arnold, pp. 129-55.
25. The Royal Society and the Institute of Mathematics and its Applications, (1986) Girls and Mathematics, p. 21.
26. ibid., p. 21.
27. Schools Council Project: Language in the Multicultural Primary School (1983) Akbar and Elizabeth: Looking at History, Broadsheet J, London: Schools Council Publications.

Chapter Eight

THE SECONDARY YEARS: MATHEMATICS AND SCIENCE

Europe Singh

THE MYTH OF NEUTRALITY

Whereas in the curriculum areas of humanities/social sciences and English there has been at least some acceptance that biases exist that reinforce inequalities in society, in the mathematics and sciences areas the notion of neutrality has held back any critical analysis of pedagogy or content: 'children who should be learning how to count are learning political slogans and 'anti-racist maths' ... Surely two plus two is always four ...?' (1) This resistance has not only come from those with a political stake in the promotion of oppressive ideas (whether they be Labour or Conservative educational spokespersons) (2) but is rooted deep in the teaching of these subjects in schools and colleges and in the 'practice' of mathematics and science in society.

The myth of neutrality rests on the premise that pure science exists outside of society. In this separate and unsullied existence 'pure science' can surely have no hint of political bias and therefore play no part in maintaining the class/'race'/sex hierarchies in society. A cursory glance at the historical record exposes this as patent non-sense. Since the earliest times science and mathematics have gone hand in hand with the development of human society in every part of the world. In the earliest societies they were the secret preserve of priests and magicians - from ancient Egypt to the Indus valley, from South America to Central Africa - and were always jealously guarded, along with writing, as a source of power. (3) Of course this elitism is still central to these pursuits today and in itself reinforces the power of those who control contemporary societies. But in addition to this attempt to lock out groups of people from participation in mathematics and science, I will argue that the content and the pedagogy of mathematics and science lessons transmit ideas that justify class society and promote racism and sexism.

In this chapter I will examine the content and pedagogy of mathematics and science and then go on to suggest some strategies towards alternative curricula.

MATHEMATICS

Content

In order to understand the biases inherent in the content of mathematics in schools and colleges we need to examine it from the following angles: in the historical perspective that is transmitted; in the attempt to abstract it from reality; and in the assumed normality of society filtered through these abstractions.

Historical perspective

All mathematics teachers will assure us that they do not teach history to their students, but in the hidden curriculum and in the odd references in textbooks, a history filters through. Teachers transmit their own patchy knowledge of a history dotted with the activities of great men - great white men I might add - and students glean a little more from illustrations and name dropping in textbooks. Newton, Leibniz, Euler, Fourier, Pascal, and the earlier 'pioneers' Archimedes, Pythagoras, Euclid; these are the makers of mathematical history.

I am not going to argue that these individuals did not play a part in developing what we call mathematics today. The problem is that only an acknowledgement of their contribution denies the massive weight of global mathematical activity in the history of mathematics. The tragedy of written mathematical histories is that they tend to follow a similar Eurocentric bias. Mike Bernal argues that the nineteenth and early twentieth centuries when most of these histories were first written down coincided with the development of 'scientific' theories on the inferiority of non-Europeans. (4) These theories extended to the 'inferior classes' and women. They represented the justifications of the 'new' scientists in the fields of human biology, psychometry, and anthropology for the sharply defined hierarchies of Victorian society at the height of empire and the most explosive growth of the industrial revolution. These theories were accepted as unquestionably true by almost every intellectual and scientist of the day. (5) No wonder then that the contributions of other societies and of women to the sum total of mathematical knowledge were either ignored, played down, or deliberately distorted: 'The history of mathematics cannot with any certainty be traced back to any school or period before that of the Ionian Greeks'. (6)

George Joseph (5) gives an example of how a contemporary mathematics historian can repeat the old formulas:

(Mathematics) finally secured a firm grip on life in the highly congenial soil of Greece and waxed strongly for a short period ... . With the decline of Greek civilization, the plant remained dormant for a thousand years ... when the plant was transported to Europe proper and once more embedded in fertile soil. (7)

This well established view of the history of mathematics, shown in the following diagram, fairly accurately represents the perceptions of the vast majority of mathematicians and mathematics teachers today:

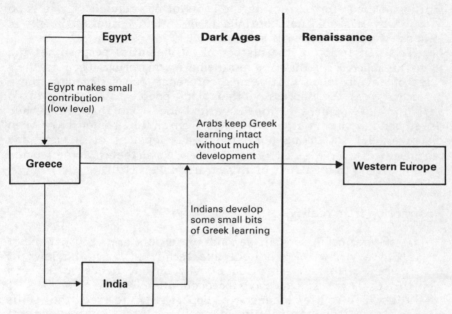

In reality, of course there was great interaction between the established societies of the ancient world - particularly Egypt and Greece, India and China, and later between India and Greece.

The most glaring distortion is in the acknowledgement, or lack of it, afforded to Arab mathematicians who drew on many and varied sources and developed the main body of content that we consider as modern mathematics. How many mathematics teachers, who could tell you much about Pythagoras, know that the word algebra comes from Arabic? Mohamed ibn-Musa al-Kharizmi (c. 825 AD) wrote 'Hisab al-djabr wa-al Muqabala' from whence the name came. His name also gave us the word algorithm from his elaboration of the Indian numerals and their uses in another book developing the work of Brahmagupta (c. 628 AD), an Indian mathematician. (8)

The depth of this process was first brought home to me when reading an article by Ray Hemmings. (9) My own mathematical education in a Manchester school provided me with the strictly-no-history-is-taught idea that the word sine originates from the undulating, nay sinuous, shape of the sine curve from the Latin sinus of course. I always worried whether the angle ratios were used before their values were plotted on a graph until Hemmings put me out of my misery. The word sine arose from the mistranslation of an Arab word meaning 'half-chord'. This word differed by one syllable from another word that meant 'the opening of a garment at the neck or bosom'. When trigonometry was transferred to Europe via Spain, Latin took over. Moreover, the triangular array of numbers that bears Pascal's name was used 300 years before his birth by Chinese mathematicians for extracting the roots of polynomials. There is no reason why it should not continue to be called Pascal's triangle as long as its earlier history is recognized.

This perception of the history of mathematics perpetuates the ideas of superiority that the mathematics historians used as their rules of thumb when writing our reference books. Reading these histories gives the impression that black people had nothing to do with the development of mathematical ideas and that there have never been women mathematicians of any note. Women have been discouraged from taking part in the development of science and mathematics over the last few centuries. Nevertheless some women have managed to break out of this strait-jacket. (10)

Abstraction from reality

Mathematics lessons in secondary schools are very often not about anything. You collect like terms, or learn the laws of indices, with no perception of why anyone needs to do such things. There is excessive preoccupation with a sequence of skills and quite inadequate opportunity to see the skills emerging from the solution of problems. As a consequence of this approach, school mathematics contains very little incidental information. A French lesson might well contain incidental information about France - so on across the curriculum; but in mathematics the incidental information you might expect (currency exchange and interest rates; general knowledge on climate communications and geography; the rules and scoring systems of games; social statistics) is rarely there, because most teachers in no way see this as part of their responsibility when teaching mathematics. (11)

This paragraph from the Cockcroft Report sums up the nature of abstractions in mathematics. Despite the passage of six years the content of mathematics lessons has changed little even if GCSE has affected the outward form. Investigations and assignments are chosen so that once again they impinge minimally on the concerns of society. Too often they bring merely a new dimension to meaningless calculations and operations and serve only as a break in the monotony of classroom routine.

The 'inadequate opportunity' to see the skills emerging from the solution of problems' is the cause of much mathematic anxiety and

the reason for widespread innumeracy amongst the adult populat......
The endless repetition of abstract skills serves not only to create
hostility towards mathematics in students, but also to disempower
them - to weaken their ability to develop their intuitive
mathematical skills as tools for understanding their reality. (12) As
Marilyn Frankenstein puts it:

> A mathematically illiterate populace can be convinced for
> example, that social welfare programs are responsible for their
> declining standard of living, because they will not research the
> numbers to uncover that 'welfare' to the rich (is much greater
> than) any meagre subsidies given to the poor.

A mathematically illiterate populace could also construe from the
distortions of the Metropolitan Police crime statistics that black
people are disporportionately involved in crime in the capital. (13)

Society as seen through the abstractions of mathematics

Class hierarchies in society are often seen as natural. Jennifer
Maxwell (15) gives the following example:

> Mr Jones owns a factory with 100 staff. He pays himself
> £18,000 a year. He pays 20 supervisory staff £10,000 a year and
> he pays 80 non-supervisory staff £8,000 a year. Find the total
> wage bill.
> The company has done well in the last year so Mr Jones
> decides to give himself a 15% rise, the supervisory staff a 10%
> rise, and the non-supervisory staff a 5% rise. Find
>
> 1)   the new annual wage for each worker
> 2)   the new total wage bill
> 3)   the % increase in the total wage bill

The questions asked reflect the political position of the author.
Alternative questions might ask: 'how much would each person get if
the good fortunes of the company were distributed equally? or 'what
means might the workers use to gain a fairer share of the company's
profits?' or a question which might require investigation and more
information, 'how did the company's profits increase?'. Of course
open-ended questioning of this nature is strictly forbidden in
mathematics lessons. Dawn Gill (16) examined one of the
unbelievably popular books by Greer (17). She looked closely at the
notion of 'interest' in Greer and commented:

> The examples used here and in other maths textbooks present
> the notion of rates of interest outside of the political and
> ideological context within which investment takes place.

Interest seems to be a concept which is entirely theoretical and context free. It is a phenomenon which occurs within a social and economic vacuum. It is presented as a neutral and value free mathematical construct. The idea of interest seems to have a clean and rational image.

The examples used are likely to encourage the student mathematicians to identify with the concerns of the investor. If we were to give the notion of interest a real-world context and content, however, students would be able to see what it means in human terms. Perhaps its image would seem less clean and rational if, for example, figures on investment in South African gold mining were used in conjunction with information about wages and working conditions for black workers in the mines. Perhaps students would be less ready to identify with the political and ideological system of which 'interest' is an integral part.

The effect of this diet of coded messages within meaningless problems is best summed up by Marilyn Frankenstein:

> Traditional mathematical education supports the hegemonic ideologies of society, especially through, what has been called, 'structured silences'. Even trivial math applications like totalling grocery bills carry the ideological message that paying for food is natural and that society can only be organized in such a way that people buy food from a grocery store. (18)

Pedagogy

Mathematics anxiety

The immediate pedagogical causes of the situation such as rote drill, taught so that it requires extensive memorization, and unmotivated applications which are unrelated to the maths one actually uses in everyday life - create a situation where people 'naturally' avoid mathematics. (19)

The majority of students fail mathematics or rather mathematics lessons fail them. The pedagogy of mathematics is designed to 'admit' a select few and lock out the majority. The more a student 'fails' at mathematics the greater is their anxiety that it is their own inadequacy that is the problem and so the student feels less confident to tackle a mathematical problem - so the student fails. Too often this becomes a vicious circle from which there is no escape.

There is such a tight bond between nineteenth century notions of intelligence and 'ability' in mathematics. An ability that is, in fact, like IQ tests - merely the skill to play certain abstract games. So failing at school mathematics becomes a sign of 'low' intelligence.

In my adult numeracy classes it is so glaringly apparent. I am confronted with students who have used mathematics all their working lives but once inside the classroom all that experience, all those self-perfected rules of thumb, become instantly redundant - the student insists on the primacy of the paper and pencil method and must perfect it. 301 - 92, a routine darts calculation, becomes a 'numeracy nightmare' with the standard algorithm. I vainly explain that the ancient Hindus used complementing (the intuitive method employed mentally by most of us: 'you need 8 to make 92 up to 100, then another 201; that makes 209') successfully for thousands of years and it is a perfectly respectable method of calculation. Mathematics lessons are also about devaluing the self-taught methods that we all develop in favour of an oppressive standardization. The most ludicrous extension of this is in forcing students from other cultures who may have been taught a different algorithm to relearn the 'proper' method.

Another oppressive aspect of mathematics teaching is an obsession with testing. Testing reinforces the elitism, deepens the anxiety, induces competitiveness. Nowhere is this more powerful in schooling than in mathematics lessons. There are certain skills that each person must be able to rehearse on their own. It is this social function of testing that is most pernicious. The practice of mathematics becomes an individual thing - the image of the child shielding answers from the prying gaze of others sums up this process of atomization. In these ways the pedagogy of mathematics perpetuates the hierarchies of class society and, as Munir Fasheh argues, is perfectly suited to authoritarianism:

> My own conviction is that in spite of the claim by educational institutions and by authorities that control these institutions that they encourage free and critical thinking, such educational institutions, in general, discourage critical, original and free thinking and expression, especially when that touches upon 'important' issues in the society ... . In short, I came to believe that the teaching of maths, like the teaching of any other subject in schools, is a 'political' activity. It either helps to create attitudes and intellectual models that will in their turn help students grow, develop, be critical, more aware and more involved, and thus more confident and able to go beyond the existing structures; or it produces students who are passive, rigid, timid and alienated. (20)

In addition to locking out so many from this elite circle of mathematics users, mathematics teaching disempowers whole groups of people. It denies them the ability to use mathematics as a powerful tool in interpreting reality.

Alternative strategies

All alternative strategies are based on a central theme: to make mathematics more accessible to the student. The conclusions of the Cockcroft report and DES suggestions for School Curriculum (21) address the same issue but stop short of the full implications of this formulation: 'mathematics lessons need to move away from the abstract rehearsal of skills. What is required is the use of mathematical concepts and ways of thinking in problem solving and investigations ...

Mathematics must certainly become more relevant to the student and it must also tackle problems in the real world rather than abstractions. However, this process cannot be confined to physical reality; it must also encompass the social dimensions of the student's reality. More than this, it must become part of the student's armoury of critical skills rather than a collection of external processes on which the student is tested.

The ultimate aim in this alternative pedagogy and content is to enable students, as Marilyn Frankenstein puts it, to problematize their own reality (12) - to formulate mathematical questions about the real world rather than always to be in the position of answering those set by the teacher. Mathematicians involved in developing alternatives are not, as our critics may claim, diminishing mathematical ideas. On the contrary, we passionately believe that maths has been divorced from reality and needs to be reintegrated with it for all our students.

The following examples come from a number of diverse sources but follow the guidelines adopted by the Association for Curriculum Change in Mathematics: (22)

1. The historical development of mathematics must become an explicit part of the curriculum ... . Mathematics must be presented as the global activity that it is integrated with the development of human societies. For example, the history of number is something that presents us with all these dimensions but is also a powerful means of reinforcing number concepts.
2. The content of mathematics must be part of a real world context, to enable students to understand and interpret physical and social reality using mathematics. In this way mathematics can be made more important and relevant to the student.
3. Part of this real world context allows students to use mathematics to challenge racist myth and stereotype, sexist ideas and other oppressive structures. Mathematics should enable students to gain a fuller understanding of local and global economic relationships and enhance the student's ability to unpick reliable and distorted information.
4. The elitism of mathematics is a barrier to all children in their struggle to learn and acquire life skills. Challenging it will not only improve maths education but also lead us to

question the whole academic system that breeds it.

Appendices 1, 2 and 3 contain examples of worksheets from a variety of sources which illustrate attempts to use mathematical skills to sharpen students' perception and are offered as examples of good practice with respect to education for equality.

SCIENCE

In a similar way to mathematics school science is artificially divorced from society. And yet it is far easier than is the case with mathematics to see the organic link between scientific ideas and the development of human societies. 'Technology' is one of the terms that is used to distance the applications of science in society from 'pure' science. The 'neutrality argument' is still plied as a cover for 'pure' research but seems feeble in the shadow of the atomic bomb. If this link between science and its consequences for society is not made explicit we as teachers are guilty of not only undermining the social responsibilities of science but are involved in indoctrination rather than education.

The substance of this part of the chapter is based on the work of the Association for Curriculum Development in Science as detailed in their publication <u>Anti-Racist Science Teaching</u>. (23)

Content

The content of science is the science that is 'done' in society. The science that is 'done' depends on the financing of research and development projects. The priorities of science therefore are the priorities of the societies in which it is practised. If those priorities are influenced by racism, sexism, and the need to maintain class privilege, then science will also reflect those biases. Robert Young in his chapter 'Racist society, racist science', (22) emphasizes the point:

> Indeed, over 40 per cent of scientists in Britain and over 50 per cent of research and development funding comes from the military ... . This is quite often expended on 'pure' science projects which might otherwise not get funded or might not get very much funding. For example, when I was an undergraduate, a professor of marine biology at Yale, Professor Talbot Waterman, got a large grant to go to Bermuda every summer to study crabs who navigated by polarized light in shallow water. This money was given because the United States Office of Naval Research wanted to be able to design ways of flying over the earth's poles, where magnetic compasses do not work.

Another large chunk of science funding comes from the cosmetics and drug industries. The drug industry also finances the bulk of all medical research - new drugs for 'Western' ailments are big business.

One would think that at least in medical research there would be a certain purity. However, Young gives us the example of funding in relation to the disease sickle-cell anaemia. This condition is specific to people who come from a certain part of Africa and their descendants. One form of this anaemia confers protection from malaria on the carrier but the more severe form leads to painful recurring crises that eventually lead to an early death. Funding for research into sickle-cell anaemia centred on describing and cataloguing the process involved. Funds for development of cures and treatments or for genetic counselling were not forthcoming. For a racist society the pain, suffering, and death of some black people does not merit a high priority.

Further examples are given of the drug industry which is based on producing expensive saleable products for the West (e.g. vitamins, growth hormone) and dumping surpluses and banned products on Third World markets. It does not develop cheap vaccines against malaria or other diseases prevalent in the Third World; as yet there is no money in it. Young leaves us with some ideas for an alternative view: 'The overall model for a science curriculum should be one that always considers all the following in their mutual interrelations: origins; assumptions; articulations; who benefits; alternatives.

Pedagogy

The pedagogy of science is dictated by the teacher's perception of ability and the idea of 'scientific method'. The desire to grade human attributes, especially intelligence, has long been an obsession of scientists. Indeed, certain sciences, anthropology, psychometry, statistics, grew directly out of the drive to establish that the white upper-class male was the 'fittest to rule'. Darwin's theories of evolution were quickly pressed into service to justify exploitation and oppression in Victorian society.

There is a direct line of descent from the theories of Social Darwinists like Thomas Galton through Cyril Burt to Hans Eysenck and more modern sociobiologists, like Wilson and Dawkins. (22) Sir Cyril Burt, in particular, was responsible for the structure of the post-war school system in Britain. It is astonishing that, regardless of the fact that Burt manufactured data and researches, his ideas about ability and assessment still dominate the practice of teachers in these areas. Burt's tripartite system of education was constructed to maintain tight class boundaries. It was superseded by the comprehensive system which, despite its aims, changed only the outward form of education. That experiment too now seems to be at an end. There is also now a clamour for 'more and better' science education which really translates into 'abstract science for the few and vocational courses for the many'.

Alternatives
Nutrition and Hunger. Liz Lindsay (25) presents us with suggestions for alternatives to teaching nutrition. She combines the analysis of diets and food composition with questions about where food comes from and who decides what we eat. After all, a McDonald's hamburger is inextricably tied up with the economics of the world cattle market. This is intermeshed with grain and soya production. One cannot be disentangled from the other. So one person's hamburger in the West is another person's famine in Ethiopia. She comments:

> The average US American gets through about 1,800 lb of grain a year but eats only 200 lb as grain, the rest being passaged through livestock, while the average Third Worlder gets about 500 lb a year, mostly eaten in pristine form.

Of course, much of the grain fed to cattle comes from the farms of the Third World. If the West at least changed to leaner meat there would be a grain surplus in the Third World, says Lindsay. She examines famine by first of all looking at the potato famine in Ireland. Another part of her course on nutrition looks at the diets of different classes in Britain - how much protein? how much sugar? and so on. What part does income play in determining diet? Do the multinationals that manufacture processed food inevitably decide what people eat in both the First World and the Third World?

Biology. Michael Vance (26) surveys current practice in school biology and human biology. He concludes that school textbooks and courses with their inadequate and misleading treatments of 'race' are part of the problem when they ought to be part of the solution:

> Good biology is necessarily anti-racist biology ... (an anti-racist biology curriculum) should aim:
> To expose and combat the way that racist, sexist and imperialist ideology is mediated through traditional curricula and textbooks.
> To provide alternative perspectives to the Western capitalist world-view which currently predominates in teaching, especially regarding poverty and 'Third World under-development'.
> To support black and 'ethnic minority' pupils whose confidence and self-esteem have been eroded by the content of biology teaching in the past.
> To draw parallels between racism, sexism, and discriminatory

practices based on social class: in this context, to foster solidarity between boys and girls and black and white working-class students by challenging the uses of IQ and other normative testing in relation to 'race', class, and gender.

To expose the concept of 'race' as a fiction devoid of scientific validity, though having a deep ideological purpose.

The integrated science curriculum. The most ambitious revision of the science curriculum was undertaken by the faculty of Craft, Design, Technology, Mathematics and Science (including Home Economics, Food Technology and Fabric Technology) at Holland Park School. (27) In 1984 they established some basic aims:

1   The pupils' physical, emotional, moral and social development.
2.   The development of pupils' awareness and the awareness of the relevance of areas within the faculty to society and the historical context of these areas.
3.   Encouraging the pupil to ask questions and search for her or his own answers.
4.   Encouraging and providing conditions through which a pupil may develop and continue to develop.
5.   Helping pupils become interdependent and independent in their learning.
6.   Encouraging and supporting individual teachers to enable them to work towards the achievement of these aims.
7.   To develop anti-sexist and anti-racist attitudes by both staff and students.

Starting from a rationale produced by Jan Harding from Chelsea College (28) they progressed towards an issues-based curriculum that attempted to integrate all the disciplines involved. They decided to produce a contents network based on SMILE (Secondary Maths Individualised Learning Experiment of the ILEA). 'The syllabus was divided up into discrete topics of work and arranged in three levels of difficulty.'

In summing up they offer the following guidelines:

An anti-racist perspective in science must address the following issues:
     the colonial history which underlies racism in British society;
     the devaluation of 'non-Western' cultures;
     development and underdevelopment;
     racism in contemporary society.
     The development of learning materials needs to be informed by consideration of the following issues:
     the links between curriculum content and its social context;

the need to examine the operation of the school as an institution, and in particular the significance of pedagogic styles on interrelationships between people and on pupil performance;

the language of textbooks (and other learning materials), which often makes subject content incccessible to students and reinforces existing ideologies of racism, sexism and social class;

the need for learning materials and classroom strategies which encourage collaborative and individualized learning and small-group work; and

the educational advantages of cross-curricular links and subject integration.

CONCLUSION

The authors of the Holland Park summary - Dawn Gill, Henry Smith, Vinod Patel, and Ashok Sethi - constantly reiterate that no amount of curriculum innovation will of itself bring about equality. Neither are they interested in the phoney equality of 'fair competition' in which the majority of students still lose out.

Curriculum innovation in both mathematics and science cannot hope to transform social relations and thus produce a classless, antiracist, antisexist society. What we hope is that such innovations will ensure that students are equipped with the mathematical and scientific skills that will help them overcome deference to experts and enable them to struggle for political equality.

APPENDIX 1

The following material is from Frankenstein, M. (1989) <u>Relearning Mathematics</u>, Free Association books: to be published.

1. Ralph Nader's Health Research Group conducted a study of smoking policies in Washington D.C. hospitals in 1976. They found "only a small fraction of those hospitals responding currently have regulations that adequately recognize and actively ensure the rights of all those who would prefer to breathe smoke-free air: 12 out of 21 hospitals do not solicit patient preferences regarding smoking in patient rooms prior to admission; 10 out of 21 hospitals sell cigarettes; 7 of 21 hospitals allow visitors to smoke in patient rooms, and 2 out of 21 even allow employees to smoke in patient rooms". Find the fraction of hospitals involved in each type of abuse of non-smokers' rights, and reduce or approximately reduce it to lowest terms.

2. In order to assure themselves of an abundant and readily available supply of low-wage agricultural workers, multi-

national corporations have "undercut self-provisioning agriculture (in the underdeveloped Third World) and thus made the rural population dependent on plantation wages ... . Plantations usurped most of the good land, either making much of the rural population landless or pushing them onto marginal soils. (Yet the plantations have often held much of their land idle simply to prevent the peasants from using it... Del Monte (for example) owns 57,000 acres of Guatemala but plants only 9,000.)" (Food First, Lappé and Collins). About what fraction of their Guatemala land does Del Monte plant?

3. "Exploring gets but a fraction of extra oil profits, study says" (Boston Globe, 6/22/81) discusses a consumer group report which shows that "after years of demanding higher profits and less regulation because they said additional means were needed to seek out more oil, the nation's largest oil companies ... are using their cash windfall to acquire competitiors, buy more land than they can possibly explore efficiently and hoard vast amounts of cash." Of course, as with all mergers, buying up existing oil firms increases the buyers' total oil reserves, but adds nothing to the country's supply of oil and gas, and does not subtract from unemployment by creating new jobs." From 1978 to 1980, America's 16 largest oil companies collected $29.3 billion in extra profits ... but spent just $5.3 billion of it on domestic oil and gas exploration and production ... at the same time, ... (they) spent $11.1 billion to buy out smaller petroleum companies or acquire businesses unrelated to oil."
   (a) About what fraction of their extra profits were spent on domestic exploration and production?
   (b) About what fraction of their extra profits were spent on acquiring companies?

4. In the 1980 presidential election of Ronald Reagan, there were 160.5 million people of voting age, 110 million registered voters, 83.7 million people who actually voted. About half of the people who voted cast ballots for Reagan.
   (a) About what fraction of eligible voters are registered?
   (b) About what fraction of eligible voters cast ballots for Reagan?

5. Use the following information to create and solve a math problem whose solution involves reducing fractions.

The United Way Isn't Any More
Over the last 30 years, the refrain that has rung in the ears of charity solicitors has been: "I gave at the office." With few exceptions, what people gave to was the United Way which has built its success as a $1-billion-a-year federated fundraiser on the right to solicit at the workplace in a one-shot campaign.

All that may change, if a new national fund-raising movement achieves some of its ends. During United Way's annual meeting in Dallas last week, representatives of some 70 dissenting charities held a counter-convention. They tentatively approved tactics for breaking what they say is United Way's monopoly: boycotts of local United Way campaigns; local drives to compete with United Way directly; persuading employers to allow other organizations to collect funds by payroll deduction.

United Way denies it is a monopoly, saying it collects only $1 billion of a national total of $30 billion a year in philanthropic giving. Dissident organizations say $1 billion is an enormous share of what is given by working individuals, and that United Way gives most of it to "safe" causes such as the Red Cross and the Boy Scouts, excluding women's, environmentalist and minority-run groups, the arts and anything controversial. Planned Parenthood, for example, has 189 local chapters, and their cause has become sufficiently noncontroversial that 47 chapters are included in local United Way drives. But in recent years, Planned Parenthood chapters have begun to offer abortion services, and the chapter in Gary, Ind., was dropped from its local United Way the year it did so.

6. "The Economics of Racism in South Africa" (The New York Times, 9/19/76) uses numbers to illustrate "the extent to which the country's 4.2 million whites have been sustained by the labor of its 18 million blacks ... the Government's own statistics ... suggest that scarcely any sector of the economy could function for long without black workers. Of the 4.9 million full time workers registered last year ... 2.7 million were black, 1.5 million were white, 527,740 were of mixed race, and 181,066 were Asian ... In gold mining, the pillar of the economy, the labor force of 380,091 included 341,575 blacks. Figures for other sectors show a similar ratio: coal mining, 190,596 (134,012); construction, 446,086 (309,094); textiles, 97,628, (66,939); and food processing, 159,577 (103,286) ... The Government's manpower survey lists the number of blacks employed in the various professions ... 11 engineers, 31 chemists, 63 lawyers, 83 university teachers, 85 doctors, 528 journalists and writers ... 74,980 (school teachers) ...

(a) About what fraction of the workers in each of the industries listed are black?

(b) About what fraction of all black workers are professionals?

(c) In contrast to their importance in the economy, "Average annual income among urban whites is estimated to be about $6,000; among urban blacks ... between $860 and $1,600 ... the Johannesburg Chamber of Commerce (estimates) that the subsistence income for a family of five in Sowetu in May 1975 was $136 a month ... 5.6 million blacks (live) in urban areas ... In 1973, the average annual income among black farm laborers was $250 ... In the tribal homelands, where nearly 8 million blacks live, the vast majority live outside the cash economy altogether, grazing cattle and bartering ...". Create and solve two math problems, using

153

this information, whose solution involves reducing fractions.

7. A <u>Boston Globe</u> article (12/5/80) reported on a study by a housing advocacy agency which led to complaints filed with the US Department of Housing and Urban Development charging that 15 out of 17 real-estate firms surveyed "treated minority homeseekers very differently than whites." "Part of the study consisted of telephone canvassing ... callers with heavy southern black or Spanish accents ... said they were prepared to pay from $300 to $350 per month for a one-bedroom apartment. They described themselves as professionals with incomes of between $14,000 and $15,000 a year ... A white caller with an identifiable New England accent then called the same company and described himself in the same way ... the total number of contacts ... (was) 42 pairs of calls. White callers were invited to visit the rental agency to look at apartments 42 times, while black or Hispanic callers were asked to come by 11 times." Compare the fraction of white with the fraction of black callers asked to look at apartments.

8. <u>Portrait of Inequality: Black and White Children in America</u> by Marion Wright Edelman (Children's Defense Fund, 1980), documents that in spite of some success, "Black children, youths, and families remain worse off than whites in every area of American life ...". In education, for example, "A Black child is almost twice as likely as a White child to grow up in a family whose head did not complete high school ... a White child is four times as likely as a Black child to grow up in a family headed by a college graduate ... Black children are suspended from school at twice the rate for White children. Over half a million of the 1.8 million students suspended were Black ... Out of some 1,264,000 American children aged 7 to 17 who were not enrolled in any school in 1976, 172,000 were Black."

(a) About what fraction of suspended students were Black?

(b) About what fraction of students aged 7 to 17 not enrolled in school were Black?

(c) Often, to compare data from groups of different sizes, we calculate <u>rates</u>, which are fractions with denominators of 100, 1,000, 100,000, etc. For example, it may not be immediately evident that the following data shows a much worse situation for Black youth:

Number of School Dropouts and High School Graduates Aged 16-24, 1977-78

	White	Black
Dropouts	640,000	172,000
High School graduates	2,747,000	347,000

(Source: US Department of Labor, Bureau of Labor Statistics Press)

In order to clarify this data, the Children's Defense Fund calculated the rate of dropouts per hundred graduates for whites and blacks. Find the respective rates and discuss why they present a clearer picture of the data.

APPENDIX 2

The following material is from 'Maths teaching materials', Association for Curriculum Change in Mathematics.

Looking at racial discrimination using statistics and percentages

Widespread discrimination against young black people applying for white-collar jobs was shown in a study by the CRE and the Nottingham and District Community Relations Council. Three letters were sent in response to advertisements for jobs advertised in the Nottingham Evening Post between 1977 and 1979. Two of the letters made it clear that the applicant was black, for example, by the name or date of arrival in Britain. In nearly half of the firms tested, employers chose white rather than black candiates with equal experience and qualifications (Half a Chance, 1980).

Here are some figures on the employment of black and white workers:

40% of white men are in professional, managerial or white collar jobs compared with 14% of black men.
18% of white men are in semi-skilled or unskilled work, compared with 45% of black men.
40% of white men at all levels have supervisory responsibilities, compared with 18% of black men.
15% of white men work night shifts of some kind, compared with 31% of black men.

(The Facts of Racial Disadvantage, D Smith, PEP)

Exercise

1. Make a bar chart to illustrate the above information, entitled Black and White Male Workers in Employment. (Note: the word 'black' is used to describe people of African, Asian, or Caribbean descent).
2. The bar chart will show a difference between the sorts of work done by white and black male workers. Why do you think there is this difference?

Now let us consider some figures about qualifications and jobs:

79% of white men with qualifications to degree standard are in professional or management positions, compared with 31% of black men with the same qualifications.

83% of white men with 'A' levels are doing non-manual jobs, compared with 55% of similarly qualified black men.

(The Facts of Racial Disadvantage, D. Smith, PEP)

Exercise

1. Make a bar chart, like that in the last exercise, to show this information.

2. Look at the two bar charts you have drawn. Do you think they show that black men suffer discrimination in employment?

Commission for Racial Equality (CRE)

The CRE was set up by the government to investigate practices of racial discrimination and to help people who claim they are discriminated against.

We are going to investigate how effective the CRE is. Below is an extract from a report on the CRE. To begin our investigation we are going to calculate some percentages.

In 1981 the CRE received 864 applications for assistance from members of the public alleging discrimination. Of these, 547 concerned alleged discrimination in employment and 317 in the provision of goods, services, facilities and education. Of the 682 applications considered by the Complaints Committee, 118 applicants were offered legal representation and 17 were offered representation by the CRE's legal officer or a complaints officer. Others were given varying degrees of assistance and advice.

(Different Worlds, Runnymede Trust Pamphlet, 1983)

Example

What percentage of applicants for assistance alleged discrimination in employment?

From the report '... 547 alleged discrimination in employment ... the CRE received 864 applications ...'. So 547 out of 864 alleged discrimination in employment: $547/864 = 547/864 \times 100\% = 63.3\%$ by calculation.

Exercise
1. What percentage of applications for assistance alleged discrimination in the provision of goods, services, facilities, and education?
2. What percentage of applications for assistance were not considered by the Complaints Committee?
3. What percentage of applications to the Complaints Committee were offered legal representation?
4. What percentage of applications to the Complaints Committee were offered representation by the CRE's legal office or a complaints officer?

Using the answers to questions 1-4, devise and complete a bar chart entitled Applications to the CRE in 1981. Show the proportions of applications (a) not considered, (b) given legal representation, (c) offered CRE representation, and (d) offered 'degrees' of advice.

The following table describes the number of applicants to the CRE alleging discrimination in employment. It describes two types of discrimination: 'direct', e.g. 'I won't employ a black person!' said the manager of N.F. Bull & Co.; 'indirect', a subtler form of discrimination: the employer does not actually say they will not employ black people, but there are no black employees in the workplace!

Type of discrimination	Completed applications	
	13 June 1977	30 June 1981
	Total	%
Direct (including segregation)	1,058	
Indirect	167	
Victimization	43	
All	1,268	

Source: Employment Gazette, October 1981.

Copy and complete the above table by calculating the percentage of: (a) direct discrimination (1,058 out of 1,268); (b) indirect discrimination; and (c) victimization.
From your table answer the following:
1. Approximately what fraction of applicants suffered direct discrimination? Underline the correct answer. Was it: (a) less than 1/3; (b) about 1/2 (c) between 1/2 and 1/3 (d) more than 3/4?
2. Do you think it should be easy to prove direct discrimination? Give reasons for your answer.
3. Would you expect many of the complaints alleging direct discrimination to be upheld in courts or tribunals? Give reasons.

157

Outcomes of complaints
Now we are going to look at the outcomes of complaints made to the CRE.

Outcome	Number	Percentage
No Tribunal hearing	150	
ACAS conciliation withdrawn	522	
Tribunal hearing case upheld	102	
Case dismissed	492	
Total	1,266	

Source: Employment Gazette. October, 1981.

Exercise

1. Copy and complete the above table by working out the following percentages: (a) applicants not given a tribunal hearing; (b) applications where ACAS conciliation was withdrawn; (c) Tribunal hearings upheld; (d) Tribunal cases dismissed.
2. What percentage of applications were successful?
3. Would this encourage people to apply to the CRE?
4. Do you think most people who apply to the CRE are satisfied with the outcome of their applications? Give reasons.

Do you think most people report instances of discrimination? Here is a final extract from the Runnymede Trust's report on the CRE: 'The CRE has concluded that "given the extent of discrimination that exists, it is clear that the majority of victims do not seek redress through the legal process" (CRE: Annual Report 1979)'.

The fact that many people have not heard of the CRE must be one of the reasons why they do not make applications. From the work you have done, could there be other reasons? Give details.

APPENDIX 3

The following material is from 'Alternative Maths Worksheets', Capetown University.

Why a Trade Union?

Standing together is the only way

It's time the bosses realized that we just can't live on the wages they give us. Bus fares are up, food is up. Prices are going up all the time. What can we do? We can't go and steal. That is a crime. We've just got to stand together. It's the only way.

A Meat Worker

To enable us to buy food and clothes and pay our rent, we have to work. Although thousands of people in Cape Town have jobs they go to every day, there is not enough work for all.

In Cape Town, only two-thirds of all Coloured people between the ages of 16 to 64 and three quarters of all African people of the same age have jobs.

Because there are always so many people looking for work, wages can be kept low. In Cape Town, wages are very low.

In seven important industries - clothing, textiles, building, furniture, baking, and the municipality - minimum wages were from R27 a week to R32 a week.

These wages are not enough for people to live on. The University of South Africa (Unisa) said a family with four children need R55 a week to live on. Even this means only R3 a week can be spent on transport and R25 a week on food.

Many workers are poorer than they were 5 years ago because prices are going up faster than wages. Since 1975, prices have gone up 62 per cent while wages in the clothing industry have gone up only 53 per cent.

This means that the wages of workers in the clothing industry can buy less than they did five years ago.

Because there are so many people who do not have work, the bosses know that if their workers ask for more wages, they can dismiss them and there will be many new people to take their jobs.

The only way workers can get more wages and better conditions at work is to stand together.

Many workers belong to trade unions. The main job of these unions is to help the workers to get decent wages and conditions.

Not many Africans in Cape Town belong to unions because, until a few months ago, Africans were not allowed to belong to registered unions. Only Coloured people could belong to registered unions.

Two important unregistered unions in Cape Town are the Western Province General Workers Union (WPGWU) which has 10,000 members of all races, and the African Food and Canning Workers Union, which has 2,000 members.

Most Coloured workers belong to unions. The biggest ones are the Garment Workers' Union - 50,000 members, the Textile Workers' Industrial Union - 8,500 members, the Food and Canning Workers' Union - 10,000 members, and the Cape Town Municipal Workers' Association - 9,640 members.

Source: Grassroots.

Questions

1. (a) What percentage of 'coloured' people between the ages of 16 and 64 are unemployed?
   (b) What percentage of African people between the ages of 16 and 64 are unemployed?
2. Mrs X is a worker in the clothing industry earning a minimum wage. What does she earn per hour if she works a 5 day week for 8 hours each day?
3. Mrs X has 6 children ...
   (a) How much does she need per week for her family to live (according to Unisa statistics)?
   (b) By how much is she short every week?
   (c) How much should she earn per hour to support her family properly?
4. Mr Y works for a building company. He earns R30.60 per week at present. How much did he earn per week in 1975?
5. Mr Y has 4 children ...
   (a) How much short is he each week (1983)?
   (b) How much short was he each week in 1975?
   (c) How much more money does he need every week now compared to 1975?
6. What is the ratio of membership of WPGWU to the African Food & Canning Union?
7. Arrange the Unions mentioned in this article in descending order in terms of the number of members in each.

NOTES AND REFERENCES

1. Margaret Thatcher in a speech to the Conservative Party Conference, 16 October 1987.
2. Jack Straw, Labour Party education spokesperson interviewed on Radio 4 after the first reading of the Education Reform Bill, scorned alternative approaches to education and attempted to take credit for the National Curriculum for the Labour Party.
3. See for instance Hogben, L. Maths for the Million, Harlow: Longman.
4. Bernal, M. (1987) Black Athena - The Egyptian Origin of Greek Civilisation, Free Association Books.
5. Joseph, G.G. (1987) 'Foundations of ethnocentrism in mathematics', Race & Class, XXVIII: no. 3., winter.
6. Ball, W.W.R. (1922) The History of Mathematics, 10th edn, London.
7. Kline, W. (1953) Mathematics in Western Culture, New York.
8. Fryer, P. (1985) Staying Power, London: Pluto Press.
9. Hemmings, R. (1980) 'Mathematics and multiethnic education part II: secondary', NAME Magazine.
10. Ruthven, K. (1980) 'Ability stereotyping in mathematics', Department of Education, Cambridge University.

11. Department of Education and Science (1982) Mathematics Counts, para. 462, p. 142 (the Cockcroft Report).
12. Frankenstein, M. (1986) 'Critical math education: an application of Paulo Freire's epistemology', Journal of Education, 165: no. 4.
13. Christian, L. (1982) in 'Policing by Coercion' (GLC). Quotes Lord Chief Justice Lane: 'So far as the (police) statistics are concerned, I propose to say nothing, except that they are mostly misleading and very largely unintelligible.'
14. Shell Centre for Mathematical Education (1983) 'Using graphs - the language of point interpretation'.
15. Maxwell, J. (1985) 'Is maths politically neutral?', Mathematics Teaching Magazine, no. 100, spring.
16. Gill, D. 'Political ideology in mathematics textbooks', to be published by ACCM (Association for Curriculum Change in Mathematics).
17. Greer, A. (1983) A Complete O Level Mathematics, London: Macmillan.
18. Frankenstein, M. (1985) Math anxiety, Boston University.
19. Hilton, P. (1980) 'Math anxiety, some suggested causes and cures', Maths Journal 1980, pp.174-88, quoted in Greer, A. (ed.) op. cit.
20. Fasheh, M. (1982) 'Mathematics, culture and authority', Bir Zeit University.
21. Department of Education and Science (1985) 'Mathematics from 5 to 16', HMI: Curriculum Matters 3.
22. Singh, E. (1985) Mathematics, Culture and Racism, ACCM, to be published.
23. Gill, D. and Levidow, L. (eds) (1987) Anti-Racist Science Teaching, Free Association Books.
24. For a fuller account of the development of these ideas see: Gould, S.J. Mismeasure of Man; Rose, S. Not in our Genes.
25. Lindsay, L. (1987) 'Nutrition and Hunger', in Gill, D. and Levidow, L. (eds) op. cit.
26. Vance, M. (1987) 'Biology teaching in a racist society'; and Gill, D., Singh, E., and Vance, M. (eds) (1987) 'Multicultural versus anti-racist science: biology', in Gill, D. and Levidow, L., op. cit.
27. Gill, D., Patel, V., Sethi, A., and Smith, H. (1987) 'Science curriculum innovation at Holland Park School', in Gill, D. and Levidow, L. (eds) op. cit.
28. Harding, J. (1987) 'The Rationale', in Gill, D. and Levidow, L. (eds) op. cit.

Chapter Nine

EDUCATION AND A SOCIAL DEMOCRACY: SECONDARY SCHOOL HUMANITIES

Doug Holly

To begin I will define my terms. 'Humanities' I take to mean that area of the secondary school curriculum around the traditional subjects of geography, history, and religious/moral education, including several newer concerns like social studies. But the term, although often used in a merely administrative sense, implies something more than a simple aggregate of traditional subjects. It is coming more and more to suggest a degree of at least collaboration if not actual integration of subjects. It is the area of the curriculum whose central concern is <u>people</u>. This concern suggests an integrative rationale and a strengthened claim for the importance of such human studies. To quote the formula offered by the Integrated Humanities Association (IHA), it is 'a core area of study in secondary schools which has to do with people - whether considered as individuals, groups, communities, societies or as a species sharing common characteristics and inhabiting the planet earth'. (1) Which makes its omission from the Baker national curriculum all the more noteworthy. In North American usage the term 'humanities' has an even wider resonance, since it refers to languages and literature, both native and foreign. Something of that wider, more liberal idea is implied in the IHA definition and is exemplified in the practice of a growing number of schools which integrate English and the social studies, in their first-year courses at least.

By 'a social democracy' I mean the original sense of those words - the completion of the unfinished business of democratic politics, the extension of equality from the purely formal sphere of elective government to the concrete area of economic/social life. This is, of course, a revolutionary project and one which requires a revolution in human consciousness. And it is this question of the level of popular consciousness which links the project of social equality/social democracy with secondary school learning in the humanities area of the curriculum. Tomorrow's social revolution has to be prepared in the classrooms of today. With the virtual total control over the means of public information now exerted by an oligarchy more powerful than any known to history, the main arena

162

for raising the popular level of consciousness becomes the schools. Humanities education is the 'core of cores', the last bastion of democracy. Without it political thinking, the necessary precursor to political action, will become even more marginalized. Without a genuinely humanist schooling the mass of ordinary people will sink deeper and deeper into the pit of resignation so carefully dug for them by the ruling oligarchy. They will understand neither the full nature of their oppression nor the possibility and methodology of liberation. They will continue to shrug their shoulders at the hopelessness of any alternative scheme of things and seek whatever fulfilment seems possible in the oligarchy's company store of credit-card consumerism.

This is very well understood by the oligarchy's Thatcherite guardians - which is why the Education Reform Act was so high on their agenda. In it they carry forward their twin objectives of strengthening the corporate state while appearing to maximize consumer choice. The local state is weakened in its main function, education, preparatory to eventual dismemberment. At the same time the authoritarian/traditionalist imperatives of the central state are strengthened by giving a minister direct control over the curriculum for the first time in British history. The populist cry of 'choice' is subtly linked to traditionalist values which actually reverse earlier appeals for contemporary relevance in the curriculum. 'Standards' is the cant word used to link popular anxieties with control and limitation of educational autonomy. It appears that the Right has a livelier sense than the Left of the real potential implied in an autonomous educational sector - an understanding further illustrated by its neofascist war of nerves against higher education.

The problem here is, typically, the confusion and lack of conceptual clarity among those who oppose the Thatcherite settlement. Many egalitarians share a version of the populist solution: the reality of life for a majority of the world's population and for a growing minority here in Britain is, indeed, the market. In this perspective education needs to be about survival in the sink or swim maelstrom of life in a capitalist-dominated world: preparation in school for the harsh realities of life outside school. Talk of a more 'progressive' education, the negotiated curriculum, an emphasis on humanities is dismissed as a bourgeois cop-out, a soft option for liberal teachers.

What this view fails to see is that no hard-nosed traditionalist education, or even a modernist technology-based one, can deliver a single extra job in the oligarchs' economy. If some teachers are 'middle-class liberals' this is something to welcome. Far better that than cynical anti-working-class authoritarians and their backers in Whitehall. But many teachers, especially humanities teachers, are gaining daily in political consciousness in the very process of their work. And more and more school students, including the most deprived of them, are learning the connections systematically

163

denied them by the mass-circulation press and TV. Which is why Thatcher aspires to control the curriculum.

What I want to argue in this chapter is the centrality of humanities education to any egalitarian/democratic politics. (2) All areas of the curriculum, if properly handled, are important in demystifying the world in which we live, but only humanities can lay bare the social and economic bases of oppression, exploitation, and the vast inequalities in social power represented by transnational monopoly capitalism and its oligarchic rivals. Again it is noteworthy that 'economic awareness' and 'political education' earlier promoted by the DES (3) have been abruptly chopped from the national curriculum. The Thatcherites have not missed the radical potential of such a prioritization. The Education Reform Act has been used to correct this dangerous slip in policy.

So how to translate an understanding of the political contest into classroom practice? How can the Baker Act's attempt to trivialize and traditionalize the humanities curriculum be circumvented? First of all, most certainly, through the experience of history - our history, the history of ordinary people, white and black, whose children are the students of state comprehensive schools. By seeing what our forebears dreamt of, what for short periods of time they actually achieved, how and why those dreams were betrayed, we can only learn. Our young need, above all, a vision. They - and their parents - need to glimpse Utopia again. Only reactionaries need sneer at utopias. If the oligarchs find a way to make us teach 'the British Heritage' their victory could turn out to be an extremely hollow one. But for that eventuality we must prepare very carefully. I purposely used the phrase 'an experience of history'. This will not be about 'History' with a capital 'H'. There must be no pageant to be glimpsed, wondered at, or shrugged away. Instead there must be a partial reliving of what once was really lived, the suffering and the triumph. It will be largely unspectacular. Momentous events, when dealt with - as they must be - will be relived as the daily experience they were for those who first lived them. But above all we will promote again the notion of dreaming a different reality - a nobler, more human reality. We will show how, for instance, the past dream of the Diggers can become the present politics of Mother Earth and a future reality very different from any that could be envisaged by souls shrunk to the size of Thatcher's.

As in time, so in space. We must extend the imaginations of our students to cope with different realities as lived today. They need a sense of place which can never be produced by ordnance survey maps or some ritual of crop rotation. Place, for instance, as experienced by native Americans, native Australians, or those who live with the rain forests. Physical geography tells us nothing by itself. It only becomes significant when we ask 'how are people dealing with mineral deposits, the savannas, the rain forests - and why?'. Herein lies a living geography. It is a geography inseparable from poetry, short story, novel, song - the means by which people tell us their experience of space. A people's geography can never be the arrogant 'science' of technocratic lackeys. It also happens to be interesting - to raise issues that even 'cool' adolescent students find fascinating. It is the necessary counterpart to historical experience, setting our history in its full context as part of the history of Planet Earth and the wider family of humankind.

Back full circle to 'humanities'. The real corrective to the Falklands Factor, that xenophobic sickness which so disables people in the imperialist countries and renders socialist/egalitarian politics almost impossible, is a humanities learning which links the past of imperialism with the present of actual ecological and potential thermonuclear disaster. This is best done through integrated, thematic, courses, but it can be done through separate history and geography. Even Baker has had to acknowledge that the 'delivery' of the curriculum (a telling expression) must be left to schools. One mechanism for this can be a modular humanities course with linked thematic modules showing the clear progression and coherence which the DES - rightly for once - insists on for GCSE accreditation. So far 'modular humanities' courses have been sadly opportunistic 'pick 'n' mix' affairs with no clear rationale. A radical humanities approach could correct this and, ironically, receive the official sanction which has so far been denied to such courses.

Rightly conceived, a radical/environmentalist approach to humanities could not be faulted as 'indoctrination'. After all, no one can deny the fact of Diggers, Levellers, and Chartists as part of our 'heritage', nor the struggles of the Maroons in Jamaica or of the movements of popular resistance in Africa and Asia. Any attempts to do so would usefully remove the camouflage of 'objectivity' from the traditionalist position and reveal the politics which already exist in the conventional curriculum of British kings and philanthropists, glacial beds and temperate zones.

The important point about a genuinely 'humanities' curriculum is that its logic is not mechanical. Issues for study in history are not chosen simply as a matter of chronology nor are those in geography chosen on any simple topographical basis. While time lines and mental maps are important they are only important if given what Jerome Bruner has described as 'explanatory power'. (4) Current talk about the importance of 'conceptual' as opposed to 'merely factual' knowledge tends to obscure the nature of concepts. Concepts are systems of significant relationships among data, i.e. we choose certain relationships in order to highlight the connection, thereby 'developing a concept'. The Diggers saw the connection between private ownership of wealth in land and political power. Their concept of 'democracy' was thereby qualitatively different from that of Cromwell and his ideological descendants. Today we can choose to illuminate the connection between beefburgers and the destruction of tropical rainforests. Our concept of 'environment' will thereby be qualitatively different from that of, say, the Society for the Preservation of Rural England. Peace Education and Political

Education, barred from entry to the national curriculum by the device of a limited set of 'foundation' subjects, can nevertheless happen through a liberated approach to 'history'. Similarly economic awareness can gain powerful entry via 'geography'. But, for this to happen, both these 'foundation' subjects must be embraced within the meaningful concept-networks of a genuine 'humanities' curriculum. Whether the GCSE integrated humanities syllabuses currently offered by three of the five regional examining groups (5) will be allowed to continue in their present form of linked themes is not clear at the time of writing, but it is likely that modularized schemes which show clear evidence of historical and geographical concerns and a clear progression of ideas will be acceptable. The salient point lies in a thematic approach being developed.

But humanities learning is not only about conceptual connections and making sense of reality, vital though these things are. It is also, crucially, about a sense of morality, a developed system of ethics and, underpinning these, a feeling - or faith - about the meanings which we discover in our universe. It would be quite possible, after all, to learn about inequalities and the possibility of righting injustice - and decide to do nothing about it. The title of this book is 'Education for Equality' not 'Education about Equality'. The idea of its editor and contributors must be, therefore, that education is going to lead to social revolution. This is certainly an act of faith. For the potentially revolutionary to become actual revolution - concrete historical action - it must be possible for such an act of faith to be communicated. No amount of education will achieve this unless such education involves, at a basic level, an ethical committment on the part of the mass of ordinary learners. The problem of revolutionary politics so far has been its implicit elitism. Always the 'leading role' of the revolutionaries has been stressed rather than the participatory-executive role of the people. A social revolution can only be brought about by an active majority of social democrats (i.e. most certainly not by the ludicrously mistitled 'Social Democrats' in Britain). For this to occur an ethical revolution needs to take place: ordinary people need to rouse themselves from terminal nihilism. In this sense 'you'd better believe it' becomes more than a catch phrase. Belief, faith, feeling - these are the things which have been systematically excluded from the consciousness of a majority in the 'developed' world. The guardians of oligarchy have mouthed sanctimonious religiosity - whether 'Christian' or 'Communist' - while cutting the mass of people off from the sort of faith which really can move mountains. A Russian joke tells of Brezhnev wanting to fill in the Moscow river and turn it into an urban motorway - because, in a dream, he saw the battleship Potemkin sailing up it. Political passion is the last thing wanted by some very important people in Moscow.

On the other hand the radical movements of the 'developing' world are now often led by priests and nuns of the various religions -- who invite the people to take the revolution into their own hands. (6)

For any such popular movements for democracy to happen here it will be necessary to re-import a felt morality into the curriculum - not the restrictive morality of Thatcher's 'Victorian values' but the expansive, combative morality of the Levellers and the Diggers, the Chartists, the Suffragettes, the black people who rose in revolt, and the dialectical materialists. For, at bottom, Marx and Engels were involved with an act of faith and imbued with a fierce passion. No one throws away the prospect of a lucrative professional career in the Rhineland to live in exile and poverty amidst the delights of Victorian values in Soho simply as a matter of superior political-economic consciousness or greater conceptual clarity. For that you need feeling and faith.

Against the daily miracles of the advertising agencies and other priests of Mammon, preaching the religion of instant gratification and institutionally sanctified greed, the only possible remedy is the encouragement in the young of a faith in common humanity. Fortunately the oligarchs with their near total control of the media of communication and entertainment have never quite been able to suppress, in the young, the primal urges of what Marx called the 'species being' of humanity. The young in schools continue to have a lively sense of justice and injustice, of outrage. While teachers and schools spend a great deal of energy trying to suppress the dynamism of youth, what a humanities curriculum can do is give it direction. Already the best humanities teachers make good use of music, poetry, and students' own felt responses to poverty, injustice, and inequality. An education for equality will be one which encourages the feelings of youth as well as the reasonings of age: both deserve to be respected.

So a form of moral education, even of religious education, needs to be saved from the Baker Settlement's exclusion from mainstream curriculum by being made an integral part of humanities. This, of course, will not be achieved by teaching Elements of World Religions. Still less will it be achieved by highlighting the currently favoured concerns of 'personal and social education'. Whether you sleep with your boyfriend or nick something from the supermarket is not simply a 'personal' consideration - it involves political understanding of the relations between the sexes and ethical understanding about self-seeking as opposed to principled actions. In both cases 'political' and 'ethical' are interdependent categories, since sexual politics implies the acceptance or rejection of a value system while the decision between principled and self-seeking action involves a choice between communal and individualistic solutions to problems which are usually social. As always in humanities, categories are problematic. Where exactly, for instance, lie the distinctions between awareness of legal process, ethical consciousness, and political philosophy?

A more fruitful approach to integrating moral feeling into the humanities is via consideration of issues like world population. In this way attitudes and feelings about the sanctity of life can both inform and be informed by understandings about the family as an economic unit in various societies today and in our own society in the past. For the same reason 'The Industrial Revolution' is better understood in relation to the concepts 'industrialization' and 'urbanization' - both of which beg questions about the real meaning and ethical status of 'development'. Young people are capable of considerable insight into the feelings and value systems of, say, native Australians in relation to the land and the family and are less prone than adults - including progressive ones - to consider such values less 'developed'.

But undoubtedly the worst separation of the Baker national curriculum is that involved between English, in the 'core', and the humanities subjects, in the 'foundation'. For the English and other mother languages, along with art and music education, are a key element in any humanistic curriculum. The good practice referred to above involving music, poetry, and students' felt responses, is likely to be most often seen in English classrooms or where English is integrated into humanities. It is for this reason that I have commented elsewhere (7) on the vital importance of having English seen as central to any curriculum area calling itself 'humanities'. This does not necessarily imply complete integration - though that should be a goal. The important thing is that the 'social subjects' of history, geography, social studies, and, I have just suggested, religious/moral education be brought into close association and planned in concert with English departments.

The importance of a thematic approach to humanities lies in its concreteness. The traditional 'subjects' of the curriculum exist as precisely that - subjects. A radical education, on the other hand, sees the learner as the subject. Subjects are technically abstract - they separate out from reality those concerns which fit the preoccupation of academics in the various traditions. It is of no concern to the 'geographer' qua 'geographer' that the planet faces ecological collapse. It is no concern, either, of the political scientist, who sees the world in terms of competing interest groups held theoretically in some sort of shifting balance. It would take a committee of economists, biologists, earth scientists, political scientists, and geographers to even contemplate such a vital question. It is highly unlikely that they would, even then, come up with ideas for concrete action. In the classroom teachers and students are better placed. For the majority of students in a comprehensive school, the preoccupations of traditional academe are an irrelevance. For the tiny minority among them who, under present conditions, will go forward to tertiary education, a far better foundation is in understanding conceptual connections between aspects of concrete reality. Only admissions tutors and reactionary politicians need concern themselves with narrowly defined subject boundaries. A humanities faculty in a secondary school can provide quite a lot of shared background for engaging students in dialogue about the environment. By involving colleagues in the science faculty, an impressive package of data and suggestive concept-networks can be produced to form the basis for some directed - and well informed - outrage and possibly even political action, like writing to the local MP or picketing the local burger joint. This will not endear the school to the Thatcherite establishment or their local bloodhounds of course, but the wise humanities faculty will have taken the precaution of involving students' families, parent governors, and others at an early stage in planning the curriculum.

The art of political-social action in education often lies in using the adversaries' own weapons against them. The shift away from university-dominated 'O' level boards to teacher-influenced GCSE examining groups was probably engineered, at least in part, to weaken the position of academics, in pursuit of the ongoing Thatcherite project of silencing the intellectuals. It has now brought an embarrassing contradiction in policy, with the Baker Act emphasizing the eternal verities of the Victorian secondary curriculum and the GCSE guidelines (8) calling for commonalities to be highlighted which link rather than separate the elements of the curriculum and, even more embarrassing, actually promote active learning strategies and - horror of horrors - 'empathy'. The GCSE is now expensively in place. Its very structure, with a compulsory minimum of one-fifth of examination being coursework-based and concepts, processes, and (presumably) intellectual skills being the aim of the tests, it undermines the traditionalizing attempt of the national curriculum. Egalitarian/democratic teachers, especially in the humanities, should occupy the line of these fortifications and prepare to defend them with parental reinforcements. Certainly egalitarians should ponder the injunction in the guidelines that testing should be criteria related rather than normative. In the past the need to 'fail' up to 50 per cent in order to fulfil the requirements of a normal curve of statistical distribution has been a powerful constructor of inequality and educational injustice. This device has now been removed. Instead examiners - more and more those who actually teach the courses - are enjoined to look for positive achievement, 'what students know, understand, and can do'. Such ideas are highly subversive of hierarchical intentions, especially in the humanities where formula knowledge is less easily defended and wide distributions of achievement far from inevitable.

In practice, of course, teachers as examiners are bewildered by the new freedom. It is my experience that even socially radical humanities teachers still cling to a 'normal curve' mentality when moderating grades - thereby quite ignoring the invitation of the GCSE guidelines to work to attainable grades based on specified levels of attainment. Teachers of humanities should be gratified rather than embarrassed by a 'bunching' of scores near the top. It is what you would expect if a larger number of students are being involved in worthwhile and relevant learning activities. There is nothing fraudulent in the idea that a majority can achieve excellence - most certainly not in the humanities. To see any problem in this suggests a secret commitment to discredited notions of inherent levels of native ability - the great god IQ whose feet of clay were finally exposed by the chicanery of its high priest, Cyril Burt. However ideas die hard, more especially ideas that offer 'explanations' of inequality as being biologically determined. The persistence of this idea among ordinary people is a continuing problem for those who want to show them that they have, in fact, been robbed of their intellectual birthright. There is probably more than a hint of self-justification in the stubborn refusal of so many to believe that there are few limits to the development of the ordinary individual. Since 'success' and 'failure' continues to be urged as a personal question, 'I'm not very clever, you know' is a way of warding off an even worse imputation of lacking will-power. A good humanities learning situation can demonstrate to students the fallacy of such notions of 'natural' incompetence. Nothing, in fact, succeeds like success, and success in humanities learning, since it is not arcane or abstract, is demonstrably attainable.

This is not, of course, to deny inequalities in basic skills, like reading. But my recent experience is of a school which expects all its students to achieve basic literacy in a foreign language together with basic keyboard competence with microcomputers and, so far, is largely seeing the expectation being fulfilled even by self-defined 'thickos' who are struggling with literacy in their native language at eleven and twelve. (9) We are not even beginning to explore the potential of ordinary young people after nearly two decades of so-called comprehensive reform. And the basic reason is the stubbornness of the conviction, shared by too many teachers, that the ordinary person is, somehow, unintellectual.

This conviction is sometimes expressed in a disguised form, even by egalitarian teachers, in terms of a dismissal of 'intellectualism' as irrelevant to the deprived and the oppressed - girls, working-class youngsters, and young black people. For such misguided radicals the only 'relevant' curriculum is a 'practical' one. This comes dangerously close to the arrogant Thatcherite presumption that 'technical and vocational' initiatives are what working-class people need, rather than education. Though those radicals - among them many humanities teachers - are to be congratulated who have demonstrated enlightened opportunism in carrying off MSC funds and using them for educative ends, this is a path that needs to be trodden lightly. Who sups with Mammon needs a very long spoon. Even paying lip-service to notions of 'vocation' and 'relevance' can end up by confusing learners who should be being disabused.

I would like to conclude by considering two issues which are essential to any humanistic education and central to any project of education for equality. They are interdependent and both emerge from this question of the nature of a 'relevant' education. They concern, on the one hand, the relationship between teachers and the community in general, more especially the families of those being educated; on the other they concern the intellectual-emotional basis of the fight for equality - the experience of power.

The problem of relevance is one which the Thatcherites have exploited because it often divides 'lay' from 'professional' opinion and is a potential source of contest between teachers and people in general. In Britain, as in other European cultures, there is a patrician tradition, often associated with the universities, which contemptuously dismisses the idea of relevance in learning. This tradition claims - against the historical record - that knowledge has grown of its own accord, promoted by disinterested seekers after truth. To look for relevance in learning, according to this tradition, is to narrow the scope of knowledge to fit a utilitarian mode. It is a view shared by many on the Left who are suspicious of the ends to which learning is being made relevant. Yet this is to misconceive the problem. All human knowledge is relevant to someone: there is no irrelevant knowledge. The point to question is - to whom is a given type of knowledge relevant? The answer in oligarchic society is predictable: in the end, the most powerful knowledge is relevant to the most powerful people. The most obvious example in modern societies is 'Science', with a capital 'S'. By and large most fundamental, 'pure' scientific research is pursued because it may have a pay-off for those whose money funds it - government and the transnational corporations. That is why science education is so energetically promoted by governments - as a training for a pool of potential profit and power generators, not in the least to help demystify the people.

The question, then, is not whether we should seek for relevance in education, including humanities education, but to whom this relevance refers. If relevance is argued in terms of, say, technology it is far from obvious that a technological bias to education is relevant to ordinary people - though it may be highly relevant to capitalism. Within humanities the question is not whether history is more or less relevant than social education but what sort of history experience is more or less relevant to the majority of learners than what sort of social experience. It is possible to devise a history syllabus that is massively irrelevant to most young people, just as it is possible to devise a syllabus in social education that is highly relevant, and vice versa. It all depends on whether the knowledge of history gained or the aspect of society experienced gives learners a greater or a lesser purchase on the reality that surrounds them. A history that explored the claims of Wilberforce to be a 'philanthropist' whose exertions freed the slaves on British-owned plantations would be relevant to the majority of people because it would enable them to see through the clouds of misrepresentation that have helped to form an institutional racist consciousness among ordinary non-black Britons, just as a study of the Tolpuddle Martyrs would help to counter the incessant anti-trade union propaganda of the mass media. In either case the young are being given back some of the reality that has been so assiduously removed from them over the generations. Traditional 'history' teaching, on the other hand, has reinforced the disinformation - as Baker and the far Right would like it to do again. The project of social equality will only be possible if disinformation is replaced by real information, since people need to realize how inequality arises in the first place and that what has been historically constructed in the interests of a powerful minority can be historically reconstructed in the interests of an empowered majority. My argument would be that this is more likely to happen where relevance is not judged in terms of the preoccupations and prejudices of the powerful men (they usually are men) who define the 'discipline' called history, but in terms of the learning needs of ordinary people - prime among which is a need to know that democracy is, in principle, an attainable object but one which has been systematically rendered difficult to attain. Such judgements may well happen within the history establishment. They are even more likely to happen where teachers do not feel themselves constrained by some intrinsic logic of a subject but, instead, operate within a people-focused logic in integrated humanities teams. I am convinced that much of the hostility within separate humanities subject associations towards integration springs from a fear of 'leftist' curriculum planning. If by 'leftist' is meant tending towards a concern for greater democracy rather than a concern for preserving undemocracy the fears are quite justified. Nor should any of us shrink from acknowledging a commitment to democracy. After all it has taken centuries of courage and self-denial to achieve the limited version we have in the 'developed' world today. If such is 'political' - fine: we should be proud of such politics.

Where teachers are on less firm ground, of course, is in justifying education for democracy and equality to parents and others. This is because of the history of mass education - something, incidentally, well worth including in any humanities curriculum. Mass education has everywhere had to be fought for but everywhere it has finally been imposed, and on terms everywhere suitable to the ruling classes. (10) Because of this, teachers on the one hand and students and their families on the other can face each other across a barrier of mutual incomprehension and distrust. An effective humanities education must address this situation, starting by acknowledging its existence. All teachers, but humanities teachers in particular, need to approach their task, their students, and the general community with humility. They must always make the effort to explain the whys and wherefores of new curricular development. It will not be easy. Given the alienated state of many peoples' consciousness in the Britain of the last decades of this century they are highly likely to demand a xenophobic, racist, sexist, and antidemocratic content to the curriculum. Argument must be patient and careful. In the end it will often have to reside in the 'proof of the pudding is in the eating' position. Much the best line of argument is to allow parents and families to share in the experience - to provide weekend and evening activities in which people can experience for themselves what a new humanities curriculum is all about. (11) The beefburger curriculum is far easier experienced than explained - how geography and economics can become very relevant to your daily life. (12) Of course this comes hard to a profession so savaged and humilitated by the Thatcherites. 'Non-directed time' is understandably precious. Yet, for those dedicated to turning the weapons of the oligarchs against them, time spent in this way may not be seen as donated to Baker exactly.

The final point is really the reiteration of one that permeates my whole argument about the humanities curriculum. One of the more encouraging developments on the Left in Britain during the 1980s has been the recognition of empowerment as the key issue. I suppose what finally distinguishes liberal egalitarians from socialist-ecological egalitarians is the commitment of the latter to the knowledge that the egalitarian project cannot be accomplished for the people - only by the people. For this to happen, for that almost unimaginable change in consciousness to take place, ordinary people everywhere have to begin to do things for themselves. The way to final democratic political and economic power is through empowerment and the way to empowerment is through the experience of taking things into your own hands, in collaboration with others - the direct experience, if often only temporary, of the power of unity. The miners' strike is a relatively recent example of ordinary people experiencing this. Jeered at and misrepresented by a lackey press, distanced by the technical incompetence of television, finally defeated by the overwhelming power of monopoly capital so ably deployed by the Thatcherite state, women and men in the coalfields nevertheless experienced again what their forebears had experienced before them through generations: the struggle to establish dignity and solidarity against owners, managers, and latterly, Coal Board bureaucrats and oligarchic hit-men.

I once attended a seminar in which a sociologist reported his experience of participant observation in a South Yorkshire school. What he had to say about the attitudes of teachers in that school towards young people from miners' families was horrific. These young people were seen as rough, uncouth, violent, and ill-mannered. The teachers saw their harsh disciplinarian methods and sharp tongues as a necessary response, the only way of ensuring a modicum of order. Yet I know at least one school in the same area where the attitude of staff is exactly the opposite to exactly the same sort of students - and these students are not seen as at all difficult young people. In this second school humanities is integrated and taught thematically and works in close liaison with English throughout, whereas the curriculum of the first school was reported to be highly traditional, employing ultra-traditional teaching methods. English teachers there saw it as their job to 'correct' the speech of their students. It is no surprise to learn that, whereas in the first school the students opposed and blocked the teachers' strike, in the second they were highly supportive. Where teachers affirm the values and experience of an exploited community, learning has a chance to grow on fertile soil. A humanistic curriculum, dedicated to ending inequality and injustice must start from the experience of the young people themselves and must afford young people the chance to experience involvement in learning. Uninvolved learning is a contradiction in terms: when students are uninvolved only ritual can take place, never learning. But for oppressed, disvalued, and, consequently, underachieving students a real learning situation, the experience of involvement and, above all, the experience of understanding are themselves empowering. What people in schools are learning when they find the connections in time and space of themselves to others is the lesson of power - intellectual power, the power that drives revolutions. Education for equality in the title of this volume implies, I take it, education to achieve equality. The humanities curriculum is at the centre of that.

NOTES AND REFERENCES

1. Quoted by Smith, D. (1986) 'The integrated humanities association, some recent history', in D. Holly (ed.) Humanism in Adversity: Teachers' Experience of Integrated Humanities in the 1980's, London: Falmer Press.
2. A similar claim is made in relation to socialist politics by Colin Lacey in Lacey, C. and Williams, R. (1987) (eds) Education, Ecology and Development, London: Kogan Page. In the same volume Geoff Whitty specifically draws attention to integrated humanities.
3. Notably in Department of Education and Science (1985) Better Schools: a Summary, London: HMSO.
4. For example, in Bruner, J. (1966) Towards a Theory of Instruction, Belknap, Cambridge Massachusetts: Harvard University Press.
5. The three syllabuses are Northern Examining Association Integrated Humanities, Midlands Examining Group Integrated Humanities, and Southern Examining Group Integrated Humanities. Of these the MEG syllabus is examined entirely by continuous assessment and schools must offer their own 'content exemplars' showing not only a variety of teacher inputs but also a variety of student activities and expected outcomes. Details of these syllabuses are available from the respective groups. (All are 'Mode 1' syllabuses.)
6. For the specifically educational implications of this see the works of the Brazilian Catholic-Marxist, Paulo Freire - e.g. (1972) Cultural Action for Freedom, Harmondsworth: Penguin Books.

7.   In Holly, D. (1986) A survey of integrated humanities in England
     and Wales, Occasional Paper One, Northampton Centre, and
     Holly, D. (1987) Integration in the new age: a report of six
     weeks' teaching in the new Greendown school, Swindon,
     Occasional Paper Two, Northampton Centre, both available
     from E. Searl, University of Leicester, School of Education, 21
     University Road, Leicester.
8.   See (1985) General Criteria for GCSE, London: HMSO.
9.   Reported in Holly, D. (1987), op. cit.
10. See Centre for Contemporary Cultural Studies (1981) Unpopular
     Education: School and Social Democracy in England, London:
     Hutchinson, for a good account of this in Britain.
11. An interesting example of this is reported on by a parent in
     (1987) Humanities Resource (the journal of the IHA) 1: issue 2,
     autumn - article 'Times, they are a-changin' '.
12. But be careful not to mention brand names - the Transnational
     Information Centre are being sued by a transnational
     corporation for publishing a book about their activities. (See
     Private Eye 18 March 1988).

Chapter Ten

AFTER BILINGUAL SUPPORT?

Ahmed Gurnah

INTRODUCTION

Although the tendency is to put too much importance on new developments and see more significance in their innovation than their contribution merits, nevertheless, we can agree with those who view the introduction of bilingualism in our schools in such momentous terms for two reasons. Firstly, bilingualism is clearly desirable for educationally liberal reasons: it will benefit and end the marginalization of black and working-class children and teachers, and also enrich the whole curriculum for everybody. However, it is arguable that, for this promise to be realized, the development of a discipline of multilingual studies should follow the introduction of bilingual support.

The second reason for celebrating the development of bilingualism goes beyond liberal education values. For, pursued to its logical conclusion, it promises another small contribution to the search for democratic, participative, critical, and progressive education. As such, it should be of interest to all those who view education as providing more than a process of socialization and training into our appropriate class categories and employment, and see it as a route to enlightenment, liberty, and equality for ordinary working people.

Lest I give the wrong impression, most local education authorities are only just disbanding language centres and have not even started to think about these issues of bilingualism. My own preoccupation with them, however, results from the problems we have been dealing with in Sheffield LEA, since we introduced a bilingual policy in the teaching of English as a second language. (1)

In the last thirty years, most open-minded educationalists have come to accept that while the comprehensive school and various adult access provisions have gone a long way to meet the educational needs of British working people, there still exists an informal, dual, state education system in this country. Sadly, the proposals contained in the Education Reform Act may well turn back the clock and treat education as prescriptive formal learning and not an activity of enlightenment. Not least, the introduction of the national curriculum, policed from the centre, and given greater emphasis on the teaching of English, is likely to downgrade dialects and varieties of regional English in favour of middle-class Standard English, whose tyranny we had spent so many years trying to discredit.

The British education system has been particularly slow in addressing the needs of the black, working-class, young women and men and has been badly served by Swann and Scarman. (2) There is a general consensus amongst black people and most academics now, that an important part of the responsibility for these young people's 'underachievement' lies firmly with the education system - with the resourcing policies of LEAs and schools, teacher attitudes, the curriculum, teacher training colleges, and so on. It is now also realized that one of the key reasons why this 'underachievement' continues for black children is to do specifically with LEA and school language and literacy policies and provision, especially with regard to the teaching of English as a second language and the relative absence of the teaching of Creole and other mother-tongue education.

In this chapter I shall concentrate on the issue of language teaching to working-class, young, black women and men. It is my belief that by focusing on these students we shall not only once again draw attention to the most glaring inequalities of the system, but, as with other equal opportunity solutions in general, they will provide good examples for the rest of the system to follow. The purpose of this chapter is both practical and egalitarian. At the very least, I hope it will stimulate further debate about another aspect of bilingualism. More ambitiously, however, I hope to make links in the struggles for language between black people and white working people. The equalitarian principle in it is that education recognizes the importance for black children and working-class children to learn Standard English which will give them access to their rights, but at the same time ensuring that their mother tongue or dialect is central to their learning experience. After all, all students and pupils have the right to excellence in and a critical awareness of both mother tongue and Standard English. The aim of the chapter is essentially practical. Multilingual studies is a serious practical proposal, but I leave how it could be developed in the classroom to those involved in the classroom. If at times the discussion appears abstract, that is only in order to clarify particular issues for this practical purpose.

THE ISSUE

Very few people will now dispute the desirability of employing bilingual teachers to give second-language and mother-tongue support to black children and students. Advocates of bilingual approaches are convinced that this would help maintain and raise the status of both black children and teachers, and end their marginalization in schools. But implicit in the more perceptive of these arguments are radical propositions which go beyond the support teaching role for bilingual and monolingual teachers. When these teachers demand that their contribution be treated with greater seriousness, as well as searching for rightful recognition, they are signalling a dissatisfaction with the support nature of their work and the desire for a new and comprehensive discipline that is capable of addressing all these issues.

While not doubting the importance of bringing in more bilingual support teachers in ESL teaching, I am therefore uncertain if that alone would improve the status of bilingual support teachers, black children, and community languages, and end their marginalization. For as long as the content of support work relies on other disciplines for its existence and effective performance, the essence of support work will remain dependent, marginal, and with low status. The fact that its work is carried out in collaboration with other subjects makes no difference to its present status; indeed, that may actually give substance to its second-order nature. Furthermore, in as much as support teachers' clientele by default remain exclusively black and bilingual children, their work is bound to involve only those children. Meanwhile, the recent introduction of bilingual support has caused some anxiety and immobilization for monolingual ESL teachers. Regardless of whether that is justified or not, the persistence of this anxiety affects both their work and the development of bilingualism.

I would thus argue here, that, as well as irreversibly laying the foundation for second-language teaching in bilingual support, support work is an inadequate instrument for bringing about the required changes. I shall argue that we need a new discipline of multilingual studies for that. I contend that this new discipline will not only change the character of dual-language support teaching, but also raise its profile, enhance its content, increase its research and in-service base, end its discipline dependence, and maybe even recruit a few monolingual students. Bilingual support teachers will then participate in a discipline without being or appearing to be dependent. It will allow many of the bilingual teachers to make use of their specialist degrees and experience, not to support subject teachers, but to utilize for the first time their knowledge of Urdu or Chinese or Indian philosophy learnt abroad, as subjects in their own right, to benefit all the children.

Meanwhile, the creation of a discipline base will allow monolingual teachers to continue to make a valuable contribution to the teaching of bilingual children, despite their limited knowledge of the children's mother tongue. Eventually, the discipline will also assist progressive teachers to continue to broaden standard English, by increasing our understanding between it and different varieties of

English. It will also put some critical sharpness into multicultural education, update social and political education, and also improve the school's curriculum as a whole.

Multilingual studies, therefore, will doubtless extend Kant's humanist project to outline our essential mutuality, or Levi-Strauss' sociologized version of it, which aims to show the coherent unity of the diversities of human existence. It is probable that it will aid sociology and development studies in concretely familiarizing students with socially common and contrastive dramas of human histories and cultures. Following which, no doubt it would sharpen up students' critical sight and encourage them to question traditional racist and hierarchical notions of social organization. The greatest value of such a discipline will be that it can start at the youngest level of educational provision.

Disciplines that arise out of new synthesis are not unknown to all levels of teaching. Language courses, degrees, and even Departments of European, Slavonic or Oriental Studies are quite commonly available. Sociology and development studies themselves emerged in the nineteenth century and the 1960s respectively. Social and political education, world studies, and multicultural education are also some of the initiatives appearing in many schools.

I shall proceed, therefore, by outlining recent developments in the teaching of English to black children, featuring why bilingual support had to replace monolingual ESL approaches. Then I shall acknowledge that while this development will improve children's learning, it also identifies further difficulties that signal the need for multilingual studies. My aim is to show that the introduction of multilingual studies will raise the standards of support teaching and the curriculum as a whole in secondary and primary schools.

EARLY DEVELOPMENTS

In a 1965 BBC publication, (3) an ILEA district inspector called A. Roy Truman discusses the problems of black children in terms of infection that necessitated fumigation during holidays (p. 99). The black child is passive when others are 'highly mobile and purposeful'. 'Left in his (sic) isolation ... he (sic) could speedily become withdrawn or aggressive in his (sic) frustration' (p. 100). The problem, according to Truman, is compounded by the child's confusion about not receiving 'corporal punishment' and the parents' cultural and religious backwardness.

Truman felt supported in this stereotype by the DES and the Home Office during the Labour administration of the time, which advocated integration and assimilation of the black child into the 'British' way of life (pp. 101-2). Black children should be 'dispersed' to avoid turning schools 'coloured', and they should be taught by English specialists returning from Commonwealth countries (p. 99).

Around the same time, June Derrick, (4) presents a more

enlightened view. She blames neither the black child nor parent for the 'problems' they face, and rather situates them in social circumstances and styles of teaching. While she recognizes that there are no short cuts to learning how to teach ESL, 'it helps very much if the teacher can begin to be aware of the language from the point of view of his pupils', and hear English 'in an entirely new way ... most of our existing ideas, both about language and about teaching, have to be modified by experience' (p. v-vi). She recognises the 'social nature' of these difficulties and appreciates the 'psychological shock' first experienced by children 'overnight' and in a new country (see Parekh (5) p. 187). The shock is compounded by 'the language problem', unfair testing, and relegation to 'backward streams'. Adolescence complicates their failure to 'comply with school rules and codes of behaviour because they cannot be made to understand them' (p. 2). Instead, she lays her emphases on the need for new curricula and materials and more precise techniques and expertise; all of which show her greater awareness of the child's needs. 'Often immigrant pupils are blamed for making no progress in English when in fact they have not been given a true opportunity of learning it' (p. 3). Though the notion of teacher racism was still not common currency then, it is possible to extrapolate that from some of these observations.

So what is the character of teaching English as a second language (TESL)? For Derrick, (4) the teaching of language must stress 'oral communication' (p. 4). She identifies strongly with the support approach by insisting that language teaching should have no curriculum content, as does geography or history. 'It is essentially a skill subject'. In fact, language is 'not a subject at all', it is rather 'an activity in which there are the four basic skills of understanding, speaking, reading and writing' (pp. 4-5). Language teaching is instruction in the acquisition of these skills, as with swimming or bicycle riding. Though she does not present it in those terms, her notion of skills learning has resonance of the later Wittgensteinian view that language use is the utilization of concepts in 'language games', rather than skills learning in the mechanical sense. Thus:

(a) For the learning process to be meaningful, it must be in the context of what actually happens in the classroom (p. 9). That will enable the pupil to 'enact' the home and wider environment. Language structure <u>and</u> content is acquired 'as parts of whole utterances or sentences used in meaningful situations' (p. 10).

(b) ESL needs special facilities such as withdrawal classes within the school. In them children will receive formal language teaching and aspects of the school curriculum (p. 15). This must be necessitated on purely educational grounds and should have no 'racial overtones' (p. 19). The number of children in any class should average between 12 and 15 (p. 18).

(c) It 'need hardly be repeated' that the purpose of these classes is to teach them English (p. 18); mother-tongue maintenance appears to have no significance at all.

(d)   The aim of (c) and of special centres for 'social training', are to help the children adjust to British life (p. 15), and through English integrate them into the school and society (pp. 18-19).

In sum, what Derrick presents in the form of second-language teaching of English is practical, skills oriented, contextual, and liberal, with strong elements of withdrawal. Her aim is both to improve the teaching of English to black children and integrate them and enhance their lives' opportunities in the British social context.

THE BILINGUAL CHALLENGE

The contemporary bilingual support approaches are as much a part of this liberal tradition as they try to escape from it. Many of the arguments used to justify this escape are collected in a book entitled English as a Second Language in the United Kingdom edited by Christopher Brumfit et al. (6) Without challenging the practical skills orientation and contextual liberalism of Derrick, these arguments support bilingual approaches by using four types of arguments: the social context arguments which emphasize the broad social and school context of black children; those which emphasize the importance and relevance of learning English while reinforcing mother tongue; the broad humanist arguments, and in small measure the philosophical arguments pertaining to concept formation.

The social context arguments

These identify the institutional and cultural racism that is daily endured by students (Ellis, p. 6, Kimberley, p. 92). (6) Apparently, the studying of language and dialect (Kimberley, p. 92, p.96) and collaborative teaching with subject specialist (Ellis, p. 11), will help dismantle this racism. TESL approaches are assimilationist, and allow withdrawal of children and are probably racist (Ellis, p. 21, Robinson, p. 32). (6) Linguistic isolation exploits and disenfranchises black people (Brumfit, p. 176). On the other hand, the 'antiracist' whole-school approach sees integration in pluralistic terms, starting from the point of view of black children and communities, both of which give prominence and power to black teachers and students. The autonomy of TESL is illegitimate, if it distances itself from 'social context and the personal beliefs and feelings of the learners'. Teachers, students, and black communities now require that English should be learnt as 'part of the development of capacities to participate fully in British society without losing essential communal and individual preferences' (Brumfit, p. v).

181

Mother-tongue maintenance

The arguments that insist that mother-tongue maintenance is part of the learning of English are as diverse as they are persuasive. They present moral, political, and purely utilitarian reasons for this coupling. But the fact that at present mother tongue is largely taught by voluntary community groups, is indicative of the low priority the education service gives it (Robinson, p. 40). In fact, mother tongues are a 'national resource rather than a problem' (p. 27).

(a) Their maintenance and the cultures that bind them will aid the learning of the second language (Robinson, p. 36). Languages complement and do not conflict and 'erode the position of another' (p. 26). By supporting the existing language base of a child, the teacher helps, rather than hinders, them in learning a second or third language (see also Skutuabb-Kangas and Toukomaa).

(b) Bilingual approaches have 'cognitive and linguistic' benefit for the child. They increase their self-esteem and confidence (p. 43) and reinforce and counter social and psychological tensions and make the embracement of another language possible with greater confidence, expertise, and enthusiasm (Ellis, p. 19).

(c) As well as increasing the status of the children and bilingual support teachers and their languages, mother-tongue reinforcement leads to collaborative work with subject teachers and helps to end black people's isolation and marginalization. The partnership brings both teachers' shared 'insights, perspectives, and experiences on the problem of how best to cater for different stages of language development within the same classroom' (Chatarin, p. 182). (6)

(d) It is also argued that bilingualism increases school, community, and parent relationship, thus facilitating children's 'communication with their parents, a vital element in the educational development of the children, ... and strengthen the links between the children's schools and their families' (Parekh, p. 188) (5) It gives educationalists the opportunity to serve the whole family, thus turning 'ESL departments, ... headteachers, local community workers' into campaigners for improved procedures and provision (Bailey, p. 75). (6)

(e) Finally, 'we recognize that language (and literacy) is the key to educational and economic opportunity', (Bailey, p. 68). Radicals, according to Kimberley, go further: they argue that language is a key to the control of the media, the government, and other institutions.

Humanistic arguments

These both emphasize democracy and internationalism, and in most part reflect classical liberal education aegis, but maybe have the potential to go beyond that.

The democratic argument concerning the bilingual issue breaks down into three sections. First of all, going by their heroic efforts to set up community languages schools on hundreds of pounds per year grant-aid monies, it is clear that black parents are extremely keen to preserve and develop their children's mother tongue, culture, and social and religious practices that bind them, while also insisting that they learn English. Second, bilingualism can be said to have democratic implications in a pedagogic context. The point is well made by Hilary Hester (6) who argues that by acting as researchers, teachers too learn from watching bilingual children in a classroom. Their association with these children becomes both an in-service and a curriculum development initiative (p. 64). Past prescriptive techniques which dictate to teachers how language must be taught give way to 'something much more open-ended and exploratory, which mirrors the way in which many primary teachers are used to working with children' (pp. 64-5). Learning becomes an investigation and the collection of evidence for the classroom and a basis for future planning. Third, I would add, students too join the educational partnership. Secondary schools particularly will benefit from this move away from didactic to a participative form of teaching. Such examples already exist in the teaching of English (Kimberley, p. 92) and in whole-school curriculum developments of some Sheffield schools. They show that participation makes pupils self-confident, interested, and successful. Thus, we can render the learning of a second language a relatively routine and unthreatening activity and make its embracement voluntary and enthusiastic. Fourth, teachers become more accountable to the black communities, in as much as they acknowledge their needs and take advice on the best ways of meeting them.

If liberal and critical education is about breaking down barriers between 'races' and cultures and fostering internationalism and cultural diversity, then bilingualism has a role to play: it can help widen the curriculum and make it more rational. Hilary Hester suggests that one way children appreciate each other's languages and cultures is by sharing them in classroom learning (p. 62). In fact, Kimberley argues, teachers too benefit when languages and cultures break out of their 'nationalisms' and 'are reformed and reinterpreted in different contexts' (p. 92).

> National languages and literatures written in them can be used to create a strait-jacket of nationalistic thinking or open up inter-cultural understanding. Students can be taught to use language within a narrow set of limits or be given access to modes of analysis and expression which give them power to act

upon the world (p. 98).

What is now emerging is that mother-tongue maintenance is valuable not just to the black bilingual student but also benefits the monolingual teacher and student while also becoming a form of a critique of chauvinism and narrowness.

The real tour de force against insularity and for cultural diversity is to be found in Claude Lévi-Strauss books, including Structural Anthropology, The Savage Mind and Totemism. (8) He completes Kant's project in philosophical anthropology which tried to show that even as individuals, all people have an intuitive sense of time and space that gives them the shared ability to judge correctly the reality that surrounds them. Lévi-Strauss makes this argument more concrete by arguing that implicit in and realizable out of the human, social and cultural symbols, myths, and totems, is a universal structuring mind which is the same for all people of different cultures and 'races'. In cultural manifestations of all communities are indicative universal meanings which underline the egalitarian origins and essential translatability of all human knowledge.

Bikhu Parekh (5) makes similar points at a less elevated level, but starting from the particular rather than the universal. He chides British people for their 'linguistic parochialism'. By viewing foreign languages in instrumental and utilitarian terms, we fail to appreciate their importance in our children's education. Seeing it as a mere means of communication rather than as

> a vehicle of culture, the way a community articulates its conception of the world and becomes aware of itself ... (until we realise) that learning them is a way of expanding imagination and deepening cultural sensitivity, we can hardly avoid seeing them in purely instrumental and utilitarian terms. (pp. 185-6)

Apparently we should consider ourselves lucky that foreign languages are at least viewed thus according to the Assistant Masters Association, (9) for a 'British parent will coyly admit to his (sic) shortcomings in geography or algebra but actually boast of his (sic) incompetence in French' (p. 2).

What Parekh is articulately observing concerns not just the welfare of the black but particularly of the white child. For him, the consequences of linguistic parochialism lead to ethnocentrism, insularity, intolerance, and ignorance. Such children think Punjabi is 'stupid jabbering', and 'Arabs cannot even write: they write from right to left' (p. 186). Parochialism limits the child's understanding and experience of the world. It 'restricts his (sic) emotional, moral and intellectual growth' (p. 186).

Knowledge of languages gives one an understanding of particular societies. For example, the egalitarian 'You' in English offends the sense of 'social hierarchy and of differential worth of different categories' used for servant, friend, or headteacher found in his language (p. 186). A similar example to Parkeh's is to be found in Swahili, where pronouns do not constitutionally carry gender identification. To indicate the gender of the subject, a gender category has to be added to the pronoun; which has made the recent necessity of inventing non-sexist concepts of personhood unnecessary. An understanding of this language and culture will lead one to recognize how Waswahilis think about gender and not show, as some thought in the past, that it indicated linguistic non-differential backwardness. As Parekh puts it, to learn English was for him:

> to learn the value of moral and social equality ... acquiring a new set of values ... an ethical system ... . Linguistic parochialism, therefore, denies the English child access to forms of thoughts and values embodied in other languages, and imprisons him (sic) within the relatively narrow range of ideas and emotions articulated in his (sic) language. (p. 186)

This child becomes convinced there is only 'one true way to describe and conceptualise the world', making the 'familiar mistake of confusing the limits of language with the limits of the world itself' (p. 186). Unable to 'transcend his (sic) language' and having no 'critical detachment from it', the monolingual child is 'overwhelmed by it, tends to mystify it, fails to grasp its conventional and arbitrary nature' (p. 187). The child is also denied the fun of learning a foreign language in uninhibited word play, music, and poetry, and is therefore probably denied the possibility of learning it.

Concept formation

By the above view, words and languages are a lot more than 'ideal names' which 'express the true forms of things in letters and syllables' as Plato had Socrates spelling it out to poor Hermogenes and Craytylas (10) (p. 55). Plato thought naming was the process of putting 'the true natural name of each thing into sounds and syllables' and thus representing their ideality (p. 54).

The assumptions behind bilingual arguments above also pose a more profound view of language than that adduced by empiricists. For though empiricists rightly dispense with Platonic essentialism, they bind language to individuals' experiences, codified in their ideas as they express them. John Locke, in An Essay Concerning Human Understanding puts it this way: (11) 'Words ... stand for nothing but the ideas in the mind of him (sic) that uses them ... words are the marks of ... the ideas of the speaker' (pp. 207-8). For Locke, language has no essential connection to the object since words do not resemble what they signify, both merely express the individuals' personal experiences in their idealization forthwith. He thus rescues language from the nightmare of Plato's metaphysics and delivers it to his own private one.

Notions of concept formation which arise from bilingual arguments must be dissociated from both these views. Here language is social, contextual, and profoundly creative. Parekh (5) insists that the parochial child who is deprived of the experience of foreign languages will also lack 'cognitive and conceptual flexibility, a diversified structure of intelligence, a strong imagination and the ability to invent as opposed to manipulate systems and codes' (p. 187). All these regrets alert us to Wittgenstein's view of language set in 'forms of life' and 'language games'- According to this view, and those against Basil Bernstein, Parekh is clearly exaggerating the monolingual child's linguistic deprivation and probably code restriction. (12)

He implies too rigid a distinction between the acquisition of 'language' as a conceptual framework and languages. In addition, he implies that learning foreign languages, is the only way we can learn about other societies, which is of course also an exaggeration. Children, monolingual or working class, clearly have conceptual flexibilities and diversified structures of intelligence and imaginations; they are simply formed differently and supporting slightly dissimilar varieties and worldviews from bilingual ones. Nevertheless, the points that Parekh makes are important on at least four grounds.

First, the views he expresses appear to defy both the naive realism of Plato and the solipsistic notion of language advocated by some empiricists. Second, they accept language represents a social process and arises out of our cultural creativities. Third, that social context does not simply compose the background setting, but also constitutes the linguistic content. Finally, these views restate the rationale of education: language acquisition results from a learning process and is not an outcome of some natural proclivities.

Many of the arguments for bilingualism and concept formation have tended to be classroom oriented and what follows may at first sight appear to be unconnected. However, even if the classroom teacher does not offer the grounding, it clearly needs to be drawn out. In the rest of this section on concept formation, therefore, I shall examine the second, third, and fourth grounds at a little greater depth in terms of Wittgenstein's notions of 'forms of life' and 'language games', and see where their implications lead us.

Social context of language

Wittgenstein ties together living, concept formation, comprehension, and language in a unitary embodiment of being. The study of language, I would then suggest, cannot be separated from 'doing' sociology of knowledge and language, because language itself is understandable only within the overall context of social and linguistic rules and organizational assumptions of each unit that speaks or writes it. Derek Phillips (13) puts it this way:

> Our form of life limits what is (conceptually) possible for us ... not only do universes of discourse, language games, and so on, available to people, influence what they think, what they will regard as evidence, as compelling, as consistent, and so on, but they also determine what people can see. (p. 99)

Meanings of words are situation specific and are related to use. 'There is not ... some correct usage for words that holds for all ... the 'same' word may be used differently and have different meanings in the language - games of poetry, philosophy and religions' (p. 29). In the Philosophical Investigations, Wittgenstein contradicts both naturalism and voluntarism thus:

> So you are saying that human agreement decides what is true and what is false?' - it is what human beings say that is true and false; and they agree in the language they use. That is not agreement in opinions but in form of life.
> (Quoted in Phillips, p.30)

For a word to be translated into another language, or maybe even be passed on in the same language, we need to transport it with its social context, emotions and assumptions (pp. 34-5). Wittgenstein summarizes the issue in this aphorism: 'every sign by itself seems dead. What gives it life? - In use it is alive' (Phillips, p.37). As Phillips puts it:

> All of us acquire a language as part of growing up; we are socialised into the use of language within a given form of life. This provides us with the conceptual apparatus (rules, meanings, conventions) which constitute our perceptual possibilities. (p. 101)

In short, language presupposes a human society and its activities. For many linguistic philosophers (see also Austin) (14) speech is an activity 'along with eating and sleeping' (Phillips, p. 29). The teaching of language to, as much as the learning of language from others, must therefore at some level presuppose the appropriation and comprehension of their social and linguistic rules. Bilingualism makes the creation and development of such a context fundamental to both the bilingual child's development and the full learning of English. The point is best illustrated by an example.

Wittgenstein insists that 'pain' is intelligible within a particular social context and given rules. Let me examine the use of this word written in three languages - Arabic, Swahili, and English - against the same experience. Let us imagine the pain that will be experienced by a wife or husband from one of these linguistic groups as they are experienced in the Yemen, Zanzibar, and Canterbury. Just by describing it thus, I have already subscribed a number of variables in connection with different languages, gender and national and cultural specificities within the same language groups. It cannot be, then, a simple matter of describing pain as people 'feel' it, for if that is to be comprehensible to the other, the mutual contexts of each other's social organizations and linguistic rules must also be gleaned. Otherwise, they will be talking to each other through dictionary definitions and understanding completely different things from their conversation; each to their own.

Let me push this illustration further. Imagine it is the wife who leaves the husband. If we accept that words like pain are complex symbolic representations of profound social and linguistic rules of particular groups, then, 'pain' to Yemeni/Swahili/English men must be as different as it is similar. Further, within each language, words assume several levels of meaning - perhaps some are core and other outer ones - which when grouped communicate 'pain'. If we imagine the core meaning as a ring, then outer rings will constitute the weaker meanings, or more accurately shades of meaning which imply subtleties, ambiguities, creativities, obscurities, and the taking of chances in pronouncements. (The purpose of using 'rings' of meaning is simply to provide a quick illustration of my argument and must not, even in a weak sense, be taken to be an analogy.) The shades of meaning stretch the life experience to the limit and make the foreign learner's life impossible. When persistently and laboriously pursued and skillfully articulated, these outer rings of meanings may be shared with other language speakers as well as the core rings of meaning. Now let us return to the pain of the dejected husband in three linguistic and national groups.

The Yemeni husband's core experience of 'pain' will probably relate to the shame of being left. Others will follow which will most likely include a sense of lack of companionship, inconvenience, diminution, anger, and betrayal. A Swahili husband will most likely feel the sense of isolation most strongly, but then experience the lack of companionship, shame, diminution, anger, and so on. An English husband will most likely first feel betrayed, then lonely and inconvenienced. Of course, the cultural and linguistic parameters are also articulated by individual preferences and biographies, which will complicate the example even further.

The point should be clear. I do not aim to represent a real situation, but to illustrate the intimacy between language rules and cultural ones, and how meanings are totally locked into each other. I shall return to the implications of these factors.

Language games

Wittgenstein's notion of language games helps us both to understand how meanings such as above are constructed within social life and how we can identify the educative process involved in concept formation. Wittgenstein makes an analogy between using language and playing games. In both cases the activities are prescribed by rules and conventions which determine permissible moves and evaluations of competence. In the acquisition of language, a child learns to use signs and words - language games. These language games train us to see and interpret the world as it is being shared by those whom we talk to and live with. When we encounter new human specialist activities like science or come up against a novel experience or word, say from another country, 'we acquire an ability to play these other 'language games' only through an appeal to and reliance upon the rules and conventions governing the language game in the form of life where we originally acquired language' (Phillips, p. 101). This would support the view that a good knowledge of one's mother tongue (13) creates a sound foundation for learning another language. These games constantly change; new ones are created and old ones are discarded.

What is relevant for our discussion about this is language games provide a multiplicity of meanings and permutations in the usage of particular words in any specific language. Existing meanings and permutations are available to indviduals through the appropriation of understood rules and conventions. New meanings are created through the extension and the use of these rules in unfamiliar contexts, through an education process. The more correct games and contexts one gets involved in, the greater becomes one's comprehension of the shared and ultimately objective world.

The process becomes both strained and creative in 'poetics', when writers and readers take licence. The situation is stressful when people fail to <u>see</u> the poet's extension, and creative when they appropriate and normalize it and thus enlarge or restructure existing permutations. Ultimately, the teaching of language that assumes social life, language games, and creativities is likely to be the one to engage young people and thus bring the best results. So even as a form of pedagogy, it is probably the most desirable.

Implications of social context and language games to concept formation

The implications of the above discussion concern a number of issues: intercommunal/interlinguistic translation, personal development, educative process, social responsibility, and so on.

Much has been made in the German cultural and philosophical debates on <u>Geisteswissenschaften</u> (see Dilthey, Gadamer and Husserl) and British social anthropology (see Wilson (3)) about the difficulties of intercultural/interlinguistic communications. Both the practical examples of bilingual learning and the above discussion undermine these artificially imposed conceptual sanctions. People do communicate and they do so because they learn about each other. As Parekh eloquently argues, language is not just exchanging words, but it is about learning of others' social and moral preferences, thought structures. and ways of life.

To learn another language is to step out of one's prescribed life-world into another's, and return to one's own a changed person, a much extended person, an enhanced and knowledgeable person. Now this person will have a greater range of ideas, with subtle or even exotic turns in them; now better equipped and raised to an orientation of life-creativity, rather than life-bound activity.

It is arguable that this context must lead to greater personal development. If we return to my construction of core and outer rings of meaning, a person superimposing various core and outer rings of meanings to form a complex stucture is bound to habituate subtlety of thinking and width of vision. It is as if the multilingual person is at any one time standing at a vantage point that allows her or him to inhabit different worlds of meaning harmoniously merged into one complex. As it were, the more languages that one speaks, or is literate in, the more conceptual muscles one has to flex in the process of knowledge acquisition.

Of all the arguments presented in this debate over bilingualism, I probably rate this aspect most highly, both for its depth and because it underlines the educative process. What is important about it is not just its humanism and internationalism but that contrary to those who overemphasize the relativity of rule governance (Winch), (21) it sees human interaction as an educative process. Other languages are total systems, it is true. But our <u>ability to learn</u> them, by definition, implies the <u>habitation</u> of other languages and cultures: the stuff real civilization is made of. Synthesis and latter innovation occurs in both host and outside societies as a result of pursuing shared assessments and critical evaluations by cross-habitors. As Lévi-Strauss would have it, the existence of contrastive systems indicate communication and not enclosure. Thus if bilingualism does not necessarily increase international understanding and harmony, it must at least improve our ability to create universal categories and bring about social and technical developments which will question the existence and continuation of oppressive parochial societies and communities. In other words, it is a process which must by definition also increase our sense of social responsibility.

As I indicated in the introduction, while it may be justified to claim all this for bilingualism or multilingualism, I am doubtful that by simply employing bilingual teachers to continue ESL support work we will deliver all of this, particularly since bilingual support work continues to be skill-based as described by Derrick (4) and thus quintessentially second order, without content and dependent on subject areas. As in TESL, bilingual teachers then become over-preoccupied with technique rather than with the content of language. They become unable to offer to children the speakers' literature, poetry. philosophy, social and political knowledge, and preferences. Thus, despite aims to the contrary, the teaching of English or mother tongue tells children little more about the peoples whose languages they are learning than does a good dictionary or textbook. Leaving aside the educational lost opportunities here, any language taught in this way becomes extremely impoverished and boring. It is then not surprising to me that the AMA representatives have overheard previously bitten parents <u>boast</u> of their ignorance of French.

Multilingual studies

Robinson (6) begins to pick up on my theme which hopes to go further than skills-based learning of language when he insists that rather than treating second-language learning as a transient 'self-eliminating' marginal activity, it should become a 'permanent feature of a bilingual education programme in a stable, multilingual and multicultural society' (p. 37).

So what is multilingual studies? In the way that I envisage it, there are already numerous models to look at and evaluate in higher education such as Classics and European and Oriental Studies. The aim is to construct an integrated subject which 'though it concentrates on language issues' can, through them, draw on philosophical, sociological, political, and historical texts of, and maybe in, those languages. If, at this stage, I suggest that the languages we should concentrate on are the mother-tongue languages of black children and various forms of English and Creole, it is not meant to bar European languages.

It is simply to recognize and respond to the neglected or special needs of these children. Once these needs are satisfied, or maybe even at the same time, it would be educationally valuable to include other European languages. But what should be recognized about multilingual studies is that it is a new subject for a new generation. It is neither merely the learning of Standard or second-language English, nor is it simply the maintenance of the parents' language - whether written or spoken. It denotes a complex new dynamic that forges languages and cultures, politics and philosophies for a new generation of keen, young, British, working-class, black people, who will make liars of those who accuse them of being caught <u>between</u> two cultures, implying confusion and lack of fulfilment <u>in their</u> lives. What these young people are in fact doing is existentially forging a new culture for their own benefit, which will integrate their parents and enrich the British community as a whole by also addressing the neglect of regional and working class English.

The aim and content of the curriculum could be to outline the linguistic rules and conventions of specific languages as well as the intellectual and concrete worlds that surround them, as are described in their poems, literature, social and political organizations, economic and cultural preferences, and religious and philosophical discourses. An important aspect of that curriculum must follow up the historical and political <u>relationship between</u> the said languages and cultures and their resolution in contemporary society. The intention of this subject would not so much be to teach students English or Punjabi, but to help them inhabit the two worlds in which these languages are spoken. It would also be an important aim of such a subject to bring about genuine integration of black children into British society, not only by teaching them to be English, but also by recognizing the fact that British culture is now a lot more multifaceted. As such, it is not just right that Punjabi children should appreciate that language and what goes with it, but white children too. Clearly, some multicultural work already addresses these issues, especially in primary schools, but it still lacks a discipline base that this subject could provide. What multicultural studies has not provided, however, is the raising of awareness of not only spoken and written English from abroad, but many working-class regional varieties from Britain. Clearly that task belongs to English departments at all levels, but their inclusion here will doubtless stimulate a creative comparative context for all students and pupils.

So the development of multilingual studies will require that there should be courses and degrees in multilingual studies. These degrees or courses should be backed up by high-level academic research in higher education institutes. Schools will need to identify posts in multilingual studies from their modern-language allocation in those areas with a large number of children speaking community languages; or they could perhaps reorganize existing teaching. Following which, LEAs and the DES will have to support schools in their in-service needs. All these developments will have resource implications. Clearly any intention to move in that direction must compute for this resource. At this point, however, the most important requirement is that we reflect and debate these matters to the full.

But what would be the consequence of introducing multilingual studies for Standard English, TESL, bilingual support, and community language teaching? In general terms, the introduction of this subject will not only help extend or include for the first time different dialects of English originating from the regions and Creole from the Caribbean, but also bring forth literary contributions from Africa and India - and elsewhere - as part of our Standard English curriculum where it is not already happening.

Specifically, as far as TESL is concerned, multilingual studies will continue to undermine its philosophical base as bilingual support has done. But now, monolingual teachers with considerable experience of TESL will not only be able to participate in the new subject with its wider base than support teaching and Standard English, but also draw on it to help them continue working alongside bilingual teachers. Monolingual children will similarly benefit, as there is no reason why some of them should not opt for such a subject in secondary school, if they had some background in primary school.

As far as bilingual support teaching is concerned, the

development of multilingual studies will clearly be of great benefit to it. My assumption here is that bilingual support work will still be necessary for those children who need to learn English and maintain their mother tongue, and will therefore have to continue as such. What would be different for the bilingual support teachers is that they will now not only have the support and benefits from a discipline base, but also can teach in it and participate in its development. As such, they will be in a better position to develop a career in the discipline area and within the school. They will have greater resources to call upon and more substantive in-service training to participate in. From their new base, they can still participate, collaborate with, and influence other colleagues, but now with great authority and responsibility. When all has been said and done, they will also have the authority to introduce new materials in the curriculum, without always being sanctioned by subject teachers.

But what about community language teaching? Will it still be required? The answer is clearly affirmative. Presumably some of the community language teachers will participate in the delivery of multilingual studies, but there will still be people wanting to learn modern languages as they are traditionally taught. There is no reason to assume that the development of multilingual studies will diminish the need for Urdu or Arabic any more than development studies downgraded sociology or politics. On the contrary, the thriving of one is bound to bolster the other.

So the consequence of developing this new discipline is more likely to fulfil several existing needs, rather than undermine current work. It is bound to strengthen both second-language and mother-tongue learning, broaden Standard English, integrate new cultures and ideas, and open up traditional perspectives and areas and involve monolingual teachers and students in a new and exciting discipline. Subsequently, a successful evolution of such a discipline is likely to have an important impact on literacy education and traditional British chauvinism.

If young people get interested in learning about languages and what binds them culturally, there is a good chance a lot fewer will leave school with literacy problems and negative attitudes towards 'foreign' languages. It is even likely that some of them will get interested following up specific languages at a higher level too. That will not only ensure the survival of community languages and dialects, but also would increase their demand in tertiary and higher education. Concurrently, a thriving interest in community languages and dialects will stimulate a creative symmetrical relationship between the young people and their parents and, subsequently, the parents and the school. In due course, if this relationship is healthy, it is bound also to benefit the parents, some of whom are in need of literacy education in their mother tongue and many in English literacy and fluency.

I am convinced that multilingual studies will also play an

important role in slowly discrediting the traditional British chauvinism and class hierarchy deeply buried in the homilies of Standard English. A lot of this challenge is already apparent in the classroom. But by making it part of an organized discipline, it will encourage classroom teachers to seek a more detailed scientific base for this challenge to require researchers in historical linguistics to provide its evidence in a convenient way. In this sense the challenge will be to colonial attitudes which fuel racism in Britain, and to class manipulation whose reduction is bound to minimize working-class racism and engender greater solidarity between black and white working people. By the same token, perhaps through the involvement of black women especially, multilingual studies is bound to provide the context through which some very interesting findings on the use of language that oppresses women can be compared with the way it exploits blacks. As such, multilingual studies will not only benefit from work done by feminists, but will make a contribution in disseminating both these ideas and their struggle.

Thus, the introduction of such a subject will have relevance for black and white children at secondary and especially primary level where it can do the most good. It would also, as did sociology, slowly work its way into all other subject areas to the benefit of other languages and the curriculum as a whole.

Two considerations are bound to be looming in people's minds by now: the lack of new resources and the Education Reform Act. First, it is my feeling that important educational discussions should not be terminated because we have a reactionary government which wishes to turn learning into the study of formal mathematics, English, and following orders. Indeed, particularly since that is the climate, we must keep raising new issues and remind one another of the traditionally important ones. Second, it is our experience as educationalists that, despite a constant shortage of funding and excess of limited imagination of the establishment, we still find ways of developing new ideas and improving our children's learning. I would therefore suggest that we also pursue the above notions if they have any merit in them. But surely there are more positive reasons for such discussions and experiments than the defence of education against recent Tory attacks? It was suggested in the introduction that bilingualism indicates the possibility of new avenues which will take us beyond the limits of traditional liberal education towards a more progressive provision. I shall turn to this aspect after dealing with some possible objections.

Some people may object to the introduction of multilingual studies on at least four grounds: (a) that it would oppose the excellent work of monolingual and bilingual teachers of language awareness; (b) that the creation of another discipline is not necessarily the best way of introducing important new ideas; (c) that subject orientation is against child-centredness; and (d) that it would undermine the learning of Standard English by black and working-class children.

The notion of multilingual studies is not opposed to language awareness; it is probably a more coherent and in-depth extension of some of its work. The experience in higher education especially, but also in schools, has proved that the introduction of new disciplines such as sociology, development studies, language studies to the curriculum in the last twenty years has been the most effective way of introducing new ideas in a system of education which is organized upon and dominated by discipline areas. I suppose that I would probably agree in principle that subject areas should slowly be phased into an integrated curriculum in schools, especially one which is student-centred. I would, however, question the effectiveness of encouraging that development by the use of vulnerable development areas of learning to lead the way. First of all, I would have thought, bilingual ESL, Creole, non-Standard English, and community languages, all need to be fully recognized, and then maybe take part in the general move away from the traditional subject base, if that were truly believed to be advantageous to secondary and especially tertiary levels. Further, it is not part of my argument that the inclusion of mother tongue or dialect should deliberately or accidentally reduce the possibilities of excellence in and criticial awareness of Standard English. Indeed, as I have already argued, the contrary is the case: mother-tongue maintenance appears to improve the learning of Standard English.

THE CONSLIDATION OF PROGRESSIVE EDUCATION

The mid and late 1980s are experiencing a different kind of educational radicalism from the libertarian and socialist ones of the 1960s and 1970s. Meanwhile, very few people are interested in the philosophical bases for our teaching and of schools. It may be that since the introduction of comprehensive education, teachers are too busy getting on with the actual business of delivering exemplary education to find time to discuss philosophy. On the other hand, that may be due to complacency, as MacKenzie (15) reminds us in those ringing tones from 1970: 'The introduction of comprehensive education meant that the school in Coal Town faced the possibility of being taken over by the traditional and orthodox grammar school' (p. 134).

It is part of my contention here that bilingualism as spelt out will not only consolidate what was achieved by those progressive initiatives, but also contribute new developments. This topic by itself deserves full treatment, but will only receive a brief mention here.

First, arguments about the need for bilingualism, as those which focus on school sexism and racism, revive debates over equal opportunities, previously conducted in terms of class. In this case educational benefits will not only be accrued to white working-class youth, but now to black and white working-class men <u>and</u> women.

Discussions about bilingualism very much raise all these issues. Second, if bilingualism will help undermine linguistic chauvinism and class hierarchy and cultural imperialism and underachievement by recognizing the importance of other languages, similar claims should be made for geography, history, English, media studies, and even science and mathematics. There is a growing body of knowledge which questions as fraudulent, class and gender oppressive, and Eurocentric the whole view that science is value free and totally unaffected by cultural and regional prejudices. (16-20) It would seem that universal categories are neither genderless, classless, timeless, nor stateless, but are a human construction which - as does language - benefit from cross-fertilization. Like language too, it is a human creative mode that is not symbolized by enduring liberal values, but is expressed through concrete contingent needs of everyday life. Only conceived thus will language and science and their teaching respond to the demands of new generations. Third, bilingualism will assist in black and working-class community development and literacy education. It will generate a creative context between the school and the community, involving parents in schools and teachers and pupils in literacy education in the community. Fourth, black community involvement in schools, as that of working people, is bound to help the development of democratic approaches in school life by making it accountable to parents and students. The participation of both sets in the process of learning and will reduce managerial and classroom authoritarianism. Fifth, this emphasis, put on bilingual education as community and not just individual development and enlightenment, mirrors an extremely progressive shift that has been taking place in school teaching. Eventually, within this framework, the responsibility for learning and dealing with social problems is transferred from the lonely individual to the whole community. Education then becomes not an accumulation of private knowledge that the privileged strategically let out to impress others, but is socially stimulating and responsive knowledge that some people may well find use for. Education thus becomes a basic ingredient for personal and social creativity and development. Finally, unfettered linguistic competence, as Kimberley pointed out, (6) will constitute a permanent critique of the establishment. When it comes from working people, it ensures a responsible use of power.

CONCLUSION

I will conclude by suggesting that after bilingual support must follow multilingual studies. Without the latter, the former will not only remain impoverished, it will continue to assist in the marginalization of black working-class children and low status of bilingual teachers, and have only a limited impact on the rest of the curriculum. If these difficulties and others already discussed are to be seriously addressed, schools and LEAs will have to rethink their resourcing and educational policies. If there is anything in the argument that concepts are enriched and understanding is enhanced by knowledge of other frameworks and worlds, perhaps to lead to the creation of an educationally relevant, egalitarian, radical, and exciting future, then we must have much to gain for our children and ourselves by the introduction of multilingual studies. Language is a symbolic expression of individual and community life. If that life reflects a multiplicity of backgrounds, experiences and languages, our education system must learn to recognize their worth, create ways of absorbing them in the curriculum, and promote sharing them with everybody else.

NOTES AND REFERENCES

1. I want to thank my brother Abdulrazak, Chris Searle, Ed Edwards, Lerlean Willis, Bill Walton, John Hull, Steve Anwyll, Pete Gibbon, and Alan Scott for reading and commenting on the manuscript. It would also have been difficult to continue this project with any sense of confidence and enjoyment but for the encouragement from a number of colleagues in the Sheffield LEA, especially those in the SUMES team.
2. Gurnah, A. (1987) 'Gatekeepers and caretakers: Swann, Scarman and the social policy of containment', B. Troyna (ed.) Racial Inequality in Education, London: Tavistock.
3. Truman, A.R. (1965) (ed.) Colour in Britain, London: BBC. Wilson, B. (ed.) (1970) Rationality, New York: Harper Touchbooks.
4. Derrick, J. (1966) Teaching English to Immigrants, Harlow: Longman.
5. Parekh, B. (1986) 'Bilingualism and Educational Investment', New Community XIII: no. 2.
6. Brumfit, C., Ellis, R. and Levine, J. (eds) (1985) English as a Second Language in the United Kingdom, Oxford: The British Council/Pergamon. All references to Ellis, Kimberley, Robinson, Brumfit, Chatarin, Bailey, and Hester are from this book.
7. Skutnabb-Kangar, T. and Toukamaa, P. (1976) 'Teaching migrant children their mother tongue and learning the language of the host country in the context of the socio-cultural situation of the migrant family', University of Tampere, Finland Research Reports.
8. Lévi-Strauss, C. (1966) The Savage Mind, London: Weidenfeld & Nicholson; (1968) Structural Anthropology, Harmondsworth: Penguin Books; (1973) Totemism, Harmondsworth: Penguin Books.
9. Assistant Masters Association (1979) Teaching Modern Languages in Secondary Schools, London: Hodder & Stoughton.
10. Plato (1974) Craytylas, printed in A. Freemantle A Primer of

Linguistics, New York: St Martin's Press.

11. Locke, J. (1977) An Essay Concerning Human Understanding, London: Dent.

12. There is an awful lot of good and bad sociological material on these issues. I chose not to review them in fear that it would have taken us too far away from the specific discussion I was interested in, without adding that much to it.

13. Phillips, D. (1977) Wittgenstein and Scientific Knowledge: a sociological perspective, London: Macmillan.

14. Austin, J.L. (1971) The Philosophy of Language, in J.R. Searle (ed.), Oxford: Oxford University Press.

15. Mackenzie, R.E. (1970) State School, Harmondsworth: Penguin Books.

16. Jarvie, I.C. (1964) The Revolution in Anthropology, London: Routledge & Kegan Paul.

17. Kuhn, T. (1970) The Structure of Scientific Revolutions, Chicago: University of Chicago Press.

18. Knoor-Cetina, K. and Mackay, M. (1983) Science Observed: Perspectives on the Social Study of Science, London: Sage Publications.

19. Barnes, B. (1974) Scientific Knowledge and Sociological Theory, London: Routledge & Kegan Paul.

20. Levidow, L. and Young, R. (eds) (1981) Science, Technology and the Labour Process, London: CSE Books.

21. Winch, P. (1958) Idea of a Social Science, London: Routledge & Kegan Paul.

Chapter Eleven

THE FURTHER EDUCATION EXPERIENCE

Beverley Bryan

Any consideration of education for equality in Further Education (FE) can only come within the context of a discussion about how black people have been viewed within this society and treated within the school system. Blame lies not within a particular section because prejudicial attitudes run deep and wide. However, much of this book has shown how this system has failed to meet the basic needs of black people. Because of racism on an individual and institutional basis, we received the very worst of what was available. The history of the black movement in this country is marked with the numerous campaigns by black parents, teachers, and students to improve the delivery of education to our community. Amongst them we would include the bussing protest of the late 1960s, against black children being 'farmed' out to white schools; the campaigns throughout the 1970s against the wholesale misplacement of black children in schools for the educationally subnormal (ESN schools) and disruptive units (sin bins); the pressure groups to improve examination results; and the development over several decades of a strong supplementary schools movement. Even though we have made an impact, through our demands, what has yet to be carried out is an assessment of the nature of that impact and how it can be used to further the aspirations of our community. We need to consider every new initiative, questioning its source and beneficiaries. It is this spirit and experience of the black education movement that informs the following contribution.

In order to make some assessment of the FE contribution, it is important to define the nature of this level of post-compulsory education. In the first instance, FE is strongly dependent on the points system that links resources from the funding local education authorities with student numbers. This has meant that, from the outset, FE has been not only strongly vocational in the substance of its provision, but also strongly entrepreneurial in its mode of operation: it has had to look for a market and nurture it in order to secure growth. Traditionally, colleges relied largely on the demands from local industry and on its links with the local labour market to

199

attract greater student numbers. In this respect, FE has been accepted as the last resort for working-class aspirations. However the nature of these courses showed little innovation and reflected traditional discriminatory work patterns and accepted gender divisions within society. Courses were largely white and male, such as building and telecommunications, or largely female, such as secretarial and nursery nursing. In every respect the colleges developed according to the political and economic realities that existed in society at large. It is not surprising, therefore that FE should have been greatly affected by the rising unemployment of the early 1980s, and increasing government overt and covert involvement in this sphere of education. Allied to these factors has been the increasing urgency of black concerns about a significant number of young people who had been failed by the statutory sector. As a result of the schools system's underachievement, black students were looking to the colleges to provide the education that they have missed, that would provide a cushion from the worst effects of the ravages of modern Britain. Many have and do enrol on the vocational courses such as those from the Business and Technician Education Council (BTEC), City and Guilds London Institute (CGLI), and Royal Society of Arts (RSA). They, because of their nationally accepted status, are seen as the route out of unemployment. These courses, however, cannot cater for the needs of all black students because not all who enter are in the traditional mode of FE students. There are a range of needs and demands from those whom the system has so far been unable to serve.

It is partly in response to the changing nature of potential recruits that new developments have taken place in FE to address the demands of this wider range in the student intake. It is two of these developments that I propose to discuss as initiatives that acknowledge the continuing failure of the system and show how the colleges have had to respond to market demand, real or manufactured. I refer to the introduction of the Certificate in Pre-Vocational Education (CPVE) and the development of Access courses. On one level, they would seem to have little in common as CPVE prepares 16-19 year olds for the transition to the world of work and Access prepares older students for higher education. However, they are both innovations in FE, where black students predominate, so it is here that the thorough examination of their purpose must begin. They can both be seen as responses to external pressure to widen the offer in FE by clearing the route to higher education and the high status vocational courses. As non-examined foundation provision, both emphasize preparation and progression to the desired goal. What we need to consider is whether either delivers this objective to the students.

CERTIFICATE IN PRE-VOCATIONAL EDUCATION

CPVE was a national initiative that came out of a debate between government and employers about poor educational standards of school-leavers and their psychological fitness for work. It was a reassertion of the historic tension between schools and industry which centred around the vocationalization of the curriculum. The focus was not on the obvious lack of jobs for young people but rather on their inability to cope with work. What this bogus criticism demonstrated was the Conservative government's reliance on, and deference to, one particular community, i.e. the business lobby, and to the political nostrum that schooling became more or less relevant only in the extent to which it contributed to the enterprise culture, whatever that might mean at any given time. It was a discussion that signally failed to involve teachers, local education authorities, parents, or students. As a result the Secretaries of State for Employment and Education, with the Manpower Services Commission, instituted in 1982 the Technical and Vocational Initiative (TVEI) to ensure the vocational preparation necessary in the last years of compulsory schooling. The underlying motivation was the need to create the reserve army of labour who might never experience real work but who were ready if the call came. This scheme was meant to provide a new full time programme in schools for 14-18 year olds, combining general with technical education, to produce leavers with the flexibility deemed necessary for the workplace. Naturally, there was some resistance from teachers and LEAs who were meant to operate this scheme and had not been consulted before its introduction. Added to this was the general mistrust of an initiative that put vocationalism at an earlier and earlier place in the curriculum. The government had to bring these recalcitrant educators to heel. Without the statutory powers for enforcing a national curriculum that the Education Secretary is now speedily, if haphazardly, accruing, money for training was used as the bait to seduce hard pressed and rate-capped councils to participate in the pilot projects.

CPVE was the next stage of the debate. It came a year after TVEI as an award for 16-19 year olds, from the joint board of Business and Technician Education Council (BTEC) and City and Guilds London Institute (CGLI), to validate the continuing curriculum development instituted by the government and the business community. The stated aim was to rationalize the existing pattern of pre-vocational courses and provide a framework of core and vocational studies to aid transition from school to work. The underlying aim of delaying entry to the job market while getting young people ready for some kind of work was wrapped in a cloak of seemingly progressive ideas that had been in educational forums for many years, going back to primary education. These ideas, however, had never been tried in the tertiary sector, but were discussed and researched in the Further Education Unit (FEU) of the DES. It was acknowledged that a large proportion of older schoolchildren were alienated from the quasi-academic and abstract school curriculum. It was also recognized that colleges could not offer a similar kind of learning experience. They suggested new methods of teaching and learning that were to be more interactive and student-centred.

The teaching for CPVE was to be mixed ability because the admissions policy was open-ended. Anyone who wanted a place on the scheme would be accommodated: from the 'A' level student to those with special educational needs. With flexible timetabling students would be able to divide their time between a wide range of vocational areas to 'taste' what was on offer. The teaching itself would take an integrated approach where subjects like english, mathematics and information technology would not be taught in discrete areas but integrated and related to practical situations and work experience. With the teacher as resource, assignments would be designed to be broad based and open ended, so that students themselves could determine their scope. The teacher's role was therefore supervisory to guide students to appropriate material and to assist them in working at whatever pace suited them.

The assessment procedure was also quite radical. It had been evolving over some years through such boards as the RSA with the help of the FEU. Its main form was profiling, which was a checklist of the skills needed to complete particular tasks. The profile statement would show the kinds of skills that had been successfully demonstrated. They could be communication skills like 'Can create and organise written material in a style suited to the purpose'; or social skills 'Can recognise the worth of other opinions'; or numeracy, problem-solving, and a range of other skills. The profile was not to be an evaluation of the student's competence but a record of individual achievement, an indication of future learning needs, and, at the end of the course, a report of attainment. At each stage, the student would negotiate through the checklist of competences what they had, in fact, learnt on completion of an assignment.

Critical to the packaging of CPVE was the idea of progression. In theory the course would open enormous opportunities to young people that varied from work to 'A' levels. The 'graduate' from the scheme would go out armed with a portfolio of work completed and the checklist of skills as a statement of what they had achieved. The portfolio was designed to replace the requirements for formal qualifications. For employers who would have had experience of CPVE, there would be no difficulty in recognizing the value of a profile. For college administrators, the situation would be much easier as they would have had first hand experience of how the assessment worked.

Significant as the scheme was in the development of an FE pedagogy, because of the source of its sponsorship and its seeming emphasis on a narrow range of skills, it met with considerable resistance from teachers who baulked at the conscriptive element in light of their recent experience of TVEI and YTS. Increasingly, the hand of government was to be seen in all the work of FE. The joint board acted with great purpose. Although it was not peremptorily introduced in Parliament, the board nevertheless gave only three months for consultation even though the new scheme meant abandoning all their own first-level foundation courses. The Inner London Education Authority which had withstood the blandishments of TVEI finally succumbed and became involved in CPVE in 1985. With such overwhelming government and educational pressure the scheme was soon taken up by the colleges. In some cases it offered the only resource for training, but in other cases, however, tutors began to see in the enterprise some possibilities for their work. Many teachers saw it as a unique opportunity to broaden and enrich the curriculum, providing more appropriate assessment procedures and courses that were more relevant to a wide ability range. Added to this was the flexibility and apparent democracy that allowed curriculum development to be directed by staff. As the profile could describe anywhere the student was at, the schemes could take any form in the colleges: the freedom that engendered was momentarily heady! However, the dubious rationale for CPVE could not long sustain what was at best a defective structure.

Criticisms of CPVE can work on many levels, be they political, pedagogical, or practical. The most fundamental is the political and nearly all other criticisms stem from, and return to this position. CPVE was constructed and is delivered as though it is not mediated by race and class. Like its progenitor TVEI, CPVE was meant to be one of those panoply of measures to deal with youth unemployment, which in many areas like the inner cities meant black unemployment. Yet CPVE makes no conscious acknowledgement of the race and class dimension or the political context in which education is located. There is great play made of the fact that it is open ended and for a mixed-ability range, yet most of the students who constitute CPVE classes in London are black, and in other regions undoubtedly working class. The rationale for the course says they are unsure of their career options and come with 'varying degrees of vocational commitment'. What is not addressed is the deep social injustice and ineptitude of the education system that has led them to CPVE. It is, in fact, a scheme for the casualties of the system and, because of racism, black students would be least able to escape the web of low-level, low-status initiatives which characterize provision for those perceived to be at the bottom of the ladder. The reality then, of CPVE, is of a course which is fairly homogeneous. The intake is largely of 16-18 year olds and significantly a large proportion are girls. They are in many ways similar to the earlier groups of students who were on general education courses. They have had a fractured experience of school, emerging with few of the required literacy and study skills. Because the school has failed them and their potential limited by low expectations and the reinforcing of negative stereotypes, they are labelled as non-academic and therefore unsure about their future. What is not appreciated is the tremendous optimism that many bring to the college, after their negative experience of school. Here is a new start and a clean slate, but it is this enthusiasm which is allowed to be dissipated by a deeply flawed pedagogy.

The CPVE methodology is faulty because there is a disjuncture between its curriculum aim, methodology, and target group. The student-centred approach which negotiates the curriculum cannot cope with students who cannot make sense of the way the learning is organized. The loose structure requires that the students have the ability to identify their own learning needs and recognize how those needs can be met. Some degree of self-motivation is expected and the skill to work with the minimum amount of supervision. The student would also need good social skills to negotiate with the teacher and to move in and out of groups as they transfer from one vocational area to another. What is being unfairly demanded is the very highest levels of commitment, confidence, and single-mindedness from the students who have had the least educational success. Students who have been debilitated by the school system, either by overt racism or the more covert and liberal kind, do not want a course that allows them to roam across the curriculum. They come with very clear, if traditional, ideas of what teaching and learning are about. In some areas it is particularly difficult and consequently CPVE has not been successful in the technical area. It is a question of class and culture that the CPVE programme has not yet addressed.

Faced with this mountain of highly personalized and sometimes intangible set of demands, it is not surprising that there is a high drop-out rate and so the spiral of failure continues. It is unfortunate that much of this failure can be masked in FE tutorial-speak such as 'counselled off the course' and 'the necessity of risk taking'. Black students have for too long been at the receiving end of every experiment that has gone on in the educational system; they cannot afford to take any more risks.

At a practical level also, CPVE is questionable in what it offers to black students. Using subjective assessments gives power to white teachers which is not inevitably used in a negative way, but is an extra burden for students and an added risk they have to take. More importantly, a black student who takes a profile to an employer has to compete with more academically orthodox certification, thereby compounding the discrimination they face. In fact, the perception of CPVE, as being of limited value, was clear from the time BTEC decided to withdraw from the joint board and set up its own First Award. How can there be confidence in a product when one of its original designers decides to develop an alternative which in practice operates in direct competition?

What finally cannot be hidden is that CPVE, in spite of its grand if cumbersome design, is at present a second-rate provision which, if offered to black students, has to be viewed with the utmost caution.

It functions largely as an incoherent in-house provision known to, and supported only by, FE providers. Even the new National Council for Vocational Qualification (NCVQ) has yet to decide whether CPVE will fall under its aegis. Who then will be responsible for it? Its piecemeal nature means that it represents all things to all people: it can be everything a teacher has dreamt of and nothing in practice that the student can take away. It is therefore the PR dream that can be marketed by colleges in whatever form they wish. If we compare the parallel and thoroughly considered development of the General Certificate in Secondary Education (GCSE) we can see the distinct contrast. For GCSE there has been a national and informed debate about mixed-ability teaching, continuous assessment, syllabus choice, and criterion referencing. Yet even though CPVE is technically available to an equal number of students, it receives no national coverage and certainly no special features in the 'quality' Sunday supplements. One must wonder if this difference in knowledge, perception, and interest is due to the fact that Cabinet ministers' children will be taking GCSE and not CPVE. The recipe for disaster is already there, if two mixed-ability courses are on offer with one given a national profile and status while the other remains the concern of the providers and a few supporters.

What then can be done with CPVE to produce a more worthwhile pre-vocational offer? The first step has to be an agreement about its practical aim and who it is for. No qualification can be very meaningful if it operates on such a wide span that it can effectively assess the competence of special needs students with moderate learning difficulties and those ready to take 'A' levels. Such a decision to come clean on CPVE and pin down the level and target group requires a more honest and genuine debate involving teachers, employers, and examination boards about how the present vocational courses are being delivered. This would give some concrete and realistic ideas about who is being ill-served by what is available and what needs to be added. The NCVQ would have to be involved if a CPVE-type course is not to be left out of the general reorganization of vocational education. Whatever decisions are made have to be accepted at a national level with proper standardization and must be delivered at a local level which is authority-wide. It is unfortunate that present government plans for cuts in the education system might militate against such a high level of co-ordination.

What is already obvious is that those who can make use of the present vocational course in FE; those who cannot are not just unsure about their career options as CPVE maintains but have been failed by the system and need a firmer, more thorough grounding in basic general education or literacy or core skills. These, in the end, are the most transferable skills that can be defined and are the most clearly required in the transition from school to work. Because of their past school experience, the students will also need more rather than less guidance, structure, and support in the teaching. This would not deny the value of integration but would seek to make it part of a tighter structure and more controllable operation. The teaching would have to be directed and interventionist but the student would be more involved, responding and commenting on a tangible contribution where both parties were concretely involved. Assignment work, for example, would be less open ended with the teacher helping the student more directly, to make the links between what they have learnt and what has yet to be achieved. When the teacher is more involved in the learning process, then that can extend to the areas of personal growth and development. It is here that the profiling statements might be most useful, as a means of self-assessment and learning. The confidence to hold that dialogue with teachers and consider strengths and weaknesses is the kind of vocational skill that lasts.

It is clear therefore that the level of provision being discussed should, if it is being offered, emphasize the 'pre-' rather than the 'vocational'. This means that although vocational elements might be involved through 'tasters', for example, the aim will be to develop those common skills that equip the students to make choices about the next stage in their lives. The emphasis should be on knowing the kinds of recruits the programme is likely to attract and catering to their needs.

ACCESS STUDIES

In this respect, the development of Access courses has shown FE as being more successful in responding to different needs or, more pragmatically, more attractive market forces. Of the two developments, Access has been clearly the more successful. Direct entry to higher education has a long tradition. The most accepted procedure was where applicants were expected to satisfy special admission requirements with perhaps demonstrated knowledge and skills, acquired through previous study. However, Access studies represent the first departure, where the system could be used in an organized way to assist black people. Nevertheless, although the programmes stemmed from a black community demand for better education, white working-class people also took advantage of the provision. Ken Millins' (5) survey showed that they represented 40 per cent of his sample.

The Access programmes, themselves, took many forms but were organized loosely on the American model. They began, in a limited way, in 1978, with a Labour government White Paper from the DES to establish special courses in preparation for entry to higher education. Unemployed people without qualifications were invited to take up places on a foundation course which, if it was successfully completed, would guarantee a place on a designated degree course. A few of these courses were run with Section 11 funding which was money given directly from the Home Office for use with 'ethnic minorities'. Although these were open only to black people, all the colleges made an effort to attract this wider clientele. The programmes offered a general foundation in communication and study skills, and an introduction to the academic discipline that the students would eventually pursue. There were no examinations built in but the students were assessed through their coursework and their demonstrated ability to cope with the academic rigour envisaged.

From their inception, Access courses were enthusiastically embraced by liberal-minded educators as a way forward. The colleges responded to an expressed need with some financial incentive from their local education authorities. These courses were very welcome because, apart from combating failure rolls and resources in certain areas, a new clientele was presented who promised to be stimulating, motivated and enriching. For some tutors, Access was seen not only as the stepping stone to a whole range of courses, but also as the beginning of a new method of assessment which discarded end testing and allowed students to be judged on their real life experiences and evidence of potential. Such was the interest that Lucas and Ward's survey (3) listed some 130 courses in 47 local authorities and 74 FE colleges, half of which had been set up in the previous two years. Similarly, the courses met with an ethusiastic response from many black people who saw them as the chance to make up for opportunities that they had missed; that would produce more goods than the first time around. This response is understandable in a community which places a high premium on literacy with a clear understanding of its value in this society and a recognition of its potential to liberate from poverty. It would be impossible, therefore, to deny what Access has done and is doing, in bringing increased opportunities to many black people thus previously excluded. However, if we are to make the programmes a success, then we must look not only at their performance but also at perceptions of what they are about.

In the first instance, it was unfortunate they began with courses in the social and welfare area: teaching, social work, social sciences, and community work. Welcome was tempered with scepticism and more than a little suspicion. Immediately obvious was the narrow range of courses available. These were the areas that were traditionally offered to women and, as was to be expected, they were taken up by black women. The prime motive for the particular area becomes clear when we realize that the proliferation of these courses coincided with the explosion on the streets of the inner cities of mainland Britain. The charge was that they were 'an insult to Black people' and 'another way to keep us down'. The black political response was that it was a cheap and easy way of acquiring an army of quasi-welfare workers to clear up the state's mess.

Harsh though this criticism is, it is important that it was made because that is how the direction of every initiative can be improved. Scepticism galvanized college administrators into continuing work on course design to widen the range of provision for black people and women. That included new areas for Access studies, such as business studies, accountancy, law, mathematics, electronics, planning, computing, and science. In some cases pre-Access courses were set up in areas where women had not been traditionally represented to ensure that teachers' stereotypical assumptions would not prove a barrier to the students' ultimate success. With these developments, consortia arrangements such as the Open College of South London began with the brief to encourage networking and monitor curriculum planning. The latter was an important area of concern and some controversy for Access planners. The requirements of the receiving institution had to be measured against the needs of the students and these could be problematic when there was no close liaison between the two institutions. Added to this, lecturers were forced to examine the Eurocentric and sometimes sexist bias of their courses, even when the subject matter was presented as neutral. Older students are more articulate and will not allow themselves to be patronized. With greater life experiences and a more critical approach to learning, they would question, even by their very presence, accepted assumptions about knowledge and its owners. As we know, non-racist and non-sexist teaching is not just about content but includes attitudes to students, classroom delivery, and assessment. In all, the process of course design and responsiveness has produced some of the best practices in FE which had been unaccustomed and quite often resistant to innovation.

What this organic approach cannot fully overcome, however, is the problem of credibility and the perceptions people still have of the nature of Access. As the Lindop Committee (4) reservations show they are still seen by many as a soft option, for those maybe congenitally unable to withstand the rigour of 'A' levels. If any higher education (HE) lecturer sees Access studies as anything less than what is required from the mainstream, then there will be perceptible differences in the way they treat ex-Access students who come into their classes. Are they seen as being of the highest calibre? Do they treat these students as though they will do anything, other than struggle through and drop out? Do they expect any of them to get a first? What is being highlighted here is the received 'common-sense' view of special provision which is bound to affect the students' progress through and out of higher education.

The students' perceptions are equally affected by what they see and hear around them. Some do complain about being treated in a patronizing manner in their degree class while others feel emboldened by the grounding they have received through Access. Nevertheless, the idea still persists that Access is an entry through the back door, especially when there are so few black students coming in through the traditional routes. What the students are in fact doing is taking the past failure of the education system as their own. This must affect self-image if one is entering an alien environment which itself has no concrete evidence of black people functioning effectively within it, as lecturers or administrators. With this insecurity, many students regret not continuing a traditional entry and some have been known to go back to take a formal 'O' or 'A' level qualification after graduating. It is not surprising, therefore, that some students insist that Access should only be a short-term measure: 'I'm on an Access course. I have to be on it but I don't want my child to have to come on one'.

There is also the view in society at large and the black community that Access is just for black people. Every black graduate is seen as the recent beneficiary of special entry and therefore form a special professional category for employment decisions. This is despite the fact that, as figures already indicated show, white students also enjoy its benefits. Past experience suggests that any programme so viewed has to be kept under close observation. Criticism of the early courses has already been addressed, but equally important is the concern that Access should not be seen as the accepted mode of entry, if this is not the route for all potential students. Many younger black applicants could benefit from the traditional discipline of 'A' levels or BTEC. These would be prospective students who had had recent experience of the school system, are unsure of specific career routes, and perhaps do not have the maturity to take on alternative patterns of learning. Some have been channelled towards Access and have been unable to handle the course and its transition to HE. Perhaps the 'A' level style of teaching has to be changed. Access practice can offer some direction. The important thing is that each kind of provision has its place. We have to guard against the drive to see these courses as the panacea for the deficiencies of the education system. That can lead to complacency, which suggests that there is a safety net that mitigates against failure that continues in all areas of the education system.

There is no doubt, however, that Access has a place in redressing the balance of inequality that exists; which means that more work has to be done to improve its record and change any negative perceptions there might be about its standard. Paradoxically, for a course that operates in an open environment, I would argue that tutors should resist any temptation to take students onto courses they are not ready for. Because of the equal opportunities ambiance in which they operate, white middle-class tutors need to overcome the liberalism that allows them to forget the kinds of demands that HE makes on students. Encouraging students who are unprepared, especially with the extended range of courses, can only reinforce and underscore earlier failures. It is a fine balance to be struck between having high expectations for students and directing them to the most enabling route, which means that in the end they do achieve their objectives.

The Return to Learning provision of courses for adults coming

209

back to education reflects the recognition that everyone who returns is not immediately ready to move into higher education. Courses with varying labels such as 'Fresh Start', 'New Directions', 'New Horizons', and 'Wider Opportunities' take the education process one step at a time. Students know that, in many cases, they have a lot to make up and are psychologically strong enough to deal with intellectual honesty, so they do enrol on courses than can and should provide them with the information needed about a whole range of Access provision, as well as other more established alternatives. That allows for greater choice, which is far better than being guided to the first, the easiest, and the quickest option.

Whatever reservations one might have about Access, there is consensus that it is a valuable initiative that has evolved through a dialogue with local communities and which has its place in a struggle for greater access to educational opportunity. It is notable that an authority such as the Inner London Education Authority has been at the forefront of this development, and recognition should be given for its achievements in this field. Unfortunately government policy will put many of those courses at risk, as well as support for the students. In the end, inequity is underlined. With resources at such a premium, it is even more important to continue a process of monitoring and reviewing whatever is on offer.

BIBLIOGRAPHY

1. Dale, R. (ed.) (1985) Education, Training and Employment: Towards a New Vocationalism, Oxford: Pergamon.
2. The Joint Board on CPVE (1985) The Certificate of Pre-Vocational Education.
3. Lucas, S. and Ward, R. (1985) A Survey of 'Access' Courses in England, University of Lancaster, February.
4. The Lindop Committee (1985) Academic Validation in the Public Sector of Higher Education, London: HMSO, April.
5. Millins, K. (1982) Progress and Performance of Students on Special Preparatory Courses 1981-1982, DES Evaluation Project, October.
6. Millins, K. (ed.) (1984) Access Forum No. 4, Centre for Access Studies.
7. Smith, G.D. (1986) 'TVEI: Replication and F.E.', in Natfhe Journal 11: no. 8, December.
8. Smith, G.D. (1987) 'TVEI and FE: "Challenges and Responses"', in Natfhe Journal 12: no. 2, March.

Chapter Twelve

THE SPECIAL ROLE OF TEACHER EDUCATION

Crispin Jones and Rosalind Street-Porter

Education for equality is a more problematic assertion than it seems at a first glance and, as in any collection of essays on the topic, the authors in this book may well conceptualize it differently. This is less of an issue if the meaning of the term is spelt out; it is liable to become an issue if it is not. Yet for much of the time in education the assumption is wrongly made that 'we all know what we are talking about' when in fact we do not. In other words, part of the problem for effective educational action in relation to education for equality is the lack of agreement over the intended goal, or worse, the fallacious belief that there is agreement. (1) In this chapter, therefore, we will take the term 'education for equality' to mean those educational policies and practices that promote notions of equality in educational institutions and the wider society, and more specifically, that help to ensure that the educational outcomes of differing groups of students will not reflect their differential location within the wider society. In other words, education for equality should mean that the range of educational attainments of, say, Turkish Cypriot working-class girls, will not significantly differ from the range of educational attainments of white, English, middle-class boys. (2) Furthermore, for reasons of both space and, we hope, clarity, the chapter will primarily concentrate on education for equality in terms of the debates over multicultural/ antiracist education. (We use the term 'multicultural/antiracist education' as use of either on its own can be confusing, given that much of the recent British debate attempting to distinguish between them has been over theory origination, often based on somewhat superficial transpositions into education of the sophisticated analysis of black scholars like Cedric Robinson.)

However, even if such educational equality were to be achieved, this would not, in itself, axiomatically lead to any significant changes in the subsequent economic and social location of such children. It has been well documented that black children who do well at school, in terms of their formal qualifications, still find it more difficult to get a job than white children with the same qualifications. (3) A similar state of affairs can also be traced in relation to physically and mentally challenged young people as well as females in terms of equality of access to employment. However, despite that depressing position in relation to the job market, equality in education is worth striving for, as its attainment would mean that the liberating potential of education would have gone a considerable way towards being realized. In other words, equality in education has an initial and difficult to achieve goal in relation to conventional attainment, but the concept of attainment must also be developed, so that it has within it notions of understanding relating to equality in the wider society.

A crucial element in the attainment of this goal in our schools is, of course, the professional practice of teachers. Although much depends on the educational climate set by central government and the LEA within which the school is located, perhaps more depends on the educational climate of the individual school and, within that, the individual classroom. And it is at this crucial school and classroom level that the influence of teachers is at its greatest. (4) If, therefore, the bringing about of greater equal opportunities in schools is not taking place, rather than blaming everybody and everything else in the system, the role of the teacher has to be scrutinized carefully, and alongside that, the initial teacher training (ITT) and continuing in-service education and training (Inset) that teachers receive. In this chapter it is these latter aspects of the educational process that will be examined. This is because it is our belief that effective work in teacher education is a key element in bringing about the changes that are necessary.

This chapter, then, looks briefly at the history of the involvement of teacher education with issues of equality, especially in relation to multicultural/antiracist education. It then examines the ways in which teacher education institutions themselves need to change in order to provide more effective work in terms of teacher education and equality, and finally, in order to demonstrate the sort of practice that can ensue from careful consideration of these concerns, some aspects of the initial training of primary teachers will be examined.

TEACHER EDUCATION AND EQUAL OPPORTUNITIES: THE CONTEXT

We would like to see every college of education in the country teaching its students something about race relations ... To say that there is no need to educate all students about such matters because, as one college has said, 'very few of our students go into schools where they are likely to meet mixed classes' is to miss the point ... Teachers should be equipped to prepare all their children for life in a multi-racial society. (5)

> The permeation of an initial training course with the principles
> underlying a genuinely pluralist approach to education should
> seek to ensure that all aspects of the course develop an
> awareness of the multi-racial and culturally diverse nature of
> British society ... (6)

This section starts with two quotations, one from a Select
Committee report, the other from a government enquiry. The tone
is similar: exhortation, pleading even, the necessary course of action
clearly stated. But they span some twenty years, the first being
from 1969, the second from 1985. Does this mean that teacher
training institutions did not listen? On the surface, it might appear
that most did not and that little has changed. Is this in fact the
case?

Almost, but not quite is probably the best answer. Maurice
Craft's survey of ITT and Inset provision published in 1981 reveals a
litany of exhortation by committees and concerned bodies laid
alongside surveys of provision that reveal, at best, snail-like change.
(7) Research that we did in 1979-80 found that much of the
provision, at both initial and in-service level, was patchy, often
dependent upon the enthusiasm of individuals rather than on
commitment by their institutions. (8) Although there seemed to be
quite a widespread desire on the part of those working in teacher
education to deal with issues relating to multicultural/antiracist
education, turning that desire into actual educational practice
seemed very difficult. Problems of resource contraction and course
validation are part of the explanation, but fall into the necessary
rather than sufficient category of explanation.

Within this context, both the Rampton and Swann Reports
stressed the importance of initial and in-service training, but
acknowledged that far too little had been achieved. (9) Indeed, the
comment in Rampton was despairing in its perceptions of the
progress that had been made:

> No teacher training institution appears to have succeeded in
> providing a satisfactory grounding in multicultural education
> for all of its students. (10)

Swann was more optimistic, albeit a future-orientated optimism,
and in a series of recommendations advocated the wholescale
adoption of what was perceived as being the best of current
practice. (11) Despite this optimism, it should be stated that little
government action followed from this or indeed any other part of
the report. This lack of response deserves closer examination
because its absence meant institutions involved in teacher education
felt (and still feel) under little pressure to change, even in the few
cases where progressive LEAs were urging the adoption of
multicultural/antiracist policies. Indeed, it is a sad irony that it was
the stance of these LEAs that strengthened this lack of response,

particularly from the DES.

The then Secretary of State for Education, Sir Keith Joseph, had as his main concern in relation to ITT and Inset the drive for greater efficiency and accountability. This drive was seen as part of the introduction of the new economic 'realism' to British society generally, and education in particular, by the government. Sir Keith Joseph had been an early and influential advocate of such views and was determined that education should not miss out in the general restructuring of the welfare state. He was also concerned by what he perceived to be the politicization of education in regard to issues of race by certain inner city, Labour-controlled LEAs. Their concern for the introduction and implementation of multicultural/ antiracist educational policies was seen by Joseph and other politicians in the DES, and elsewhere in the government, as an ill-thought-out hotchpotch which, they claimed, antagonized many parents and failed to bring about any improvements in the quality of education in the LEAs concerned. Joseph, in particular, was offended by the manner in which the term antiracism was being used, thinking it inaccurate, and saw little validity in concepts like institutional racism unless an explicit legal and administrative policy and practice could be demonstrated. As a result of this 'my neutrality, your bias' attitude, racism had almost become a forbidden word in the DES; antiracism certainly had. In this educational/political atmosphere, it is not surprising that the Rampton and Swann Reports had a flavour to them which was unlikely to appeal to the politicians at the DES. This lack of ardour was not confined to the two reports however, but spread and affected other institutions concerned with teacher education.

Thus attempts by the Council for National Academic Awards (CNAA) to ensure that the teacher education courses that they validated were explicit in their commitment to preparing students for work in a multicultural society were watered down, perhaps due to pressure from the DES. The CNAA's Committee for Education, which oversees about half the initial teacher training courses in the country, set up a working party of experienced teacher educators which recommended that the CNAA should take more of a lead in advocating a multicultural, antiracist perspective. (12) The term 'antiracism' used in the working party report was considered too extreme and the CNAA's response to the working papers avoided its use as well as putting down the working parties' suggestions by implying that they were 'simplistic solutions'. (12)

Another major potential avenue for change, the Council for the Accreditation of Teacher Education (CATE), whose criteria were binding on all ITT institutions, made little of these concerns, although they merited a brief mention. Of the 45 criteria by which a course was to be judged, only one, 5.8, made specific reference to equal opportunities issues:

Students should be prepared for the diversity of ability,

behaviour, social background and ethnic and cultural origins encountered in ordinary schools; and in how to respond to that diversity and guard against preconceptions based on race and sex. (13)

Given the all-embracing and draconian nature of the CATE criteria and the HMI visitations that accompanied them, it is not too surprising that the ITT/Inset institutions were not enthusiastic about radical reform of practice in relation to multicultural/antiracist education in relation to part of 1 out of 45 criteria that they were endeavouring to meet. No matter how long overdue and important, if changes in practice did not clearly help to bring courses into line with the CATE criteria, it was often seen as diverting of effort best reserved for more 'acceptable' areas. Again, given that courses could be closed down if they failed to meet the criteria, this concern can be understood if not accepted. However, as few courses were closed down, it must be assumed that in CATE's judgement the criteria relating to equal opportunities just quoted was usually met in some way or other.

It should be noted that, at the same time, despite the often negative pressures resulting from CATE, the HMI were trying to move practice along. But their findings, too, replicated those expressed in the Swann and Rampton Reports:

> About a third of the institutions gave considerable time and emphasis to preparing students for work in a multi-ethnic society, and a substantial number were reviewing their policies in this area and adjusting their course content, although a minority gave it insufficient attention. (14)

At first glance the comment seems encouraging, which in a modest way it is. What it is actually saying is that two-thirds of all training institutions have not really done anything, and of the third that have done something, there is no real evaluation of the quality. It also makes one wonder as to how seriously that particular CATE criteria was being pursued, either by the institutions concerned or the investigatory bodies like CATE, the CNAA, and, indeed, the HMI.

As the army of threatening acronyms bore down on most teacher training institutions in relation to their work in ITT, attempts to encourage developments through Inset in relation to certain aspects of equal opportunities in education made less headway than they might have done. Part of this was due to yet more changes, this time in relation to funding arrangements, in which yet more acronyms were spawned, producing, as in nature, very few froglets. However, just as teachers, schools, LEAs, and the teacher education institutions started to make sense of the new system of Inset provision, the new Secretary of State for Education, Kenneth Baker, decided to make his mark on education. This aim is one which he is manifestly achieving, for the massive changes to be brought about by the Education Reform Act mean another period of chaos, particularly in relation to Inset. As a result, equal opportunities issues will continue to have to be fought for, in Inset and teacher education generally, as they will have to be fought for elsewhere in the education system. (15)

It is difficult to be optimistic in such an educational climate and one should not be if the facts do not justify it. However, good and exciting practice in teacher education relating to multicultural/antiracist education has taken place and continues to do so, despite current uncertainties. And, it is important to note, such practice is being supported by elements within the DES and HMI, despite the current preoccupations of the politicians based there. The rest of this chapter looks at some of this current practice to demonstrate what can be done, even in difficult circumstances. This last point is important as circumstances are unlikely to change for the better, at least not in the short to medium term.

CHANGING THE INSTITUTIONS: THE LONG MARCH THROUGH

A less stressed aspect of work on equality in education relates to change in the teacher education institutions themselves. For, if teacher training institutions were to adopt equal opportunities policies in relation to their own practice, many of the issues discussed in this chapter that assist in the denial of equal educational opportunities to black and other racial and ethnic minority students could be more readily overcome. Where such policies do exist, it is often as a result of initiatives taken by LEAs which have encouraged initiatives in institutions that are either located in their area or are funded by them or both. In many such institutions, it should be remembered, ITT and Inset are only a part of what they do and are often regarded as of low status by the rest of the institution. Yet much of the internal impetus for change has come from education departments and faculties, mainly because the nature of their work has made them more aware of the issues involved than it has for other departments and faculties.

From the experiences of institutions that have worked on such policies, it would appear that an effective policy should have six major strands, namely:

(a) A clear definitional statement about the nature of the issues involved. This would clarify terms such as 'racism', 'black', and 'equal opportunities'.
(b) Policies to help bring about equal opportunities within the institution; these would mainly relate to the administration of the institution in terms of matters like admissions, staffing, and disciplinary procedures in the case of racist incidents.
(c) Policies to help students to understand the issues in relation to their professional practice; such policies would have as one of

their major areas of concern the courses that are taught.

(d) Staff development policies and processes; of particular importance in relation to teaching staff, but also necessary throughout the institution.

(e) All the above should grow from as wide a consultation process as possible. Equally, formal approval should be given to the policy by all relevant decision-making bodies in the institution including its governing body or equivalent.

(f) The implementation of the policy needs to be formally monitored and evaluated. Such feedback needs formal institutional modes of response and reaction.

As can be seen, to bring such a policy to fruition demands the work and support of more than a few people, particularly in the large institutions under consideration here. (16) Some of the more significant issues can best be explored by looking at the six headings just outlined in a little more detail.

As was mentioned at the start of the chapter, definitional issues are a potential problem in this area. The problem is of two kinds. The first is the intellectual difficulty of clearly conceptualizing terms like 'black' and 'racism'; the second is that clarity of the sort some people demand is probably not possible, as is so often the case with the social sciences. (17) The danger about protracted definitional arguments is that that process can be used as a further excuse for inactivity or opposition. More, if the definitions used are too loose, opponents of the policy will use it as a stalking horse to destroy or delay the policy. Too precise and it will tend to leave out those groups of people the policy is aimed at. (18)

If definitions are difficult, changing the way an institution works is as difficult, albeit in a different manner. Modern teacher training institutions are bureaucratic and rule bound, and it is at that level of rules that much of the institutional racism takes place. There are certain key areas to be addressed. Admissions of students should be closely monitored, both at application and acceptance stages; the same is true of staff appointments. If few black people apply, the institution should take steps to remedy this, not accept the position passively. If few black students are admitted it should be clearly known why this is so; the same, of course, applies to the appointment of new staff. The inequalities of the past cannot readily be undone, but there is no reason for their continuance. Equally complex is the issue of racist incidents within the institution. The way in which they are investigated has to be fair and clear to all. Any disciplinary code that contains sanctions almost certainly will have to involve the unions of people likely to be involved. Again, there are likely to be problems of definition. An example of this is the code of an urban LEA which distinguishes between 'acts of racism' and 'serious and/or repeated acts of racism'. How can one make an agreed distinction between an act and a serious act of racism? But if the first carries the threat of a formal written warning and the second dismissal, the distinction is crucial. Additionally, attention needs to be given to support for black students experiencing problems within schools on placement, where it is apparent that racism is a factor in negative staffroom treatment, comments by children, assessment of professional performance.

Similar difficulties crop up when what is taught is looked at. Current attacks on the concept of academic freedom make the examination of courses a most difficult area. Yet many people who work in teacher education would want their courses to be more reflective of the concerns of this book. For these people there is the need for advice and support to enable any necessary changes to take place, including strategies for utilizing the course validation process to support change. (19) For those who either do not wish to change or who positively oppose the spirit of even the modest proposals put forward in, say, Education for All, there is not a great deal that can be done in the short term. This is not a note of despair, however, as there is so much to be done in relation to the larger group. What the senior management of the institutions have to accept is that such change costs money in that it has considerable resource implications, not least of all on the already overcrowded time loads that many in teacher education bear.

Clearly, emphases on these concerns are likely to necessitate staff development for both teaching and non-teaching staff alike. Taking the issue of development for teaching staff, such a process is important in terms of providing and/or updating information about diversity and black experiences within Britain; providing firsthand experience of working in schools with children from a variety of backgrounds (which may not have occurred during a previous career as teacher); supporting developments to permeate and resource the curriculum offered students in terms of equal opportunities; sensitizing staff to the ways in which the daily experience of black students within the institution can be negatively affected by casual comment and styles of interaction which are racist. To be effective, such staff development has to move beyond voluntaristic attendance, but also avoid the moral pressure endemic in 'awareness' courses, which tends to alienate the reluctant or disinterested. As with students, the responsibility rests within the professional arena. Such staff development might seem an impossible task, particularly with the range of competing demands for increased research expertise, recent and relevant teaching experience, knowledge of information technology, etc. Experience would indicate that it is difficult, but not impossible: enabling factors including an instrumental element for those undertaking such development (contact time remission, reduction of student drop-out rates, for example); linkage of this educational aspect with research and/or with recent and relevant classroom updating; course team development meetings for review and development purposes.

Because of these extra demands that the introduction of such a policy entails, it is essential that the process through which the policy is created involves as many people in the institution as possible, and that every attempt is made to include significant representation of groups currently treated in an unequal manner. In addition, this policy creation process has to involve students, teaching and non-teaching staff, and, if it were thought to be helpful, people who do not work in the institution but who have expertise to bring to the task. Examples of these could be governors of the institution and local community leaders, particularly from minority communities. Such a consultation process is time consuming and not for the impatient. However, it is the best process by which a policy can become 'owned' by the people who have to work it. And if it is 'owned', it is likely to be effectively implemented. Perhaps more importantly, the policy should reflect the educational concerns of those whom it is intended to benefit. This can really only be effectively done where representation is significant rather than tokenistic. This is not so much an issue of numbers, although that can be important. It is more that the expressed concerns and policy priorities of the concerned group(s), in this case primarily black groups, must have a significant place in any policy that is to have credibility.

A policy statement, however derived, is only an initial step. Even in a favourable institutional climate there is still a need for formal procedures to ensure that implementation of any policy is effective, that lessons that are to be learnt are learnt, and that the policy is reviewed in the light of those lessons. This probably needs quite formal mechanisms, involving senior decision-makers within the institution. It is not a job just for a group of committed junior staff; without committed senior staff the implementation will slowly halt, the impetus lost, with all that remains being a sheaf of documents to show, and perhaps impress, visitors. Success is, indeed, a long march through the institution.

INITIAL TEACHER TRAINING AND EQUAL OPPORTUNITIES

The political context of the debate on equal opportunities in education that was examined in an earlier section has tended to set the framework and the tone of much of the work that is conducted in the field and the orientation of both teachers and students within it. To amplify one aspect of this context, the policy confusion has led to an overemphasis on moral exhortation, either in the way the ideas are introduced to students, or in the way the students perceive their introduction. For too many students, it appears to be their professional responsibility to assist children in developing mathematical concepts, but to be their moral (and voluntary) responsibility to assist black and other disadvantaged children to come to terms with the education being given them by an institution that is all too often ignorant or dismissive of their legitimate educational needs. The problem lies in the failure to locate concerns about equality in education securely enough within the general educational theories underpinning courses or within the realm of professional responsibility.

As a consequence of this 'bolt on' attitude, much of the debate within ITT has been largely concerned with the mechanics and style of implementing policies for equal opportunities, or about the inclusion within courses of recognition of equal opportunities issues. Over time, emphasis has increasingly shifted to the need both to permeate all course content together with the need to include some more detailed and specific work, a position endorsed in the Swann Report. (20) At the level of primary courses this could mean, for example, addressing criteria for the selection of story books, the examination of issues relating to dialect and languages in the classroom, recognition of differing musical traditions, a consideration of multi-faith issues, all within the main body of the course. In addition, a specific part of the course would examine in more detail issues relating to equal opportunities in education with an assignment attached. Complementing this would be the placing of students in schools which contain children from a diversity of cultural backgrounds to make the reading and discussions in the course more real and relevant to their professional practice. This is particularly important as many intending teachers still have little real experience of living and working in such environments.

For those who have worked in this way, there is still too often a disappointing disjunction between input and output; at the end of the day, on the final teaching practice, students may demonstrate their ability to work effectively with children in the classroom on aspects of education they have internalized as the important, professional ones, (language, mathematics, science, topic work, etc.), but often still give only superficial recognition of equal opportunities, as if they remain a moral option. It would appear that several factors operate to make the process of affecting the student's classroom practice (as opposed to their discussion and essay writing) more problematic than the permeation model would appear to suggest. These factors need to be understood more clearly if ITT is to be more effective in the area of equal opportunities.

Fundamental to such an understanding is the necessity of exploring with students the theoretical frameworks which explain why particular groups within this society fail to achieve at the same level as others, an exploration which demands more than simple resorts to descriptive labels of racism, sexism, and so on. One such framework is to be found in the extensive work on education and urban social theory. (21) The processes by which urban areas have grown from discreet towns to the sprawling masses within which the majority of the population now live are important to understand, given their educational consequences. Such an understanding, particularly of the increasing economic and residential segregation in British cities and their schools, a process confused but not altered by neighbourhood revitalization ('gentrification'), is most pertinent. In a similar fashion, it is important to examine and to understand the timing of post-war immigration to Britain in relation to economic shifts and changes of fortune for specific urban areas and those living/working within them, given the widespread misconceptions surrounding such phenomena. (22)

Such a study of crucial urban processes firmly shifts the explanatory frameworks relating to reduced opportunities (or disadvantage) away from deficit, pathological models which blame the victim, to a more positive range of structural explanations, which locate the issues in their wider societal context. As an extension of this field of enquiry, the reasons why educational concern has been generated about the consequences of these urban socio-economic processes on girls, black, and working-class children, also require investigation. Among the issues to be examined in this respect would be the range of reasons that cause concern about such groups of young people (economic, civil unrest, humanitarian, educational, etc.) and the make-up of the concerned people and/or groups (internal pressure groups, educationalists, politicians, etc.). In looking at these, the structural explanations are reanimated in the sense that the actualities of educational reform and the possibilities for its furtherance are addressed, with attention firmly paid to the actions of the 'victims' themselves.

This kind of approach allows students to understand the reasons for equal opportunities policies and practices in education and the context within which they operate. It provides the historical dimension which reveals particular emphases within equal opportunities at different times and places, as well as the conditional relationships between the various groups concerned, both important for an understanding of the contemporary scene. As a consequence, it encourages students to take a more positive and better informed stance towards the client groups and their education. Of particular importance, it firmly delineates equal opportunities as an integral part of the educational debate and consequently of concern to all who teach. Finally, it enables students to understand that 'starting from where the child is', 'enabling all children to achieve to the full extent of their potential' must incorporate an understanding of who the children are and where they are located in society.

It may seem that working through the conceptual issues outlined here is too major a task within the time allowed (particularly for PGCE courses) or too complex for the initial training level. We would argue, however, that such an exploration with students is neither of these; rather it allows students to make sense of what is all too often disparate bits of course learning. Without it, there is a real danger of giving students the fallacious notion that race, gender, class, and special educational needs issues are somewhat peripheral to the main task or are only for those who teach in particular areas.

Several courses have worked on the development of such an approach, most particularly those training teachers for the secondary level. It has been more difficult to introduce such an orientation within courses for the primary level, due no doubt to the continuing influence of various child development theories which concentrate on the individuality of children and their learning needs to the exclusion of the interaction of children with their environment in its widest sense. Such more structural explanations for children's development and learning still encounter resistance when proposed for inclusion in pre-secondary school age initial training courses; the younger the age group being prepared for, the more that seems to be the case. However, changes can be made. To illustrate this, some aspects of a primary PGCE course which utilizes an urban theory base will be described, as examples of practice which has the potential to shift students from a rhetorical position on equal educational opportunities towards adopting an interactive and constructive theory/practice response.

The course explicitly sets out to be a training for teaching within urban areas, with specific reference to teaching within the inner city. There are two reasons for this, the first being that most teachers will at some point in their career work in an urban school and the second that there are currently greater employment opportunities in inner city primary schools, a circumstance unlikely to change in the medium term. Geographically, the course is located close to the centre of a large urban conurbation, allowing for its inner city specificity in terms of practical experience offered. However, the course takes as its definition of 'urban' that of the Standard Metropolitan Labour Area (SMLA), which, by focusing on functional aspects of 'urban' life, perceives 96 per cent of the British population as affected by urban processes. (23) The conceptual framework of the course is as relevant, therefore, for teacher training across Britain.

The course begins with a two-week introductory unit, providing an intensive, shared experience for students and tutors. Apart from more general aims (for example, providing a common reference point for the course as a whole, assisting the development of group cohesion and co-operative learning, confronting at the outset worries about working with children in front of tutors, etc.), the unit aims to introduce students to urban processes and their implications for schooling at the levels of both theory and practice. It does this through a focus on the urban environment (in this case, inner city) as a curriculum resource for children's learning. The basic structure of the unit involves groups of about fourteen students, working in pairs, in a week-long exploration of the environment of a particular school, culminating in an exhibition of the environmental aspects of interest to them mounted within the school. Sharing the exhibition with the four or five children with whom each pair work in the second week becomes the starting point for the school-based work to follow.

The second week is spent working with the children in and around the school, investigating some aspect of the local environment selected in discussion with the children. All the work done by the groups is brought together and discussed in the school in a work-sharing assembly. Some examples of the work done have been examinations of play facilities, a building site, waste ground, wildlife, street sounds, local transport, diversity of produce in shops; the range has been enormous.

In addition to this intensive practical work, there is a significant input of theory and other information useful for the students. Structured into this fortnight is a carefully organized set of lectures and seminars which take place in the faculty and the school. As well as perhaps more obvious ones such as recording techniques, children's talk, mathematics in the environment, there are others that focus on processes of urbanization and their implications for schooling, the history of immigration and educational responses to post-war immigration, and concepts of disadvantage and equal opportunities. Additionally, students meet with various individuals/groups within the local communities to discuss issues related to the families sending children to the school. Such contacts include community workers, housing officers, police, community arts groups, social services, parish priests. Differing perceptions of the needs of and problems associated with families living in the inner city are thus highlighted and discussed.

The intensity and depth of the learning for the students (and tutors) is difficult to convey, apart from the easily imagined exhaustion. The urban theory base that has been provided challenges many students to reassess their judgements about the poverty-stricken inner city neighbourhoods they are exploring and about those who live, work, and go to school within them. The backgrounds, experiences, life-survival skills, and creativity of the children they meet both disturb complacency and personal experience and raise expectations of possibilities. The children's views on their own environment takes the disruption of preconceptions a stage further. The background information on the immigration and experiences of ethnic minority groups within Britain gives a reality to the ethnic and cultural diversity of the children encountered in the schools, projecting the students into a more proactive stance on the issue than might otherwise be the case. In other words, the explicative framework is used to illuminate the descriptive and vice versa.

Apart from forming the substance of the first assignment, this unit sets the theoretical and practical framework for much of the course that follows. Its timing is a crucial factor here. Too often in primary courses urban/equal opportunities elements are introduced after an initial grounding in child development, for example, has been explored. Once initial conceptual frameworks for analysis have been set (in this case individualistic ones), other frameworks appear as afterthoughts and less essential to consider. (As many students enter primary teacher training with an initial conception of young children as relatively unaffected by socio-economic processes and status the apparent theoretical reinforcement of this confirms rather than challenges, thus rendering subsequent reconsiderations more problematic.) The memory of the experiences of the unit prompts students to raise equal opportunities issues with tutors working with them across the various curriculum components if not raised by the tutors themselves, thereby acting as a constant reminder of permeation needs. As one outcome, it is illuminating that a significant number of students choose an educational issue relating to equality for their education studies seminar group presentations later in the course, focusing on such topics as integration of children with special needs within the classroom, gender issues and children's stories, the role of religious education in a multicultural society, playground interaction between different social groupings, all done within an explicit multicultural/antiracist perspective.

The design of the rest of the course follows a more orthodox pattern, with a model of both permeation and specific work in relation to equal educational opportunities. Considerable emphasis is placed on peer group learning and sharing of expertise and experience, enabling crucial learning to take place where personal experience may be lacking, for example in relation to working with children with a variety of mother tongues or with particular special needs. Of considerable importance, however, is the mechanism used for ensuring both the maintenance of understanding and commitment and also their translation into practice in schools, namely the inclusion among criteria for all assessed items of the explicit recognition of race, class, gender, and special needs issues. This recognition is thus built into shared criteria for profiling personal professional development by the student, specialist curriculum work, general essays, and crucially, assessment of performance on the final teaching practice. Clearly such an inclusion in critieria for assessment has the additional advantage of keeping these concerns at the forefront of tutors' minds too.

CONCLUSION

This chapter has looked at the political context within which teacher training operates, change within teacher training institutions, and, as an antidote to a possibly depressing scenario, some ideas for development within ITT. The lessons to be learnt from this analysis (such as they are) are ones that precipitate teacher trainers back into issues of quality of provision and what that entails and away from current preoccupations with student numbers and of marketing courses in a climate of economic pseudo-realism, a change back in emphasis all would welcome. In the past, consideration of equal opportunities issues has been challenged for diminishing quality; the concerns it now illuminates allows the assertion that its consideration enables a return to a focus on quality of provision of value to all involved in the schooling process. After all, ultimately teacher training is supposed to be concerned with offering education of quality to all children/young people in schools in a way which develops to the full the potential of all. As over 50 per cent of our school population are not being offered this currently, this should be a professional concern of the highest priority. Given this concern, there are four final points to be made.

First, the kind of work necessitated in the discussion above within the teacher training institutions themselves and within their courses demands a high level of communication between varying participants: teaching and non-teaching staff, tutors and class teachers, tutors and students. Effective change and development relies on partnerships between all these interest groups. At the ITT level, for example, the disjunction often experienced by students between course and school policy and practice (23) can be surmounted by a collaborative approach to training students which is of obvious benefit to all.

Second, the pedagogy advocated for those working with children in schools by both HMI (25) and teachers and trainers involved in antiracist and antisexist work needs to have an emphasis on discussion, problem solving, flexible thinking, and confident and independent learning. Equally importantly, this pedagogy is equally applicable to work with students. 'Learning 'em' in Ratty's inimitable phrase returns us to the moral imperative and is ineffectual. Students need time to discuss, experience, read, think, and discuss again, which is itself demanding of tutor time and organization for learning. The qualities this provision engenders benefit all aspects of education, however.

Third, much of the successful work in this field has underlined the need for an iterative approach to theory and practice. Previous debate on whether theory should proceed practice, or practice proceed theory, is superceded by a recognition that these two aspects of effective teaching need constant intermeshing for real learning to take place. The effectiveness of the introductory unit outlined above rests on that iterative approach. Clearly the demands of such an approach are expensive in terms of tutor time, in that its effectiveness relies in part on the involvement of tutors at more than the obligatory theory input/lecture time. Experiences in the Inset field would support the value of such an approach, however. The current desire within the DES to see real change in schools as a validator of monies spent on Inset have led to the provision of courses with a school-focused and school-based element. In our experience, in the field of race and education issues, change in schools is facilitated by a model of course design which alternates time in the training institution with time in school, allowing discussion and planning time on the relationship between work in each sphere. The involvement of course tutors in the school-based work enables the more theory-based time to be pitched at an appropriate level.

Finally, as an extension of the third point above, practical experience for students/teachers of children from a diversity of class, gender, ethnic origin backgrounds can, by itself, rarely be enough. Provision of diversity amongst children does not, of itself, provide the learning which is paramount in education for equality. The inexplicit theories we all carry with us will remain unchallenged unless presented with alternative and at times opposing ways of viewing the world. The children themselves are a necessary but not sufficient stimulus for progression. The task for teacher education is thus significant and potentially of great value in making our schooling system one where equality has real meaning.

NOTES

1. A simple confusion is the way in which some LEAs use the term 'equal opportunities' to refer to policies and practices relating to the elimination of sex discrimination in one context, and to a much wider range of antidiscriminatory policies and practices in others.

2. Of course, different groups may perceive a different range of educational attainments and there may well be differing perceptions within any group. However, the broad principle is clear in that groups (whether defined in terms of race, ethnicity, class, gender/sexual orientation, language, religion, etc.) should not be denied access to educational attainments which they and other groups (or elements within them) perceive as being important to their educational fulfilment. In addition, in the higher-order valuations of many such groups would be concern for education in terms of equality, although there are considerable difficulties with the operationalization of this without invalidating imposition. Equally problematic is the concept of range of attainment - in crude terms the location and distribution of pupils on scales such as bell curves, and as to how such location and distribution both replicates and reproduces the hierarchical nature of the wider society.

3. See, for example, the work of Smith (1974, 1981) and that of Jenkins (1986a, b) for detailed investigations and explanations of the role of prejudice and discrimination in the labour market for young black people.

4. The changes to be brought about by the Education Reform Act of 1988 are unlikely to change this, despite what many teachers fear. The experience of teachers working in more centralized systems, such as Sweden or France, indicates the continuing educational importance and pedagogic independence of teachers in more centralized systems (c.f. Jones and Kimberley (1986) for examples of practice in such centralized educational

environments). Those LEAs in England who still test children frequently do contain classrooms that reflect this; they also contain classrooms that do not. The pressure on teachers there is as much from parents as from the LEA. It is interesting to note the semantic shift that takes place in such discussions. Parental demands that are perceived as progressive are community demands; demands perceived as reactionary remain parental ones, and by implication selfish and middle class.

5. Quoted in DES (1985b), p. 545; it is from a Select Committee on Race Relations report (1967).
6. DES (1985b), p. 557.
7. Craft (1981a) in Craft (1981b).
8. Jones and Street-Porter (1980)- Even when institutions appeared committed across the board, closer investigation usually revealed a similar individualistic initiative pattern, with the individuals in these cases being in positions of considerable influence within their institution. able to affect more than the courses they taught on.
9. DES (1981) and DES (1985b).
10. DES (1981), p. 61.
11. DES (1985b). Like much of the rest of the report, the section on ITT and Inset is curate's egg, and thus both frustrating and helpful (i.e. it can be used to justify most things).
12. CNAA (1985), p. 2.
13. CATE (1985), p. 5.
14. DES (1987), p. 15.
15. The Education Reform Act has little to do with equal opportunities, or with reform in the usual sense of the word. It has references to religion and to the Welsh language, which are retrograde rather than reformist, and makes no mention of multicultural education issues.
16. Street-Porter (1985). A more detailed exposition of work and personnel involved in changing a teacher training institution is outlined here.
17. It is the same with the natural sciences too, as even a partial acquaintance with particle physics demonstrates. In the social sciences, such pretensions are arrogant and ignorant. See Culbertson (1971), p. 110.
18. Note that Swann (DES 1985b) ducks key definitional issues while pretending that it is not. See, especially, the discussion of 'racism' in Chapter 2.
19. The 'Training the Trainers' project, co-ordinated by Professor Craft from the University of Nottingham, is an attempt to help in this area. Sadly it has received only modest support from local and central government.
20. DES (1985b), pp. 556-64.
21. C.f. Bash (1985) and Grace (1984) for details of this approach.
22. ibid and also Street-Porter (1978).
23. For more detail on the concept of the SMLA, see Bash (op.

cit.), especially Chapter 2.
24. This is further developed in Jones and Street-Porter (1983).
25. DES (1985a) is a strong advocate of developing the orientations towards learning discussed here.

REFERENCES

Bash, L., Coulby, D., and Jones, C. (1985) Urban Schooling, London: Holt, Rinehart & Winston.

CATE (Council for the Accreditation of Teacher Education) (1985) Criteria for the Accreditation of Courses of Initial Teacher Training, London: CATE.

CNAA (Council for National Academic Awards) (1984) Multicultural Education: Discussion Paper, London: CNAA.

CNAA (1985) Multi-cultural Education, (Document reference 0148E). London: CNAA.

Craft, M. (ed.) (1981a) Teaching in a Multicultural Society, London: Falmer Press.

Craft, M. (1981b) 'Recognition of need', in Craft, M. (1981a) Teaching in a Multicultural Society, London: Falmer Press.

Culbertson, J. (1971) Macroeconomic Theory and Stabilization Policy, New York: Wiley.

DES (Department of Education and Science) (1981) West Indian Children in our Schools (The Rampton Report), London: HMSO.

DES (1985a) Better Schools, London: HMSO.

DES (1985b) Education for All, (The Swann Report) Cmnd 9453, London: HMSO.

DES (1987) Quality in Schools: the Initial Training of Teachers, London: HMSO.

Grace, G. (1984) Education and the City, London: Routledge & Kegan Paul.

Jenkins, R. (1986a) Racism and Recruitment: Managers, Organisations and Equal Opportunities in the Labour Market, Cambridge: Cambridge University Press.

Jenkins, R. (1986b) 'Education, employment and policy: "racial" disadvantage in the United Kingdom', in Weis, L. (1986) Race, Class and Schooling, Buffalo, NY: Comparative Education Centre, SUNY.

Jones, C. and Kimberley, K. (eds) (1986) Intercultural Education: Concept, Context, Curriculum Practice, Strasbourg: Council of Europe.

Jones, C. and Street-Porter, R. (1980) Educational Disadvantage: Implications for the Initial and In-service Education of Teachers, Manchester: Centre for Educational Disadvantage.

Jones, C. and Street-Porter, R. (1983) 'Anti-racist teaching and teacher education', in Multicultural Teaching, 1: no. 3.

Robinson, C. (1983) Black Marxism: The Making of the Black Radical Tradition, London: Zed Press.

Select Committee on Race Relations and Immigration (1969)
    Report. The Problems of Coloured School Leavers, Cmnd 413-
    iv, London: HMSO.
Smith, D (1974) Racial Disadvantage in Employment, London:
    Political & Economic Planning Broadsheets.
Smith, D. (1981) Unemployment and Racial Minorities, London:
    Policy Studies Institute.
Street-Porter, R. (1978) Race, Children and Cities, Milton Keynes:
    Open University Press.
Street-Porter, R. (1985) 'Initial Teacher Training and the Swann
    Report' in Multicultural Teaching, 111: no. 2.
Weis, L. (ed.) (1986) Race, Class and Schooling, Buffalo, NY:
    Comparative Education Centre, SUNY.

INDEX

234